THE PUBLIC RELATIONS HANDBOOK FOR NONPROFITS

THE PUBLIC RELATIONS HANDBOOK FOR NONPROFITS

A Comprehensive and Practical Guide

Art Feinglass

Foreword by Naomi Levine

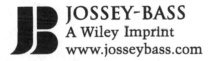

JOSSEY-BASS
A Wiley Imprint
www.josseybass.com

Published by Jossey-Bass
A Wiley Imprint
989 Market Street, San Francisco, CA 94103-1741   www.josseybass.com

Jossey-Bass books and products are available through most bookstores. To contact Jossey-Bass directly, call our Customer Care Department within the U.S. at 800-956-7739, outside the U.S. at 317-572-3986, or fax 317-572-4002.

Jossey-Bass also publishes its books in a variety of electronic formats. Some content that appears in print may not be available in electronic books.

Readers should be aware that Internet Web sites listed in this work may have changed or disappeared between when this work was written and when it is read.

Library of Congress Cataloging-in-Publication Data

Feinglass, Art, date.
  The public relations handbook for nonprofits: a comprehensive and practical guide / Art Feinglass; foreword by Naomi Levine.—1st ed.
    p. cm.
  Includes index.
  ISBN-13   978-1-118-33607-6

  1. Nonprofit organizations—Public relations. I. Title.
  HD62.6.F447 2005
  659.2—dc22

                              2005006219

FIRST EDITION
HB Printing   10 9 8 7 6 5 4 3 2 1

CONTENTS

EXHIBITS

FOREWORD

This remarkable book, *The Public Relations Handbook for Nonprofits*, makes it crystal clear that public relations is the key to survival for nonprofit organizations. PR is essential for effective fundraising, attracting members, energizing supporters, and fulfilling an organization's mission. Without being known in the community—in other words, without public relations—a nonprofit institution cannot attract volunteers and certainly cannot raise money.

How to achieve this high profile with a limited expenditure of money is the story that Art Feinglass tells so astonishingly well. The book not only discusses theories but also shows how these theories can be put into practice with very specific examples—dramatic, entertaining, and informative examples that make the book far more interesting than other texts of its kind. Feinglass writes in a light and engaging fashion that is simply a delight to read.

The book is extraordinarily specific and thorough, covering every aspect of public relations. It explains how an organization must target its markets, set its goals and messages, create a public relations plan, and find the right PR fit. It discusses the importance of writing and placing releases and demonstrates how to prepare press releases, brochures, newsletters, and annual reports. And it examines the roles and uses of direct mail, advertising, and the electronic media—television, radio, the Internet, videos, and DVDs.

In short, no aspect of public relations is overlooked. Everyone working in the nonprofit sector—especially fundraisers—should place this book at the top of their reading list.

March 2005   Naomi Levine, Chair and Executive Director
George H. Heyman, Jr. Center for Philanthropy and Fundraising
New York University

PREFACE

The American Red Cross: "We're There"

On a gray November afternoon, I was standing at a podium looking down the length of a long, gleaming wooden conference table at the expectant faces of the senior staff and board members of the American Red Cross in Greater New York (www.nyredcross.org). They had gathered in the fifth-floor conference room of the group's massive headquarters building in midtown Manhattan to hear what I had to tell them about developing new public relations (PR) strategies for their organization.

I had been inside this building before. On September 11, 2001, I was one of hundreds of New Yorkers at the organization's headquarters, volunteering to give blood and do rescue work at what came to be known as Ground Zero. I had received a certificate of appreciation that now hangs in a place of honor on the wall of my office. I had also received a red-and-white American Red Cross lapel pin reading "9/11 Volunteer WTC." I regularly use both the certificate and the pin as examples of nonprofit incentives in the classes I teach at New York University (NYU) on public relations for nonprofits. Now I was on the Red Cross Communications Advisory Committee, trying to define and reach new target markets for support.

It was a familiar situation for me. As founder and president of Access Communications, a New York–based training and public relations firm, I begin most projects with a series of conversations. I speak to as many people as I can within the organization in order to understand my client's goals and to get a sense of how the client organization goes about achieving those goals. Every organization is different.

Tolstoy opens his novel *Anna Karenina* with the lines, "All happy families resemble one another. Every unhappy family is unhappy in its own way." I've found that every organization, whether a nonprofit or a Fortune 500 corporation, is unique in the way it deals with the challenges it faces.

The two dozen serious-looking people seated around the table smiled at me, waiting for me to begin my presentation. I smiled back, wondering what I could tell these veteran leaders of one of the best-known of all nonprofit organizations. *Everyone* has heard of the Red Cross.

To my left, a couple of feet from the podium, was a big red, white, and blue American flag, and next to it was an equally large white flag upon which was emblazoned the organization's famous red cross. To my right, a framed plaque bearing the organization's mission statement hung on the wall. It seemed a good place to start.

I took a deep breath and began reading aloud. "The mission of the American Red Cross in Greater New York," I read from the plaque, "is to help people avoid, prepare for, and cope with emergencies; to enhance self-reliance and concern for others; to improve the quality of human life." I was beginning to run out of breath but I continued reading. "It fulfills this mission through services that are led by its volunteers and guided by its congressional charter. . . ." With another line still left to go, I had run out of breath. I stopped reading.

"So, can someone tell me," I asked the people seated at the table, "just what exactly it is that you people do?"

They began telling me, and what they had to say was impressive. On an average day, the American Red Cross in Greater New York responds to eight emergencies throughout the five boroughs of New York City, ranging from fires, building collapses, and water-main breaks to blackouts, blizzards, and hurricanes. Just a few days earlier, the organization had handled fifteen such emergencies in one twenty-four-hour period.

"The media knows us and respects us," says Leslie Gottlieb, director of communications and marketing. "They know we're there whenever there's an emergency. Our people usually arrive at the same time as the Fire Department. We're usually on the scene by the time reporters arrive."

Media visibility is not a problem for the organization, which recently got 244 mentions in the local media in a six-month period. And there is no shortage of willing hands to get the word out. Gottlieb oversees a staff of four full-time professionals and twenty volunteers.

The American Red Cross in Greater New York is a sizable operation. Overall, 175 people are on staff at the organization's Manhattan headquarters, and their efforts are augmented by another four thousand volunteers throughout the city. The organization's operating budget is over $6 million.

"The volunteers are incredible," says Gottlieb. "In a blackout or a blizzard, when we're called on to meet a difficult situation, our volunteers make their way through the dark or the snow to give of their time and expertise to help us help the people of the city."

I was impressed. Who wouldn't be?

"Who do you see as your target market?" I asked the board. "How are you getting your message to that market? What other target markets would you like to reach?"

We settled down to review the components of the organization's PR campaign. Together we explored a variety of new approaches to branding and positioning the organization that would enable it to reach new target markets. Like every other organization with a complex story to tell, the Red Cross works hard to make its mission and its message easily comprehensible and compelling to the public.

The American Red Cross in Greater New York is a large organization with a dedicated staff for public relations—and considerable success, as evidenced by their coverage in the media.

"But," says Gottlieb, "you use the same PR tools and skills whether you're working for a large organization or a small one, for a nonprofit with a big budget or one with no budget at all. You plan and follow professional standards, you push and push and push, and you get the media coverage. It's not just about being big and having resources. It's about having the skills and being persistent."

Many of the PR challenges faced by the Red Cross are rooted in the vast scope of its operations. Although all nonprofits strive to get their messages out, different organizations face different challenges.

The Adoptive Parents Committee: "Creating Families"

The Adoptive Parents Committee (APC) (www.adoptiveparents.org) can be described fairly as a small nonprofit. An all-volunteer organization founded in 1955, it is the oldest adoptive-parent support group in North America. Dedicated to improving all aspects of adoption and interim (foster) care, it receives no grants, no endowments, and no funding at all aside from what its two thousand member families throughout the tri-state New York area are able to contribute.

In marked contrast to the Red Cross, APC has neither staff nor budget for public relations, and yet every year, on the Sunday before Thanksgiving, nearly a thousand people attend APC's annual conference to learn about the challenges and rewards of adoption. People come by car, bus, train, and plane, often traveling for many hours, to attend workshops and seminars and learn from over one hundred experts about how adopting a baby can create families and change lives.

With no promotion budget, what brings all those people to APC's annual conference, held at the Brooklyn College campus of Long Island University? The answer, according to the organization's president, Alan Wasserman, is publicity—lots of publicity, and all of it free.

"We are an all-volunteer not-for-profit," Wasserman says, "and we work on a shoestring. We pay nobody. We ask people to volunteer from their hearts. The media responds to that."

Effective PR doesn't have to be about big budgets. It can also be about heart. A look at how APC and its annual conference get into the news is instructive. It reveals how nonprofits can use the tools and techniques presented in this book to fulfill their missions.

With no salaried public relations people on staff—or, for that matter, any unsalaried ones—public relations at the APC is a homemade operation. If members of the organization decide to promote an upcoming chapter meeting or event, they go ahead and do it as best they can. A case in point: to promote APC's twenty-fourth annual conference, Wasserman worked with his brother, a retired radio announcer, to prepare a series of radio public service announcements (PSAs). To maximize the chances that their PSA would be read on the air, he wrote it in the three standard lengths radio stations prefer, crafting spots of ten, thirty, and sixty seconds.

"My brother helped me time it out," Wasserman says, "and it was tricky. He taught me that you can have fifty-eight seconds, and that's OK for the sixty-second spot because it's close enough, and some announcers read a little faster or slower than others. The longer version was the easiest to prepare. I found I was adding adjectives to lengthen it. The shorter versions were trickier. It's hard to hit just the right number of words and still include the important information, like the name of the organization and details about the conference and the Web site and phone number. But it worked. The spot ran on many area radio stations, and we got a lot of response to it."

The APC also got the conference listed on the calendar of events of a local cable-access TV station, New York One, as well as on many local radio stations and in local newspapers.

Wasserman says, "One of our members contacted every media outlet she could think of, found out how they preferred to get the information, and then sent it out to them and followed up with phone calls. She said she didn't care if they thought she was a pain in the neck; it was important to get the conference listed. I told her not to think of herself as a pain in the neck but to consider it perseverance for a good cause."

The APC was also able to get free ads placed in local newspapers—for example, the Brooklyn section of the *New York Daily News*—and in magazines targeting parents, such as local editions of the magazines *Parents* and *Big Apple Parent*, again relying on no-cost PSAs. (In fact, placing print PSAs is a tactic used to great effect by many savvy nonprofits.) The APC promoted the conference on its Web site, which featured descriptions of the various workshops and a list of exhibitors so that visitors to the site could clearly see how they would benefit from attending. The APC site addressed concerns about the various methods of adoption available (the APC advocates for all legal forms of adoption) as well as about postadoption and parenting issues. The APC conference also received free postings on the Web sites of related organizations. Another tool used to promote the conference was the APC newsletter, *ADOPTALK,* which goes out to the organization's two thousand member families.

Wasserman says the organization has found that letters to the editor are effective in fostering awareness of adoption issues in the public consciousness. He has also found it helpful to link stories about the organization to events in the news, and to calendar listings.

"November is Adoption Month," he says, "so that's when the media is most receptive to our stories. Holding the conference the week before Thanksgiving fits in nicely with their schedules."

The Adoptive Parents Committee, with no PR staff or budget, employs a range of public relations tools to get the word out. It provides a good example of how basic skills combined with commitment and perseverance can have a real impact.

PR for nonprofits differs from PR in the for-profit world, and at the APC, a typical nonprofit with a mission, the bottom line has more to do with a sense of purpose than with fiscal goals. Wasserman, who adopted a baby boy himself nineteen years ago, sums up why he puts so much effort into furthering the organization's mission: "There's nothing that makes me feel as good as helping people form families through adoption."

Wasserman is convinced that "a small group of people can make a difference. If you have dedicated people and some basic skills, you can get people's attention. People want to help, and they will if you give them an opportunity. Media is not something negative. It's not something to be afraid of. If you can't afford professional PR, you can roll up your sleeves and do the job yourself. If you don't have the money, you have to have the sweat. Either way, to get the public's attention, you have to touch their hearts."

Making a Difference

The sense of satisfaction that comes from working for a cause is typical of people who work in the nonprofit world. Whether a nonprofit is large in scope and resources, like the American Red Cross, or more modest in both, like the Adoptive Parents Committee, working for a cause has a power all its own. Even though day-to-day realities sometimes get in the way of idealism, the core motivation remains.

One of the things that makes PR for nonprofits special is that it taps into that core of dedication and commitment. The resulting energy can move mountains. It can also generate great publicity.

In the PR classes and seminars I teach at NYU, I show people how to put the skills of public relations at the service of nonprofit organizations. Many of the people in my classes currently have well-paying jobs in corporate America but feel the urge to put their talents to work for causes in which they believe. Others are already working at nonprofits and want to learn skills that will enable them to advance within their organizations. Still others are involved with nonprofits as volunteers and want to bring more to their work or are thinking of moving from volunteer roles into staff positions. Some are preparing for a first job, and others making a midlife career change. Whatever the reasons behind their wanting to master the skills of public relations for nonprofits, they all have something in common. They all share an inner drive to do good, an irrepressible urge to fix the world. You can see it in their eyes and hear it in their voices when they speak about why they are involved with their organizations' missions. No matter the specific cause, it soon becomes clear that all of them are motivated by an inner need to accomplish something meaningful with their lives, to bring their time, energy, and talent to bear on something that has value for them personally. They feel compelled to make a difference.

Whether the focus of a nonprofit is on issues of health, the environment, religion, education, the arts, social action, or community, or some combination of several, or something altogether different, the ability to mobilize people on behalf of the cause comes down to effective public relations. PR in the service of nonprofits is the essential, invaluable, and irreplaceable tool on which everything else depends.

In my classes, I teach people how to use the tools of public relations to rally support for a cause and accomplish an organization's mission. I present guidelines for using each tool, along with plenty of actual case histories. This book follows the same pattern.

What You Will Learn from This Book

The book, designed as a kind of "apprenticeship between covers," includes step-by-step guides for creating and using essential PR tools. It also presents a host of revealing real-life examples illustrating how people at a broad range of nonprofits have handled a variety of PR challenges. Taken as a whole, this book comprises a handbook and comprehensive guide to the field of PR for nonprofits.

The book is structured in three parts. Part One, "Getting Started," consists of two chapters and deals with creating a PR plan. This is the section of the book that lays the groundwork for everything that follows. Chapter One looks at identifying target markets—determining who you want to reach. Chapter Two looks at setting goals and shaping the key message points that will be communicated. The chapter also looks at choosing the most effective ways to get your message to your target and creating an effective PR plan.

Part Two, "The PR Toolkit," is the largest section of the book. Chapters Three through Sixteen explore a variety of PR tools and skills for getting your organization's message out. The skills considered range from writing and placing media advisories and news releases to pitching a story to radio and TV stations to dealing with satellite uplinks and handling special events.

Part Three, "Monitoring the PR Campaign," like Part One, consists of two chapters. Chapter Seventeen deals with reviewing and revising the PR plan and looks at measuring the plan's success and making necessary adjustments. Chapter Eighteen looks at the importance of keeping stakeholders informed and reveals how PR practitioners handle that vital task at a variety of nonprofits.

The purpose of this book is to provide the essential tools and skills necessary to mount an effective PR campaign. The techniques presented are based on many years of hands-on experience by PR practitioners at scores of nonprofits who have used them with great success. Any organization—big, small, or in between—can create and run a successful PR campaign by using the principles in this book. All you have to add is the perseverance.

People at nonprofits do not dream small dreams. Their goals, like their dreams, are writ large. Effective PR can help those dreams become realities.

New York, New York   Art Feinglass
March 2005

To my lovely daughters, Ronit and Dannah, who have always filled my life with joy. And to Lynn, with deep gratitude for everything. Without her this book would not have been written.

THE AUTHOR

Art Feinglass is the founder and president of Access Communications, Inc., a New York–based firm doing public relations and training for nonprofits and corporations. An adjunct professor at New York University, he teaches courses in Public Relations for Nonprofits at the George H. Heyman, Jr. Center for Philanthropy and Fundraising.

Feinglass has more than twenty years of experience in the nonprofit world. He currently serves on the Communications Advisory Committee of the American Red Cross in Greater New York and was formerly director of public relations for American ORT. His company's nonprofit clients include the Association of Junior Leagues, the Brooklyn College Foundation, and the Episcopal Theological Seminary of the Southwest.

Feinglass and his programs have been featured in numerous media, including *The New York Times, Business Week, Crain's, Entrepreneur*, and the Fox television network. A member of the Dramatists Guild whose plays have been produced off-Broadway, he has also written for the Comedy Central television network. His articles have appeared in *Consulting Today, Nation's Business, Training and Development, Sales and Marketing Excellence*, and *Successful Meetings*.

He can be contacted at www.artfeinglass.com.

THE PUBLIC RELATIONS HANDBOOK FOR NONPROFITS

PART ONE

GETTING STARTED

Many organizations undertake public relations campaigns out of the conviction that they are the best-kept secrets in their fields. The common cry is something like "Nobody knows who we are or what we do. We need visibility!"

If a public relations campaign does achieve greater visibility for an organization, can the results really have a positive impact on the nonprofit's bottom line? The answer is definitely yes.

Pat Smith, executive vice president at Rubenstein Associates, Inc., likes to quote a college president for whom he managed a PR campaign. "Publicity does not make my phone ring," the president said. "But publicity does make people more ready to take my phone call." Effective PR enhances the ability of a college to attract the best teachers and the brightest students, the superior coaches and the most talented athletes—things that are the stuff of winning appeals to alumni associations. Effective PR can have similar bottom-line results for every nonprofit.

The tools and techniques outlined in these pages are the basis of any effective PR campaign. The real-life case histories provide instructive guidelines on using PR to achieve media recognition and motivate supporters. Nonprofits have important missions to accomplish; effective PR can help them do it.

Part One of this book is appropriately titled "Getting Started." It consists of two chapters and begins, as any discussion of public relations should, with a chapter on identifying target markets. To create an effective PR plan, every nonprofit, whether large, small, or somewhere in between, must be very clear about who it is trying to reach.

Chapter One provides guidelines for determining exactly who are the people that make up an organization's target market and for designing a PR campaign to reach them. Like all the other chapters in the book, it combines step-by-step guides with actual case histories that illustrate how people at a range of nonprofits practice PR in real life.

Chapter Two takes the next step. After you have identified the people who comprise your target market, what, exactly, do you want them to know about your organization, and what, exactly, do you want them to do? This is where goal setting comes in—and, again, it is important to be specific. If you don't know what you are trying to accomplish, you will have no way of measuring success or failure and no way to make needed adjustments to your plan. Having decided on your target and your goals, you need to be very clear about your message. Chapter Two looks at the importance of crafting a message that will resonate with the target audience. It also explores how to build an effective media list and establish relationships with the media. Then, with the groundwork laid, it is time to create the PR plan, and Chapter Two also provides guidelines for doing that. Each part of the plan must be broken down into its constituent elements, with timelines established for the various steps along the way. Responsibility for each part of the plan must be assigned so that all the people involved know exactly what they are expected to do and when they are expected to do it. It has been said that a plan is a dream with a deadline. A PR plan is a series of very specific deadlines, a plan that enables a nonprofit's dreams to become reality.

CHAPTER ONE

IDENTIFYING TARGET MARKETS

Saving Lives: New Jersey Search and Rescue

At 2:30 on an unseasonably chilly October morning, Oren Levin was awakened at his New Jersey home by his emergency beeper. The call from the Bergen County Office of Emergency Management informed him that two hikers were missing somewhere in the wild reaches of Campgaw Mountain Reservation.

Earlier that night, park police had found the couple's empty car in the camp parking lot—the only car still there, long after all the other hikers had left. Following standard procedure, and recognizing that finding the lost hikers was going to require people with special capability, the Parks Department had contacted the Bergen County Police, who in turn brought in the Bergen County Office of Emergency Management, which immediately alerted Levin.

Levin, a lieutenant in New Jersey Search and Rescue, Inc. (NJSAR) (www.njsar. org), quickly put the word out via the emergency Swift Reach Program. By 3:00 A.M., twenty members of NJSAR, all highly trained and experienced in wilderness survival and rescue skills, had rendezvoused at the park to begin the search for the lost couple.

With a professionalism born of long experience and training, the NJSAR team entered the woods to begin executing a standard search pattern. The temperature was dropping, and a storm was on the way. The missing couple would be at serious risk of exposure if not found quickly. Time was the enemy.

New Jersey Search and Rescue is a nonprofit organization whose ninety members meet at the Bergen County Law and Public Safety Institute. NJSAR receives no funding from any private or governmental agency. Members supply their own equipment and train for rescue missions in their spare time. One of the largest search-and-rescue teams in the state, NJSAR is a member of the Search and Rescue Council of New Jersey (www.sarcnj.org), which has thirty search teams statewide. Because search-and-rescue groups regularly call on each other for support, NJSAR has worked in wilderness areas throughout New Jersey and in neighboring New York and Pennsylvania.

Despite the life-and-death nature of the service the organization performs, the public generally does not know that NJSAR exists—not surprising, since the organization does not conduct any public relations (PR) operations targeted at the public.

"We don't respond to a request for a search unless the request comes from a government agency," Levin says, "so we've worked to establish relationships with police and fire departments and other agencies that may call on us."

And NJSAR has been very successful in reaching out to that target market. The organization regularly has a display table or a booth at conferences of the New Jersey State Emergency Management Association, at the annual New Jersey First Aid Conference, and at the annual Bergen County Law and Public Safety Exposition. NJSAR hands out fact sheets about the organization to people who may one day call on NJSAR's services. NJSAR distributes pocket calendars bearing the organization's name to New Jersey park police and police chiefs. And the group relies heavily on its Web site, www.njsar.org.

"Getting the Web site up is important," says Levin. "Government agencies in need of rescue teams have told us they found us through our Web site. We also use it a lot for internal communication with our members, posting meeting notices and other information on the site where everyone can access it easily. As for publicity in the local media, to tell the general public about what we do—basically, there isn't any."

This lack of visibility in the media is not due to any shortage of great stories to tell but, as for many other nonprofits, to a lack of focus on public relations. In this all-volunteer group, whose members all have jobs and families and countless demands on their time, the feeling is that no one has the necessary leisure to devote to public relations. But this is certainly not to say that a wealth of raw material for public relations doesn't exist. For example, a TV station in Albany, New York, shot and aired footage of a NJSAR team engaged in a dramatic search for an elderly man lost in the woods. CNN taped and aired scenes of NJSAR on a wilderness training exercise. In both cases, NJSAR has been offered the footage. The professionally shot material could be used to make promotional videos for screening at conferences and expositions. It could also be used for public service announcements (PSAs) to be aired on local television stations. Another use would be as a B-roll (that is, background footage) provided to TV stations interested in doing stories on the organization, to save them the time and expense of shooting the footage themselves, and to make the prospect of doing a story more appealing. But no one at NJSAR has the time to deal with recycled video.

NJSAR also has a wealth of great human interest stories that would be perfect for local print and electronic media. As a case in point, a local kindergarten class was studying good deeds. The class decided that every time a pupil in the class did a good deed, that pupil would put a penny in a jar. As part of their class project, the kindergartners studied search-and-rescue dogs. Eventually the kids collected $84 in pennies and decided that they wanted to use the money to buy a search-and-rescue dog. Levin and another member of NJSAR came to the class with a dog and talked to the kids about the role that dogs play in the search-and-rescue process. The kids sat listening wide-eyed, and at the end of the talk they all gathered around the dog, hugging and petting him. It was a scene that begged to be photographed and run in a local newspaper along with a story about NJSAR. TV loves pictures, and the story would have made a great segment on the evening news. But no story appeared in the newspapers, and no segment ran on TV. No one was interviewed on any of the local radio stations. There was no media coverage at all.

For nonprofits of all kinds, this is an all-too-common story. Many nonprofits have equally compelling stories that go untold in the media. These organizations are not getting the public recognition they deserve for the good work they do, and they often refer to themselves as well-kept secrets. But nonprofits find that being PR-savvy pays. Getting stories in the press, or on radio or TV, can boost an organization's visibility and credibility, help increase membership, and enhance fundraising.

The basics of PR are fairly simple and straightforward. PR does not have to consume inordinate amounts of an organization's time or money. Public relations can help an organization achieve its goals. This book shows how.

As for the couple lost in the woods on that cold October night, NJSAR found them later that day—cold, hungry, and frightened, and scratched and bruised from too many close encounters with tree branches in the dark woods, but otherwise safe and sound . . . and very grateful to the men and women of New Jersey Search and Rescue.

Carousels for Ants

I teach a class at New York University on PR for nonprofits, based on my twenty-five years of experience in the field. For fifteen of those years I was director of public relations for American ORT, a nonprofit organization that supports vocational training programs for young people and adults in fifty countries around the world. I founded and am president today of Access Communications, Inc., a New York–based public relations and training firm that works with corporations and nonprofits in the areas of health care, education, the arts, and community service. My class is based on real-life examples of public relations in action.

The students are either working in nonprofit public relations or very much want to be. Some work at small neighborhood nonprofits that help homeless children or counsel inner-city teens or support dance troupes. Others work at larger organizations like the New Jersey Symphony Orchestra, the American Cancer Society, and the United Nations. Some make a living in the for-profit sector but feel a need to use their talents and abilities to work at something they feel is more personally meaningful. In my class, they seek the skills to help them make a change in their lives. They come from all over the United States and also from overseas, eager to learn how to use PR to mobilize support and raise money to help disaster victims in Armenia, train doctors in Poland, care for unwed mothers in Chile, and support the aged in Japan. Over the course of several recent semesters, I've had students from a Catholic high school in Connecticut, an Episcopal seminary in Austin, a Jewish synagogue on Manhattan's Upper West Side, and a Moslem cultural organization in New Jersey. They all want to learn how to use public relations on behalf of nonprofit organizations they care about. Many hope that PR will help them generate the money their organizations need to continue operations. Others need the publicity to bring in grants and municipal support. Still others urgently need to expand their groups' membership. They all believe that PR can help them achieve their goals. It can, and I show them how.

I begin the first class every semester by getting to know the students and their goals. And then I hand out the eggbeaters.

The students gather in groups of five or six, and each group gets one eggbeater. The assignment is to spend three minutes coming up with every possible use they can think of for an eggbeater—except beating eggs.

There is always a moment or two of hesitation while they exchange looks, trying to figure out what eggbeaters have to do with public relations. But then someone cranks a handle and says, "You could use it as a fan." And someone else asks, "How about a hair curler?" Another person tentatively suggests, "Maybe a back massager?"

Soon ideas are flying fast and furious. "A cat toy." "A wrist exerciser." "A carousel for ants." One silly idea leads to another, and soon everyone is laughing and tossing around off-the-wall suggestions. Even after I call "Time," people keep coming up with new ideas. And that, of course, is the point.

As I collect the eggbeaters, I point out that the class has just engaged in an impromptu brainstorming session. When you are brainstorming, any idea, no matter how seemingly silly or illogical, can be put forward without fear of ridicule. Most of the ideas people come up with are unworkable. And that's fine; that's what is supposed to happen in a freewheeling brainstorming session. But among all the impractical ideas are always several that are actually pretty good. Unconventional, perhaps, maybe even weird, but good nonetheless. That is what comes from thinking "out of the box."

The Nonprofit Difference

PR for nonprofits has things in common with PR in the for-profit sector, but some aspects are unique to the nonprofit world. The mind-set of supporters and professionals alike—that they are engaged in fulfilling a significant mission, as opposed to increasing a corporate bottom line—influences the choices that are made and how those choices are implemented. There are other differences as well.

"Nonprofits often face greater hurdles in getting their messages heard," according to Howard J. Rubenstein, founder and president of Rubenstein Associates, Inc. (www.rubenstein.com), one of the nation's largest independent public relations firms, whose clients range from the New York Yankees and BMW to the New York Philharmonic and UJA-Federation. "Because they usually have fewer resources, nonprofits need to find creative ways to get out their message. And they need to be persistent when it comes to pitching stories."

Ken Sunshine, founder and president of Ken Sunshine Consultants, a leading public relations firm that handles celebrities like Ben Affleck, describes the "nonprofit difference" in starker terms: "When it comes to publicity, many nonprofits don't have a clue."

Limited resources are a reality for many nonprofits. But many nonprofits, despite sometimes being looked down on by the for-profit world as "not ready for prime time," have an impressive record of success in getting their messages out to the media.

To be effective, a PR campaign for a nonprofit organization must take into account the goals and expectations of everyone involved: supporters, volunteers, staff, the population being served, and the media. With sound planning and some out-of-the-box thinking, an effective PR campaign can play a major role in helping an organization accomplish its goals.

PR: The Essential Element

There are 1.2 million nonprofit organizations in the United States, and they all need good public relations. PR is the key to survival for nonprofits, especially in hard economic times. Effective PR is essential to raising money, attracting members, energizing supporters, and fulfilling the organization's mission.

With the proliferation of charities in recent years, all pursuing the same sources of support, competition among nonprofits has become fierce. As resources shrink and needs continue to grow, that competition has gotten tougher than ever. Whether the goal is running a successful bake sale or launching a $10 million campaign, effective PR can mean the difference between success and failure.

Most of the support for nonprofits—76 percent—comes from individuals. In a weak economy, individuals cut back on their support. And they aren't the only ones. With profits down, corporations have also devoted less to philanthropy, as have the foundations that contribute to some 700,000 public charities, since their assets are tied to the stock market. The needs of a larger population must now be met with resources drawn from a shrinking pool of contributions. The result is increasing competition among nonprofits for limited resources.

Beating the Competition

One obvious goal of any public relations campaign is to stand out from the crowd. And when it comes to nonprofits, there is always a crowd.

People in the nonprofit world often don't like to think of themselves as being in competition in the way that businesses are. But the competition is there just the same, and it can be ferocious.

No matter what your organization's field of activity—health care, community service, education, the arts, environmental protection, promotion of cultural activities, historical preservation, or any other worthwhile cause—you are, in effect, in competition with all the other organizations that specialize in the same area. And not only are you competing with your sister organizations, you are also in de facto competition with organizations that operate in other areas. Despite the focus of your efforts, the odds are that you and your competitors are reaching out to many of the same people.

The reality is that people usually don't support just one organization. More typically, they support concerns ranging from the local to the global. It is not unusual for one person to support his local library, homeless shelter, and symphony orchestra while being involved with organizations that protect whales in the Pacific or support medical research in the Amazon or care for orphans in Africa. And then there is your organization, trying desperately to be heard above the clamor. That one individual may receive letters, appeals, and newsletters from literally dozens of organizations, all asking for attention and support. Therefore, one obvious job that your public relations efforts should accomplish is to help your organization stand out from the background noise by making a personal connection. In more hard-nosed terms, public relations can be a tool to help you beat the competition.

The Public Theater

Like many performing arts organizations, the Public Theater in New York (www.publictheater.org) is a nonprofit that seeks to bring performers and audiences together. Originally founded by Joseph Papp as the Shakespeare Workshop, it is "dedicated to embracing the complexities of contemporary society and nurturing both artists and audiences." According to executive director Mara Manus, doing that places the Public Theater in the ring with some stiff competition. "So many cultural institutions are nonprofits operating with limited funds for marketing and publicity," she observes. "They often find themselves competing with much larger and better-funded operations like Hollywood films and Broadway shows."

Manus knows the "competition" at first hand. She was a studio executive for many years at Universal and also served stints at Warner Brothers and Columbia. Compared to the marketing budgets for Hollywood films, the promotional resources available to an off-Broadway theater are, to be kind, modest. "To achieve any visibility," she says, "requires creativity and developing personal relationships with the media."

Hitting Your Targets

Before you can hit a target, before you can even take aim, you have to be clear about what you want to hit. For a nonprofit, that means realistically identifying and defining its target markets. Note the plural: an organization doesn't have just one market; it has several, each market with its own specific needs that must be addressed. The first thing, then, is to clearly identify those target markets and understand exactly what they need.

For each target market, ask who are you trying to reach. Who do you want to get your message to? Identify the people who care about what you do, or who would care if they knew about your organization. The more you know about the people you are trying to reach, the better job you'll do of reaching them.

Kathryn Kimmel is vice president of marketing and communications for the Gemological Institute of America (GIA) (www.gia.edu), a large nonprofit in the jewelry industry. Her duties include responsibility for GIA's considerable public relations campaigns. Her advice is to focus the PR message on what she calls "key constituents, or stakeholders." According to Kimmel, "Audiences, communities, individuals, and organizations that are affected by what your organization does, or who have an interest in your organization, are your constituents or stakeholders. They must be your primary, though not only, focus of communications. Know who they are, what their needs and interests are, and the various ways you can best communicate with them."

To return to the example of New Jersey Search and Rescue, NJSAR's target markets are fairly typical for a nonprofit organization. One market is the people being served—in this case, people who need to be found and rescued. Another market is the police and fire departments and other agencies that call on NJSAR's services. Still another market comprises the volunteers who deliver NJSAR's service—the club members who actually go out on the search-and-rescue missions. Then there are the organization's supporters and potential supporters. Plenty of people would be happy to write checks if they knew about the group. Others would be pleased to donate equipment and supplies. It may be possible to generate substantial corporate support and find companies that would be willing to supply equipment in exchange for some of the favorable publicity the group can generate. Still another market is the media, always hungry for good stories. Meeting that need, providing the stories, would mean getting coverage in local and regional newspapers as well as on radio and TV. That coverage in turn would make people aware that New Jersey Search and Rescue is available to help whenever there is a need, and that awareness would lead to more of the rescues that are the organization's mission.

Being clear about your target markets and about how to reach them allows you to focus your public relations efforts for maximum effect. The results can be quite remarkable, particularly where local publicity is concerned.

Variety of Target Markets

It is not unusual for a nonprofit to deal with a variety of target markets. Lynn Uhlfelder Berman, senior media relations manager at YAI/National Institute for People with Disabilities (www.yai.org), concentrates on getting her organization's message out to them all.

"Defining our target markets can be tricky," Berman says, "because there are so many audiences that we have to reach. There are two types of audiences for our materials—internal and external. I consider the internal target market to be our existing consumers and their families, our staff, current donors, people who are already connected to us. We also want to reach external targets, like families who have a child with a developmental or learning disability, and organizations that make referrals, such as hospitals and professionals in the field, so that they can learn from our expertise. This is an important part of our mission, since many of our programs serve as national models. We also want to reach potential donors and foundations, medical professionals, and government officials."

To reach her various markets, Berman targets the mainstream media and has had consistent success placing stories in major metropolitan papers like *The New York Times* and the *New York Daily News* as well as on local TV stations like WABC. She also targets selected professional journals in order to reach the medical community.

Berman isn't alone in confronting a variety of target markets. Cedric Bess, PR manager for the Public Relations Society of America (PRSA) (www.prsa.org), says that the association offers the following definition of the role of public relations: "Public relations helps an organization and its publics adapt to each other." Bess's group identifies no fewer than seven different target markets, or "publics," with which nonprofits must communicate: employees, members, customers, local communities, shareholders, other institutions, and society at large. And the message often needs to be shaped differently for each of those markets.

Internal Markets

An organization's "internal market" is also very important and should not be neglected or overlooked, advises Alicia Evans, president of Total Image Communications, a New York–based PR consulting firm. Evans, who is also president of the New York chapter of the National Black Public Relations Society (www.nbprs.org), says, "Even a small nonprofit with limited resources can do a simple newsletter, either printed or online, for distribution to internal staff and volunteers. You can find free templates online that are simple to use and look attractive and serve well as excellent communication vehicles. Whatever vehicles are used, keeping up an ongoing communication is essential."

Pooch Publicity

When a municipal animal shelter in New Jersey was informed that budget cuts would force it to close its doors in just eight days, the operators despaired of finding homes for the shelter's 103 dogs. Any dog not adopted in those final eight days would be put to sleep. A local resident, Dr. Paul Hartunian, decided to help.

Hartunian, a veteran publicist and an avid dog lover, is also the cofounder, with Mary Cody, of a dog shelter called Aunt Mary's Doghouse (www. AuntMarysDoghouse.com). With time running out, he wrote a one-page press release and sent it to all the local media. The response was immediate, as it had to be, and in the shelter's final week of operation, all but four of the dogs were adopted by local residents, and rescue workers took those four. In the end, not one dog was put down. Such is the power of knowing how to use local publicity.

Kathryn Kimmel of GIA also encourages the use of internal newsletters: "Remember your internal audience. Some of your greatest advocates and communicators are within your organization. They have family members, neighbors, friends, and relatives who they constantly share information with." Newsletters, she says, because they ensure that the organization's internal audience is frequently updated, "can help to form a significant sphere of influence. Members of the organization should be the first to know, as much as is appropriate."

In summary, then, it is the job of a good PR campaign to identify the nonprofit organization's markets, recognize the specific needs of those markets, and then effectively meet those needs. Not every nonprofit is involved with matters of life and death, but many do touch people's lives in very significant ways. It takes planning, organization, and an appreciation of how the process works, but the nonprofit organization, by defining its various markets and understanding what they need, can develop PR strategies to accomplish its mission.

The Media as a Market

The *Weekly Reporter–Chronicle–Herald News–Examiner*

To be effective, a nonprofit must serve the needs of the media. The media are focused on the need for good stories to tell, and for reliable sources of information to tell them. Media professionals appreciate people who help them to do their job. To get a better appreciation of what media people want, try putting yourself in their shoes.

Imagine, for example, that you are the editor of a small-town newspaper. Say it's a weekly. Maybe it is called the *Weekly Reporter* or the *Chronicle* or the *Herald News* or the *Examiner* or some combination. Let's call it the *Chronicle-Herald*. What does the editor of the *Chronicle-Herald* want? Well, for one thing, she wants to sell advertising. Lots of advertising. As much advertising as possible.

But why would someone want to advertise in a relatively small-circulation local paper like the *Chronicle-Herald*? Why, for example, would a local hardware store choose to run an ad week after week? The obvious answer is that potential customers will see the ad, which is why all the advertisers in the paper have chosen to spend part of their advertising budget with the *Chronicle-Herald*.

Advertising is a tricky thing, as much art as science. In a later chapter, we'll look at the mechanics in greater depth. For now, a brief quotation will help make the point. The department store mogul Sam Wanamaker once said, "I know that 50 percent of my advertising is wasted. I just don't know which 50 percent." This is a problem for all advertisers. Part of the advertising budget is wasted. But which part? In the uncertain world of advertising, the local hardware store can be sure of one thing—many of its potential customers read the *Chronicle-Herald*.

Why? Take a look at any local paper. You'll see stories and photos, lots of photos, about local people. There will be articles about the high school football team, the local fire department, area museums, the library, the Founder's Day parade, the yachting regatta, and the annual flower show. You'll find flattering profiles of retirees with interesting hedges around their property, and photos of kids flying kites in the park. It is a natural tendency of people to want to read about themselves and their neighbors. And so the editor runs those stories and photos in the *Chronicle-Herald* to make the paper appealing to local readers. The editor works at building up a large readership because that is what gives the paper its appeal to local advertisers.

What the editor wants are stories that will interest readers. Stories about people. Human interest stories. Warm, funny, touching, interesting stories that will keep readers reading and advertisers advertising.

"The local press can be an invaluable resource for nonprofits," observes Howard Rubenstein. "People really read their local papers. Placing a story in a small neighborhood weekly can result in a lot of visibility for a nonprofit that needs to be noticed in the community. Never underestimate the value of such a placement. In addition to the local impact, such stories can be leveraged into national coverage in the print and electronic media."

The Montclair Historical Society, or Why Is Everybody Smiling?

Understanding exactly what an editor needs is the first step in knowing how to meet that editor's needs. In the case of the *Chronicle-Herald*, locally slanted human interest stories are the ideal. All you have to do is provide them.

A good example is provided by Kathleen Zaracki, a trustee of the Montclair Historical Society (www.montclairhistorical.org). Montclair is a New Jersey town blessed with a rich local history. The town was founded when New Jersey was one of the thirteen colonies, and Zaracki finds its history fascinating. But she realized that the average resident of the town, and the typical reader of the town's weekly newspaper, might not fully share her enthusiasm for local history. Wanting to get the historical society some publicity and lay the groundwork for the spring fundraising campaign, she decided that she needed to get the organization into the local paper with a story that would excite local interest.

Working with executive director Alicia Schatteman, her first step was to create an event that would get local kids onto the site of one of the town's historic houses. They invited the press, of course. At the event, they arranged groups of adorably photogenic kids listening with rapt attention to a storyteller dressed in a quaint costume of the colonial period. They also held a colonial crafts fair, where other kids learned how to make model birdhouses and corncob dolls. They worked with the paper's photographer to make sure she got a lot of appealing photos.

White Gloves and Pearls

When I gave a seminar in Orlando, Florida, on public relations and marketing for two hundred presidents-elect of the Association of Junior Leagues International (www.ajli.org), I asked the attendees who they considered their target markets to be. The women had flown in from cities all over America and were a sharp, savvy group determined to be effective as new presidents of their local Junior Leagues.

We began by looking at the mission statement that appears on the organization's Web site and literature: "The Junior Leagues are organizations of women committed to promoting volunteerism, developing the potential of women and improving the community through effective action and leadership of trained volunteers. Our purpose is exclusively educational and charitable."

Very impressive. Then I asked the new presidents about the organization's image: "What do people in your communities think of when they hear the name 'Junior League'?"

The answer came back, in an assortment of regional accents, from women throughout the room. "White gloves!" A few voices added to the chorus: "White gloves and *pearls!*"

All the women in the room were laughing now and nodding to each other as they agreed that, whatever the official wording, the image of the Junior League was the white-gloves-and-pearls set. What, they asked, could they do about that?

We continued identifying the chapters' various target markets. A woman from Atlanta suggested that one target market for the Junior League message was the organization's members. I wrote "Members" on my flipchart.

"Potential members," a woman from Boston proposed. I wrote down "Potential members."

A woman from the Midwest said, "Supporters." That was followed by "Potential supporters" from a Seattle woman. Then the suggestions slacked off.

"Any other target markets?" I asked. "Who else do you want to get your message out to?" A local Orlando woman put her hand up and hesitantly asked, "The media?"

I wrote down "The media."

We spent the next twenty minutes coming up with answers to the question of why the media should be interested in what the local Junior Leagues were doing. The answers focused on the projects that the Junior League chapters carried out in their communities, and on the fact that so many people were touched by these efforts and benefited from them. We looked at how stories could be shaped and pitched to the media, stories about things that the Junior Leagues were already doing.

> Then we addressed the white-gloves-and-pearls question. Did it matter to the media? Wasn't the real story the tremendous impact for good that the local Junior Leagues had on their communities? How could that message be conveyed to this "other" market, the media? By providing the media with good stories in a form that could easily be used.
>
> The rest of the presentation dealt with PR tools, but the presidents-elect had begun to see the media for what it is—another important target market.

Editors love warm stories and photos of local residents because they know that their readers like them, and if readers like them, so do advertisers. In this case, the photos worked so well that in addition to photos that appeared on the front page, another series of photos ran inside the paper along with a profile of the historical society, which got it some much needed attention around town. These pages also made wonderful reprints for later promotional use. Because Kathleen Zaracki understood the specific needs of her market, she was able to meet those needs and get her organization a valuable spotlight that helped launch that year's fundraising campaign.

What holds true for small local papers works equally well for the large metropolitan dailies. The circulation of *The New York Times* or the *Seattle Post-Intelligencer* may dwarf that of the small-town *Chronicle-Herald*, but understanding an editor's needs and knowing how to meet them works the same way for the major press.

The same basic principles operate for coverage on radio and television as well. Understanding what the media need and packaging the materials properly can get your organization the support it deserves, and that support can work miracles. It can even put a man on the moon.

The Wisdom of Sun Tzu

The Chinese philosopher Sun Tzu, who wrote *The Art of War* around 500 B.C.E., is frequently quoted in business books. Many of his principles for running a war are adapted for the executive running a business. His goal was to teach generals how to win a war through wise maneuvers rather than costly battles.

Sun Tzu's writings also provide valuable insights for nonprofits. "Know your enemy and know yourself," he wrote, "and in one hundred battles you will never be defeated."

In place of the word *enemy*, try substituting other words. Try the word *volunteers*. Try *supporters*. Try *media*. They all work. Not that volunteers, supporters, and the media are your enemies, but they are on the other side of the equation from you.

Boxes of Love

Every Thanksgiving, in eighteen cities nationwide, an organization called Here's Life Inner City (www.hlic.org) distributes "Boxes of Love," containing the ingredients for a Thanksgiving dinner with all the trimmings to families in need. Meredith Gandy, who helps to run the New York operation, notes that Here's Life Inner City works with two different kinds of volunteers for the Boxes of Love project.

"One group of volunteers," says Gandy, "comes from inner-city churches. They are a part of the workforce that assembles the boxes, and they are the ones who deliver them to needy families in their own communities, often their own neighbors. The other type of volunteers at the 'packing party' are the non-inner-city people. They come to help because they are following their religious convictions to care for the poor. They are generally more affluent and more educated; they don't usually go out to distribute. Sometimes they are also donors, but not necessarily."

What the people being served need is relatively simple: to connect with the turkey dinners. To meet those needs, Here's Life Inner City has to let them know the turkey dinners are available and how they can be obtained, something that is generally done through local churches.

Now consider the volunteers who give their time to the organization, assembling Thanksgiving in a cardboard box. They need the tools to do the job. In this case, the term *tools* can mean the turkey dinners themselves. Tools may also include the actual physical spaces where those turkey dinners are assembled and the tables and the boxes too. In a sense, the volunteers themselves are also tools, providing the willing hands that get the turkey dinners out to where they are needed.

The volunteers have needs, too. They need to know that their efforts are valued and appreciated. Although they are not being paid a salary, they are not working for nothing. They are working for the sense of accomplishment and pride and fulfillment of their religious convictions that comes as a result of helping others less fortunate.

In addition to the volunteers who literally roll up their sleeves to get the job done, Here's Life Inner City counts on a nationwide network of supporters who provide the funding. As Gandy notes, an organization's volunteers and its supporters are not always the same people. In the case of the organization's Thanksgiving project, many of the supporters do actually show up each year to pack Boxes of Love and see that they are delivered to the people that need them. But most of the organization's supporters neither pack nor deliver. What they do is write checks. Those supporters are another market that the organization has to consider, and they are as vital as anything and anyone else in the whole operation.

To reach that market of supporters and potential supporters, the organization needs another set of tools: information tools to help raise the funds that keep all the wheels turning. The organization needs materials that will get people excited and enthusiastic about the organization's goals. That can mean printed materials like brochures, flyers, newsletters, and annual reports. Information tools can also include electronic and digital tools, such as videos and DVDs, the organization's Web site, and e-mail news releases.

The media can be seen as another market. Media coverage is essential to letting the world know about the Box of Love project. Getting the word out makes it possible to raise more money for turkeys, to enlist more volunteers to help with the packing and distribution, and to attract more supporters and more contributions to make all the rest possible.

The media need good stories to tell. Here's Life Inner City has to meet that need by preparing the kind of material the media can readily use. By doing it right, the organization vastly increases its media coverage. Increased media coverage generates increased support, which makes it possible for the organization to reach more of the people it serves.

How Public Relations Put a Man on the Moon

When President John F. Kennedy announced that the United States of America was going to put a man on the moon, he turned to the National Aeronautics and Space Administration (NASA) to get the job done. The people at NASA realized their first task was to raise public support for the program. A journalist who asked the heads of NASA what actually got those huge rockets off the launch pad and up into outer space probably expected a complicated explanation having to do with the laws of physics. The answer he got was far simpler: "Funding." The funding came from Congress, and what got Congress to vote for those funds was the public's enthusiasm for the space program.

That is why NASA decided to make national heroes of the astronauts in the space program. Tom Wolfe tells the story in *The Right Stuff*. John Glenn and Gus Grissom and the rest of America's first astronauts became household names because NASA knew that the public would not respond to abstract theories of aerospace and higher mathematics and geopolitics. People respond to stories about people—people they feel they know, people they have come to care about. NASA excited the public's imagination about the space program, and the resulting support made it possible to put a man on the moon, ahead of schedule. It was public relations that put a man on the moon, and if public relations can do that, think of how far it can take your organization.

New York Cares: Understanding the Market

Supplying what supporters want, giving that market what it needs, is the job of an effective PR campaign.

New York Cares (www.nycares.org) is a nonprofit that has great success in New York City every year mobilizing thousands of volunteers, who give time on weekends and evenings to help New Yorkers in need and to clean up, repair, and paint schools and community playgrounds around the city. According to Colleen Farrell, senior director of communications, approximately twenty-seven thousand New Yorkers volunteer with New York Cares each year. Volunteers come to New York Cares by word of mouth, the Internet, and traditional marketing and also through partnerships with local corporations who send employee teams to serve on corporate service projects. The agency's Web site is the primary tool New York Cares uses to engage and manage its large corps of volunteers.

New York Cares' team-based volunteer projects are especially popular with young, single New Yorkers. While working on a project, volunteers have an opportunity to spend informal time together in a pressure-free, nonwork setting. The good works of New York Cares are made possible in part by the agency's recognition that people tend to get involved with a nonprofit for many reasons, some of which involve giving back to others, while others focus on meeting other people and building social connections.

The agency has many supporters, from foundations to government, individuals to corporate donors. Major corporations in New York City have their own reasons for getting involved. Being involved with New York Cares enables corporations to demonstrate that they are good corporate citizens of the city, both through financial contributions and through direct service done by their employee volunteers. In addition to providing substantial financial support, corporations are a source of new ongoing volunteers, who may join New York Cares on their own after participating in corporate service.

Community service projects lend themselves to great photos that ultimately appear in company newsletters and local newspapers. Local TV likes the stories because they are visually interesting and show people coming together to help others. New York Cares gets significant media coverage for its work every year and that, in turn, fuels the support the organization needs to operate.

Because it understands the appeal of its programs to its corporate market and individual volunteers, New York Cares' brochures and marketing materials include information about the impact of its projects, as well as photos of smiling volunteers—typically young, attractive New Yorkers looking cool in their T-shirts with the red New York Cares logo. Marketing materials demonstrate that volunteers are having fun as they spend a day working on behalf of their community. Furthermore, there are several examples of volunteers meeting Mr. or Ms. Right through their volunteer work with New York Cares. New York Cares' model of flexible, team-based volunteering for busy New Yorkers became the model for scores of other organizations around the country. Due in large measure to an understanding of what its various markets need, New York Cares continues to grow and attract new volunteers and new corporate supporters.

The better you know the people you are trying to reach, the better you will be able to reach them. Take the time and effort to do research and find out about the people in your target markets. The kind of information you're looking for is often called *demographics* and includes things like age, sex, educational level, profession, annual income, marital status, number of children, number of cars owned, political affiliations, religious preferences, number of vacations taken annually and to where, credit cards used, magazines and newspapers subscribed to, pets, hobbies, favorite charities, memberships in clubs and professional associations, and likes and dislikes.

You need to know enough about the people you are trying to reach in order to reach them effectively. You need to shape your message and your materials to appeal to the people who are your target market. This is not a one-size-fits-all world. People expect your message to be customized to their unique sets of interests. A thorough knowledge of your target markets is essential.

Your side of the equation is summed up by the phrase "Know yourself." It is essential that you realistically assess your organization, its strengths and weaknesses, its potential, and limitations both real and imagined. What is called for is an honest evaluation of what you can and cannot do, what you have and have not done in the past and why, and what you may be able to accomplish in the future.

Now is the time to get out the eggbeaters.

Gather a group of people whose judgment you trust and start brainstorming. No idea is out of bounds in a brainstorming session. Encourage everyone to suggest whatever comes to mind. Set a lively pace, and write down every suggestion, no matter how crazy. That is phase one. When you are done, stop and take a break. Go out for lunch, take a walk, and put it all out of your mind.

When you come back, you're ready for phase two. This is the time to review the list of things you wrote down in the earlier brainstorming session. As you go over your list, seek out the diamonds among the pebbles. Pull out three ideas with potential. Discuss how they can be implemented. Compare their relative potential. This is the time to be cold-blooded and logical.

Once you have determined your markets and their needs and decided how you can best meet those needs, and once you have realistically assessed your organization, its mission, and its capabilities, you can select the best PR strategies to meet your goals so that, in Sun Tzu's words, "in one hundred battles you will never be defeated."

CHAPTER TWO

SETTING GOALS, CLARIFYING THE MESSAGE, AND CREATING THE PR PLAN

How to Begin: Setting Goals

To create an effective PR plan, a nonprofit must begin by identifying its organizational needs and setting specific PR goals. Needs and goals can vary widely.

A look at the goals of three very different nonprofits will illustrate the point. A campaign goal of the New York Urban League (www.nyul.org) was to attract a big turnout to a special event in Manhattan. The goal of the Richard David Kann Melanoma Foundation (www.melanomafoundation.com) of West Palm Beach, Florida, is to educate local residents about the dangers of skin cancer. The ongoing goal of the Episcopal Theological Seminary of the Southwest (www.etss.edu), in Austin, Texas, is to establish the seminary's identity in the religious community. Different goals, and yet all are aimed at similar needs. In each case, the need is for the organization to achieve heightened visibility and name recognition, to foster increased public involvement, and to support fundraising—all of which in turn enable the organization to accomplish its mission.

How do you know when your goal has been accomplished? That is not always an easy question to answer.

According to Melvin Taylor, media specialist for the New York Urban League, "One way you know you're successful is when people show up to your event." The crowd of seven thousand who attended the annual conference that Taylor organized attests to how well he fulfilled his particular goal.

Emily Painter, whose official title is special events/community liaison, handles public relations for the Richard David Kann Melanoma Foundation in her "spare time." Painter measures success in lives saved.

"We arranged for dermatologists to provide a screening for people at the Office Depot Corporation in Boca Raton and were able to screen fifty people in one day. We found seven cases of skin cancer and two cases of melanoma, the most serious kind, the kind that can spread like wildfire and kill you. We saved lives that day. We definitely count that as a success."

For Bob Kinney, director of communications at the Episcopal Theological Seminary of the Southwest, success means getting feature articles placed in media ranging from *Episcopal Life,* the national newspaper of the Episcopal Church, to the *American-Statesman,* Austin's leading local daily newspaper. The appearance of such articles helps enhance the reputation of the seminary as a center of excellence.

"The visibility in the religious press raises awareness of the seminary within our target market," says Kinney, who has directed communications at the seminary for eighteen years. He sees a definite relationship between public relations, on the one hand, and both enrollment and development, on the other. "Public awareness of the seminary helps us to attract more students, better faculty, and increased levels of support."

For each of the three organizations, fulfilling these goals was not an end in itself but a means to an end. Effective public relations serves the organization, and in all three instances cited here, PR success was part of a continuing campaign in support of the organizational mission. It is always nice to revel in a PR coup, but staying focused on the organization's mission is essential.

The Mission Statement

The purpose of a mission statement is to provide direction. Everyone involved in the organization, at every level—leadership, staff, and supporters alike—should be clear about the organization's mission. A mission statement should answer basic questions about the organization: who you are, what you do, where you do it, how you do it, and, most important, why it matters.

A mission statement serves as a standard against which to measure actions. Does taking this action further the organization's mission? Answering yes to that question may not always mean that the action should be taken, but a "yes" does carry weight in the decision process. Similarly, if an action will not further the organization's mission, then what is the reason for taking it?

A mission statement should resonate with everyone involved, and a good way to begin creating one is to get everyone around a table for a brainstorming session, says

Alicia Evans, president of the New York chapter of the National Black Public Relations Society. Evans, who is also president of Total Image Communications, a New York–based PR consulting firm that works with the famous Apollo Theater, recommends including people from every level of the organization. "It may also make sense to include people from the neighborhood," she adds, "especially if they are going to be affected by the actions of the nonprofit."

To be useful, a mission statement should be simple, clear, and direct. Nevertheless, organizational mission statements tend to run long and be fairly convoluted, especially when created, as they often are, by committees. Indeed, the mission statements of some organizations read as if they were all written by the same committee.

"The mission statement is often drawn up by the development department and is intended to resonate with grant officers," observes Gary Lewi, executive vice president at Rubenstein Associates, Inc. "But that is just not how you should market yourself to newsrooms and editors."

In fact, a mission statement, by reason of its inclusive nature, may be too unwieldy to serve effectively as the organization's message. To serve that purpose, the mission statement may have to be transformed into a message that is short and easily comprehended.

The Message and Key Message Points

If an organization does not have a clear message about its purpose and objectives, then that message will not be effectively communicated. Ultimately, it will not be understood. The solution is to hone down a dry or convoluted mission statement to its most key elements. Shorten it so that the final message answers the essential questions—what you do, where you do it, and, most important, why it matters—in no more than two or three sentences, and in only one, if possible. Be clear about the key message points you want to convey. What makes you special? What makes you unique? What makes you significant?

For example, the mission of the Richard David Kann Melanoma Foundation is "to save lives by educating the public on sun safety and the prevention and early detection of skin cancer, especially melanoma"—a long sentence, but the foundation's message is clear, simple, and easily understood, and it is conveyed in all the foundation's public relations efforts. The key message points included in public relations initiatives offer tips on becoming what the foundation calls "sun smart." PR materials also include announcements of specific events, such as free skin screenings to which the public is invited. To accomplish the organizational mission, the foundation must communicate its key message points. If a public relations effort gets an organization's name into the media but does not convey its key message points, that effort is not effective.

Once an organization has a clear, concise message, it should be widely disseminated throughout the organization and included in all the organization's literature and all its media outreach efforts. Key message points should be especially well ingrained in leaders, whether professionals or volunteers, who are involved in any form of communication on behalf of the organization—to internal or external audiences, and as guest speakers, presenters, representatives at various events, or media spokespersons.

The Statement of Goals

A clear mission statement makes it easier to formulate the specific goals that need to be accomplished in order for the organization's mission to be fulfilled. The statement of goals can be seen as an extension of the mission statement. The mission statement outlines the organization's purpose, and a statement of specific goals outlines exactly how the organization intends to carry out that purpose.

In creating a PR plan, Gary Lewi of Rubenstein Associates stresses, it is important to ask, "What is my goal? Is it to assist with development? Increase attendance? Make a good impression with the numbers for grant applications? Show potential patrons how effective the organization is? Is the goal to highlight board members in the media, to encourage their ongoing and increased support? The PR person looks at the statement of goals and immediately begins thinking, How many different ways can I get the organization into the media?"

Once goals have been clarified, it can be helpful to produce and disseminate a statement of the goals. A goals statement is a declaration of intent, a laying out of just what the organization intends to do. It lets supporters know exactly what they are

---

Starting at the Top

Kathryn Kimmel, vice president of marketing and communications for the Gemological Institute of America (GIA), a large nonprofit in the jewelry industry, is responsible for GIA's public relations campaigns, among her other duties. Kimmel firmly believes that public relations, to be effective, must start at the top.

"It is imperative that the organization's leadership understand the PR function," she says. "The organization's top leadership must set clear, achievable communications goals that the PR program will support. Once the specific communications objectives have been set, it is up to the PR practitioners to translate the plan into action steps. The PR function should be organized, staffed, and funded to support those goals. Leadership must then be prepared to become continuously and closely involved."

signing on for, and what to expect. One danger of stating specific goals is that you run the risk of turning off potential supporters. Someone who dislikes or disagrees with just one of your goals may hesitate to support you. Therefore, considerable thought needs to be given to the formulation of the goals statement. Stating a few of the most important goals, rather than a "laundry list" that invites people to quibble, is often the best course.

With the passage of time, a list of goals may become dated. Some of the goals may have been accomplished, or situations may have changed to make them less compelling or even irrelevant. It is important to review the statement of goals regularly, to ensure that it remains in touch with current realities. Goals need to be evaluated and reassessed on a regular basis to ensure that they continue to conform to the organization's mission. They should be revised and restated as necessary.

Creating the PR Plan

In preparing a public relations plan, the first step is to consider the organization's mission. What are you trying to accomplish? What short-term and long-range goals need to be met in order for you to fulfill that mission? What target markets must you reach to accomplish your goals? In the initial stages of formulating the plan, possibilities are considered and objectives are refined.

Next you consider your options. How can you best reach your target audience with your message? Consider the available media outlets, and choose the specific publications, TV and radio stations, and programs you will target. Develop a media list, with contact information for each outlet on your list.

It has been said that what turns a dream into a goal is a deadline. The same can be said of a PR plan. Nothing happens until specific dates are attached to each task. Decide when you are going to take each specific action in your plan.

Develop a detailed production schedule for each project that is part of the PR plan. Make the schedule as detailed as possible. In determining dates, it can be helpful to start with the end result and then work backwards. Consider every step along the way in every project, and assign a date for it. For each outreach to the media, decide in advance what media outlet and which journalists will be contacted, and when. Determine who will be responsible for each aspect of the plan and how you will track and follow up on each part of it. Try to consider everything, and set it down with a date. Ask others to review the schedule to see if you've left anything out.

Even the best-laid plans sometimes go down the tubes. But if your plan is well thought-out and well constructed, you will have created a blueprint, a campaign guide to direct all your efforts—an essential tool for achieving your goals.

The following eight rules summarize the process of creating a PR plan:

1. Know your audience. Be clear about who you want to reach.
2. Know the results you want. What do you want your audience to do?
3. Develop a clear message. Know what you want to communicate to your target audience in order to achieve the desired results. Develop key message points.
4. Choose the appropriate media. Different media reach different audiences.
5. Target specific individuals within each media outlet.
6. Develop the tools to reach out to the media and individuals you have targeted.
7. Develop a plan for using your outreach tools.
8. Review, reevaluate, and refine the planning process as necessary, for maximum results. Set concrete goals and objectives. To gauge your level of success, you must be able to measure results.

We'll look at each of these rules in turn.

Know Your Audience

There are many ways to learn about your target market. These range from informal research techniques, such as personal contact, community forums, and advisory committees, to more sophisticated techniques, such as the use of mailed questionnaires, online surveys, focus groups, and polls conducted by organizations like Harris Interactive. Every organization should maintain a computer database of donors, volunteers, and other supporters. It is also important to meet supporters face to face, to gain an appreciation of their interests and needs. Most successful public relations programs are a combination of the high-tech and the traditional.

Know the Results You Want

Is your goal a higher level of fundraising? If so, how much higher? How will you know when you've achieved your goal? Set clear and defined objectives that can be measured. Maybe your goal is to make your organization better known and better appreciated among health care providers. Perhaps you want to increase attendance at a rally or influence legislators about key social or environmental issues. If you know exactly what you are working toward, you will be able to shape your campaign to achieve those goals.

Develop a Clear Message

Create a concise, well-stated mission for the organization and a clear way of expressing it. This is what is known as *messaging*.

"We're Not in the Publicity Business"

A complaint voiced all too commonly by people working in nonprofits is "We're the best-kept secret in the field." This remark is generally followed by something along these lines: "Other organizations are getting the headlines, the front-page stories, the TV specials, and the huge contributions. And us? Nobody even knows we exist."

Obviously, not every nonprofit can be the best-kept secret. But people in many nonprofits certainly feel that their organizations are not getting the notice and the appreciation they deserve. No matter what a nonprofit's specific field of operations is, there will usually be a number of other nonprofits—often *many* others—working in that field, all of them competing for the support of the same people.

Why do some nonprofits get more notice than others? In the competition for publicity, the organization's size is not always the determining factor, as David Greco discovered at the headquarters of the National Wildlife Federation (www.nwf.org) in Reston, Virginia, just outside Washington, D.C.

As Greco, who was the organization's corporate and foundation relations manager, recalls, "We were always getting our clocks cleaned by the smaller environmental groups when it came to publicity. Some of them would regularly take credit for the things we did." When Greco pointed that out to people in his organization, the response was typically something like, "We're not in the publicity business. We're in the business of saving animals."

"They were biologists," Greco says, "animal people. They didn't get it until they finally understood that visibility for the organization translates into dollars raised, and that makes it possible for you to save more animals."

To get noticed, you need publicity. There are things you can do to get it. Some require time and effort, and others require money. Some don't require much of anything—except a plan. Without one, you are unlikely to accomplish much.

Messaging begins with a simple, easily comprehensible message that conveys to the public what the organization does and why it matters. You must know exactly what your organization's message is and what your key message points are. What do you want the media to say about you? Shape your message, hone it, and be sure everyone in the organization presents it. Keep your spokespersons on message. Keep your press releases and other publicity materials on message, too. If your organization is getting lost in the crowd as "one of those environmental organizations" or "some agency that deals with women's issues" or "just a church group," you need to work on your messaging.

> ### "Plan Your Dive, and Dive Your Plan"
>
> The Professional Association of Diving Instructors (PADI) drums a simple rule into novice divers: "Plan your dive, and dive your plan." Most beginning divers wonder about the need to spell out the obvious. Veteran divers explain that diving is always inherently dangerous. It is easy to become distracted in an uncertain environment, where things can happen suddenly and unexpectedly, so you need to plan your objectives thoughtfully along with the steps you will take to accomplish them. Obviously, you need to allow for some flexibility and changing circumstances, but it is important to stay focused on your objective. A diver without a plan is at serious risk of losing her bearings, running out of air, and getting into serious trouble—just like an organization without a plan. Like a diver getting ready to take the plunge, you need to be clear about where you are going.

"Staying on message is the job of the public relations person, not the job of the media," says Pat Smith, executive vice president of Rubenstein Associates. He uses a fictional example. "If a nonprofit group that organizes art programs for children were considering sponsoring an event featuring Britney Spears at a popular night spot, I would advise against it," he says. "The organization's message would get lost in the club atmosphere and among the paparazzi shooting Britney Spears in her sexy outfit. Instead, I would recommend staging a morning activity at a school, with Britney Spears wearing a smock and painting pictures with disadvantaged children—a much better idea for the organization, and one that stays on message."

"Messaging is also a matter of consistency and branding," says Lori J. Greene, director of special events at Relay for Life of the Eastern Division of the American Cancer Society (www.cancer.org). "The consistent message, along with the logo, should be on every communication that comes from the organization, from business cards and press releases to banners and T-shirts."

"In looking for stories to send to the media, try to find those that reflect the meaning of your organization," advises Deborah Sturm Rausch, director of public affairs for the New York State Office of Mental Retardation and Developmental Disabilities, Albany (www.omr.state.ny.us). "Consider issues that are germane to the community, and look for possible connections to what your organization or the people it serves does, and connect the dots. Tie your story to a current event, issue, or idea, and develop the story along those lines. But," she cautions, "be sure to stay on message."

The Elevator Pitch

To grasp the difference between a mission statement and a message, imagine that you are in an elevator and that you are carrying a briefcase featuring the name and logo of your organization. The doors of the elevator open. A man steps in, smiles, looks at your briefcase, and says, "Nice logo. What does that organization do?" You begin to recite the mission statement, perhaps beginning with the founding date and the core principles. Before you get very far, the elevator stops, the doors open, and the man smiles again and says, "Nice meeting you." He steps out of the elevator, and you're left with a half-spoken mission statement. As for the man, he has no idea what the organization does.

What you need in this situation is a brief, succinct statement that includes the name of your organization, what you do, where you do it, and, most important, why it matters, and you have to be able to deliver it in the time it takes for an elevator to travel a dozen floors—less than twenty seconds. This is the elevator pitch, and creating one puts you through a good exercise in brevity. And you need to be brief: an elevator isn't the only place where the organization's message has to be conveyed quickly and in an easily understandable way.

Choose Appropriate Media

One of the first things a public relations firm does for a new client is create a media list for that client. If you don't already have an appropriate media list, you need to create one. If you already have one, review it, and update it regularly.

Your media list should reflect your target market. Who do you want to reach? Who is your target market? What do people in your target market read? What do they listen to on the radio and watch on TV?

Rick Frishman (www.rickfrishman.com) is president of Planned Television Arts (www.plannedtvarts.com), an independent division of Ruder Finn, Inc., a leading public relations agency. "Every day," Frishman points out, "ten thousand guests appear on four thousand radio and TV shows. The potential for nonprofits is virtually unlimited."

Frishman, with smart outreach to the media, promotes a client roster that includes the American Diabetes Association, CARE, and the National Geographic Society. The author of *Guerilla Publicity, Guerilla Marketing for Writers,* and *Networking Magi,* he is also a firm believer in the importance of local media, especially for nonprofits with limited resources.

"Get on local radio and TV programs," Frishman urges, "and into local newspapers. To do that, you need to have a hook. Whatever you are doing, there are almost certainly four or five or twenty other organizations doing the same thing. What is it that makes you different? *Stress* how you are different."

Local Press: Suburban Community Newspapers

Suburban sports provides a good example of how local newspapers function to publicize community events.

The Watchung Hills Soccer Association (WHSA) (www.whsa.org), in northern New Jersey, runs neighborhood soccer programs for fourteen hundred kids from elementary school through high school. Stories about WHSA teams that appear in the local press help stimulate enthusiasm and involvement on the part of the kids and their parents. According to WHSA president Steve Finkel, the association has no publicity chairperson and no formal arrangements for handling public relations. It relies on its Web site to provide kids, parents, and fans with "latest news, events and hot topics." WHSA does not publish a newsletter but does send e-mails to kids and parents to alert them to important items on the Web site.

"Getting stories to the press is all done informally," says Finkel. "News stories about teams and games are sent in by parents at random, by e-mail and fax, to the local newspaper, the *Echoes-Sentinel,* which runs the stories on its local sports page. Photos are usually sent digitally by e-mail or delivered on a disc."

At the *Echoes-Sentinel* (echoes-sentinel@recordersnewspaper.com), Phil Nardone notes that this is pretty standard procedure for community sports teams. Nardone is assistant executive editor of Recorder Community Newspapers, which owns seventeen New Jersey community papers including the *Echoes-Sentinel,* which covers Long Hill Township, Warren Township, and Watchung.

"We only send out a reporter or photographer to cover the major things, like the high school football games," says Nardone. "For the rest, we rely on the teams and leagues to send in stories to us. Usually volunteers send the information. We get press releases from the parents of kids on the teams, mainly by e-mail. Most photos come in from the teams, about 80 percent in digital format. In the case of a soccer program or a Little League baseball program, for example, we prefer that one person send us stories about all ten teams in a league rather than getting separate material from each team. It makes things easier to manage."

Like most other community papers, the *Echoes-Sentinel* must cover a lot of activity with very little staff. This means that the less work the paper has to do to prepare a story for publication, the more likely the piece is to be published. And that is a basic rule of publicity: the easier you make it for a journalist to use your story, the better your chances of success.

"Keep it brief, and keep it well written," Nardone advises. "We prefer getting the information by e-mail, one page maximum. For sports events, we advise that the piece summarize the game and include a few key plays without

> trying to present a detailed, blow-by-blow account. Don't try to get your kid's name in every week, or the name of every single kid on the team."
>
> Nardone offers an important piece of advice to nonprofits: "Make contact with local editors. You can do it via phone calls and e-mails. It's fine if someone wants to come in to introduce themselves, but it's always a good idea to call and check first."

Frishman believes in using a variety of approaches to help the organization stand out from the crowd.

"You must have a good Web site. But you can't stop there. Get a big magnet with your logo on it, and have your members put it on their cars. Ask for a free ad on the placemats of local diners and bowling alleys. Put on events that will make news. Do a car wash, a fundraiser. Bring in speakers. Hand out flyers. Get the local community involved. Do things that get you into the local media, and build from there."

If your audience is defined by geography, an ethnic or religious affiliation, a profession, or a passion, make it your business to find out what media outlets your audience favors. Your media list should include all of them.

Be thorough. When is comes to publications that your audience reads, don't settle for a quick glance at one issue. Read through several issues, cover to cover. Look at the news that is reported, the subject matter and style of the articles, the regular columns, the letters to the editor, the photos and ads. The success of the publication is determined in large measure by how well the editor shapes it to the tastes of its readers. You can learn a lot about a publication's readers by studying several issues closely.

Don't scorn the local media. The smaller dailies and the neighborhood weeklies can be highly effective vehicles for your publicity. Compared to placing a story in *The New York Times* or the *Washington Post*, getting into local papers is easy. And local media have another advantage over the national outlets—credibility.

According to Pat Smith of Rubenstein Associates, "People trust their local media more than the national media, so local press and TV can often work best for you. A story aired on a local affiliate, or a story in a local publication that is picked up by the Associated Press and run nationally, seems more credible to many people than news that comes from the national media hubs in New York."

Being PR-savvy often comes down to knowing who in the media to contact, knowing what they need to do their jobs, and then packaging your materials accordingly.

Local press can be a great publicity resource in the big city, too. The category of local press also includes free papers and penny savers, which are typically desperate for local stories. If you provide a solid, well-written story, chances are good that it will be picked up and even prominently featured.

The "Mystery Shopper" Approach

For a small nonprofit with limited resources, the task of developing a PR plan can seem a little overwhelming. New York–based PR consultant Cynthia Horner suggests a shortcut.

"You really don't have to reinvent the wheel," she says. "You can take advantage of the fact that there are other organizations already out there. Find an organization that works in the same field you do, and see what they have done. That can serve as a model for what your organization needs to do."

Horner works with North General Hospital in Harlem, where she stages a community health and wellness fair to acquaint neighborhood residents with the resources available to them at the hospital. To minimize the strain on the hospital's limited budget, Horner regularly partners with other organizations, including the March of Dimes, the Lupus Foundation, and the New York City Health Department.

Knowing what the competition is up to is an important element in any plan. Retailers have long made use of "mystery shoppers," people who visit the competition to check out their goods and services. A standard practice in retailing, "mystery shopping" can work equally well for public relations, Horner believes. She uses the Internet to research the competition.

"Go online to Yahoo or Google, and see what similar nonprofit organizations are doing, where they are getting placements in print and electronic media. And copy them. Visit the Web sites of organizations like yours, and look at the articles posted on their sites. See which journalists at which papers are writing about them, what radio and TV programs have covered them. You can begin to compile a media list by seeing who has covered the competition. See what other organizations have done, and then go and do it better."

When New York publicist Cynthia Horner was working on a health and wellness fair at Harlem's North General Hospital (www.northgeneral.org), she sent a press release and an accompanying photo to the newly launched *Harlem Times*. The paper ran the story and photo on the front page. Even better, the story was continued on the inside of the paper with a second photo, this one of a hospital official happily shaking hands with a representative from the governor's office of community affairs. Everybody concerned was very happy.

Target Specific Individuals

Make a point of finding out which areas are covered by particular reporters and editors in the various media outlets. If your story will appeal to an audience concerned with health issues, identify the reporters and editors who cover that area. Try to develop relationships with the people at media outlets.

There was a time when a public relations practitioner communicated with the media by mailing a press release and following up with a phone call. Some journalists complain that today the PR professional calls, writes, faxes, and e-mails—and then does it all over again. As a result, journalists suffer from information overload. It can be a challenge to get your organization's voice heard above all the background noise. In fact, more and more journalists have simply stopped looking at their PR-related e-mails; they don't return phone calls from PR professionals, and they routinely toss press kits into the trash.

Ronni Faust, a New York–based PR consultant, says, "Calling a reporter to follow up an e-mail of a release is a good idea. Reporters get so much e-mail that your release could get lost in the shuffle. I will always call and leave a message just to be sure my release is seen—but I do this only with reporters I know would ordinarily cover that beat. Having a relationship with the reporter will always help you get that second look."

Like many public relations practitioners, Faust looks for opportunities to connect with journalists in her field at networking events, professional conferences, symposiums, and panels. She regularly interacts with journalists, with and without her client, over a meal or coffee, and she speaks with them on a regular basis to ask if she can help them with anything they are working on. This ongoing communication keeps the connection alive.

Develop the Tools to Reach Out to Targeted Media and Individuals

In some cases, a simple one-page media advisory, AFI (available for interview) notice, or news release may be your PR tool of choice. At other times, the ideal vehicle for your message could be a PSA on radio or TV. Pitching a radio or TV interview might call for a press kit and sample audiotape or videotape of previous interviews. Having B-roll on hand could encourage TV news coverage for your organization. A good Web site is an essential tool for any PR campaign. Consider all these options carefully, and then use the combination of tools that best enables you to achieve your goal.

Develop a Plan for Using Your Tools

Devote time and energy to developing a PR plan that will enable you to communicate often and everywhere. The goal of the plan or campaign is to see that your organization and its message get as much coverage as possible in every print and electronic media outlet and by word of mouth, to enable you to effectively reach your target markets with your message.

Establish a detailed schedule that indicates when you will implement the various aspects of your plan. Consider, too, who will be responsible for which details. Leave

---

Miss Shelley's Upward Prep School

The process of building relationships can be pretty basic—for example, sending out holiday cards to all your media contacts. Alicia Evans of Total Image Communications makes it a point to remember journalists' birthdays.

"You build relationships with the media the way you build them with anyone else," she says, "by being human, thoughtful, and considerate. If someone mentions that their mother is sick, the next time you speak to them, remember to ask how she is doing. If you know they are interested in something that may have not any connection with what you do, and you run across an article on it, send it to them with a note: 'Thought this might interest you.' When you remember to be a person, not just a mouthpiece for your organization, you are involved in building relationships. Never feel that it's a waste of time. You are planting seeds that will bear fruit in the future."

In one instance, the seeds bore fruit for Evans when she was doing PR for Miss Shelley's Upward Prep School in Roosevelt, Long Island. At the time, it was the only African American prep school in the area. Evans connected with a noted artist, LeRoy Campbell, who agreed to an art show/auction of his work to benefit the school. To maximize the impact, Evans needed television coverage of the event, and for that she called on David Ushery, then at New York's WNBC (Channel 4), with whom she had established a working relationship.

"I was able to call him and say, 'David, I need a favor. Can you work with me on this?' His answer was a noncommittal, 'I'll see what I can do.' You can't hound them," Evans cautions. "It's an ongoing relationship, and you can't be a pest. But you also have to be persistent. It's a balancing act."

In the end, the station did the story.

---

nothing to chance—too much depends on the successful application of your public relations plan.

In communicating with the world at large, do not neglect the internal audience composed of staff, members, and supporters of the organization—local, regional, and national. Be sure your colleagues and supporters know what a great job you're doing.

Review, Reevaluate, and Refine the Process

Regularly review the campaign and its various components. Measure your success against your stated goals. Identify elements that are working well and things that can be improved. Avoid becoming complacent. Always be alert to new ideas, techniques, and strategies that can enable you to bring your organization's message to your target market.

Hiring a PR Consultant or PR Agency

Not all organizations can do it all themselves. There may be times when it is a good idea to consider hiring a PR consultant or the services of a PR agency to handle some or even all aspects of a PR campaign.

PR consultants do not guarantee that they will get their clients in the media. They don't guarantee it because they can't. It is impossible to be 100 percent sure that a story will be picked up. What consultants can and do promise is that they will devote their best professional skills, skills that have brought positive results in the past, to the project.

The usual measure of how well a consultant or an agency has succeeded is the amount of coverage the client gets. That can be measured by the number of news clips and pickups in the electronic media.

PR consultants can be hired for the specific project or on the basis of a monthly retainer. Fees depend on what you want the consultant to do: write a news release, send it out, follow up with the media, and so on. PR professionals can be found through professional public relations associations like the Public Relations Society of America (www.prsa.org).

For specific segments of the media, there are similar organizations, such as the National Black Public Relations Society (www.nbprs.org), which describes itself as a "one-stop shop" for African American professionals in public relations, public affairs, communications, media relations, community affairs, and government affairs. Alicia Evans, president of the organization's New York chapter, recommends that a nonprofit carefully review perspective publicists' track records before bringing them on board. "Ask to see samples of work they've done for other clients, such as press releases and news clips, to get a sense of how effective they are at placing stories in the media."

The American Jewish Public Relations Society (www.ajprs.org) is another niche PR association specializing in one specific segment of the media. When I served as the society's president, I made it a point to invite to our monthly meetings journalists from niche media outlets like *The Jewish Week*, in New York, as well as from mainstream media like CNN, in order to help our members establish personal contacts with the people they were pitching stories to. Members of the society are public relations professionals working at nonprofit organizations that serve the Jewish community or freelancers familiar with that world and the media that serve it. Their expertise enables them to routinely place stories in what is called "the Anglo-Jewish press" as well as in major local and national media outlets.

Although the basics of public relations are essentially the same in every area, each niche has its own cast of characters, and publicists tend to develop their contacts in one or two specific areas. It can be helpful to know the extent of a prospective consultant's media contacts in the relevant area. Freelance writers, editors, and publicists can also be found through such Web sites as elanceonline.com and www.wordsmitten.com.

Sometimes a PR agency will work with a nonprofit at no charge, on a pro bono basis. Off the record, however, PR agencies will admit that pro bono work often isn't very good: you get what you pay for.

What a firm supplies on a pro bono basis is usually more along the lines of advising than actually doing the work. Since a nonprofit typically has not established relationships with journalists, the advice alone is often not of much help. What the nonprofit needs is someone with an understanding of the tools and techniques needed to get the organization into the news.

When the idea of bringing in an outside consultant is being considered, says Melvin Taylor of the New York Urban League, a nonprofit should be sure that the prospective consultant really knows and understands the organization and its specific target markets. Experience counts.

When discussing a possible assignment, experienced public relations consultants will typically ask a prospective client, "What do you have that is really newsworthy?"

"To know the answer to that, you have to understand how the news cycle works," says Gary Lewi of Rubenstein Associates. "I have sat in countless meetings where people from nonprofits have berated the media for not covering the organization's black-tie gala. That just shows a complete lack of understanding of the news cycle. If you are not working to the news clock, not appreciating the basic components of journalism, you are not getting on the air."

Lewi believes that most nonprofits do not understand how to get into the news. "Ideally," he says, "there should be someone on the organization's board who has an understanding of journalism, but that is not always the case. People at most nonprofits are driven by their love for the organization and what it does. But that is not the concern of a news reporter. They want a good story.

"The fiction is that you just write a release, and it becomes news. But you need to know how to write a press release so that it will be viewed as news. PR consultants and agencies exist to apply that level of knowledge to getting an organization into the news."

In considering a PR agency, it is a good idea to choose one with both an interest and a track record of accomplishment in your field. David Fenton, president of Fenton Communications (www.fenton.com), a large public interest agency in New York, agreed to work for a minimum fee with Riverkeeper, an environmental group, because of his strong affinity with the organization's cause. Cathy Renna, media relations director at Fenton, recommends choosing a firm "that cares about what you are doing, has experience in that area, and will work with you and fit into your budget." She says the usual procedure is to charge according to the services the nonprofit is interested in. "We have a minimum retainer, and we assign a mix of junior and senior staff to a project. When possible, we try to keep the staff mixed, to keep the costs down. We don't take on a client unless we care about the issues and then we put our heart into it." For Renna, working on behalf of issues she believes in comes naturally. Before joining Fenton Communications, she spent fourteen years, first as a volunteer and then as a staff member, with the Gay and Lesbian Alliance Against Defamation (GLAAD) (www.glaad.org), a media advocacy organization.

The PR Budget

When it comes to the public relations budget, resources among nonprofits can vary widely. Large national-level nonprofits will typically have much more money to spend than small neighborhood-level organizations. The number of hands involved in the process can also vary widely. Some larger organizations have many people on staff, with different departments assigned to specific aspects of the campaign. Smaller organizations fly by the seat of their pants, with people from the organization taking whatever time they can steal from other operations to deal with PR.

As director of public relations for American ORT (www.aort.org), my responsibilities included developing the annual PR budget. I began by listing all the things that were already in place and scheduled, starting with the number of staff people for the PR department (never enough, of course). Scheduled projects included the annual report, a quarterly newsletter, an annual conference, direct-mail campaigns, brochures, posters, banners, promotional videos, news release distribution, invitations, journals, special events, and the like. I tallied the costs involved in each item. Later, I would develop a detailed production schedule for each project, as part of the PR plan.

I then worked up a rough budget estimate for additional PR projects I thought the organization should be doing and listed each item with its estimated cost. Like most people in my position, I included things I was fairly certain would never be approved. In doing so, I was following a time-honored budgeting principle: "It never hurts to ask." Having checked and rechecked my figures, I submitted my proposed budget.

My proposal was reviewed, and the numbers were trimmed down from what I had requested. I was given a figure that the organization had decided to allot for PR and told to spend it for maximum impact. On occasion, I was able to lobby for extra funds for a special project, but whatever the number I finally ended up with, my job was to get the most bang for those PR bucks.

Most public relations people developing budgets follow a similar process. Most find themselves asking for more money than they ultimately get. And most end up working with what they have.

For special PR projects like a new video or an elaborate annual report, a special grant would sometimes be made by one of the organization's supporters. A not uncommon practice among nonprofits, such windfalls afford "angels" the opportunity to underwrite pet projects. However, such random generosity also presents a special challenge to the budgeting process, since such grants cannot always be counted on.

Nonprofits that do not appreciate the importance of the public relations role are often reluctant to allocate funds to the PR process. Gary Lewi of Rubenstein Associates feels that the same lack of understanding for what makes a good news story carries over into the process of creating a budget. "Some nonprofits are simply unable to develop a realistic PR budget," he says. "It's like matter and antimatter. Boards are reluctant to spend money, and yet it is essential. A nonprofit that puts some money into the process and spends it wisely can get good results."

Cathy Renna of Fenton Communications agrees. "Nonprofits must realize that if they want publicity, one way or another, they need to spend some money."

Establishing Relationships with the Media

Like many other nonprofits, the Richard David Kann Melanoma Foundation does not have a full-time public relations person on staff. Its entire full-time personnel roster totals just three people. The foundation manages a contact list of some five thousand people in the West Palm Beach area and puts on an impressive array of events during the year, from school programs to dinners to golf outings to luncheons and fashion shows. The foundation's Emily Painter says, "None of us has any training or real experience in PR. We fly by the seat of our pants. When I began working at the Melanoma Foundation, I asked everyone on the board, and all the committees, who they knew in the media. Then I made it a point to follow up and introduce myself to everyone I could in the local media. I would drop by to tell them about the organization and to give away a T-shirt and some sunscreen. They get a sense of the organization through the personal contact. Whenever someone does a story on us I always call to say thank you. Just by maintaining ongoing personal communication, I've developed relationships with local media people, with the press, and also with radio and TV."

Much larger organizations also appreciate the necessity for establishing personal relationships with the media. Kathryn Kimmel of GIA manages a considerable staff to deal with public relations. She places great emphasis on media relations. She reminds her people that in dealing with the media, "It is important to be as prompt and accommodating as possible in responding. Remember that you need them more than they need you. The key is to deliver your message while giving journalists material that they can use. Appearing too promotional or guarded will turn off reporters. Journalists will call again if they feel that they have been helped in doing their story."

Leslie Gottlieb at the American Red Cross of Greater New York agrees. "Every PR person, whether working for a large organization or a small one, has to develop relationships with the media. You have to develop a solid reputation that you can be trusted and that your information is true and accurate. It's important to connect not just with reporters and editors but also with producers and other media people."

As a good example of the importance of developing and maintaining such relationships, Gottlieb recalls an idea she had for a TV story on preparing for emergencies, an area in which her organization has considerable expertise. Over the course of several months and many conversations, she repeatedly proposed the idea to a producer she knew at WNET (Channel 13), the PBS station in New York. "It took six months of pushing before he agreed to do the story and another three months until the story was actually done. Since then it's been broadcast a dozen times and it always gets a tremendous response."

It is important to note that the story would not have been produced and broadcast at all if Gottlieb hadn't had the ear of the producer and a solid reputation for knowing what makes a good story. She was also known as someone who could be counted on to follow through on getting the station the materials it needed to do the story. The reliability factor, coupled with her persistence, ultimately tipped the balance in her favor.

"Let Us Know What You're Up To"

A look at the process from the media side underscores the importance and potential benefits of knowing how to present a nonprofit's story to the media. Anna Carbonell is vice president of press and public affairs for WNBC (Channel 4) and WNJU (Telemundo 47), based at Rockefeller Center, in New York. An Emmy Award–winning veteran of thirty years in television, Carbonell advises nonprofits to do their homework before approaching the media with a story.

"Nonprofits are often frustrated because they send a press release to the news department at a station and nothing happens," she says. "But often their stories tend to be more features than hard news. A story about another parade, when every little organization in the world has a parade, is not news unless there is something unique about it, some kind of hook. For example, did someone leading the parade, or in the parade, have to overcome some terrible obstacle to be there? You have to have a hook."

Carbonell advises nonprofits to contact the station's community affairs director. The initial contact is usually made by e-mail and followed up with a phone call. "Let us know what you're up to. Establish a relationship."

NBC bought the Spanish-language Telemundo Network several years ago, and today Carbonell estimates that WNBC and WNJU combined reach 95 percent of the New York tristate-area population. That is a lot of reach for any nonprofit.

"We have media relationships with several major nonprofits' events every year," she notes, "including the Puerto Rican Day Parade and the AIDS Walk. The Colombian Festival is another huge event that we cover. We do live weather reports from the festival at Flushing Meadows Park. For each of those organizations, we also produced a PSA that we aired according to a regular schedule, all at no cost to the nonprofits."

All that media muscle is available, essentially for the asking—if you know how to ask. Meeting the right people, or networking, can be a good way to start.

Networking

It is always a good idea to establish an ongoing relationship with the reporters and editors at the publications you are reaching out to on a regular basis. Find ways of meeting them on a one-to-one basis. Join and attend meetings of community and professional associations, go to conferences, and take advantage of every networking opportunity that presents itself. People respond to people, and a reporter or an editor is far more likely to take your call and consider your release if she knows who you are and can put a face with your name. Make a point of getting to know people in the media and of letting them get to know you.

Organizations such as the Public Relations Society of America, the Publicity Clubs (with chapters in New York, Los Angeles, the San Francisco Bay area, Chicago, and New England), the Association for Women in Communications, the National Black Public Relations Society, and the League of American Communications Professionals provide excellent forums for meeting other people engaged in reaching out to the media. Media professionals are frequently guest speakers at chapter events, where you can meet them face to face and pick up hands-on tips for pitching story ideas.

Find out the names of the reporters and editors who handle your area. Call—but not when they are on deadline—and offer to meet with them to tell them about your organization. All reporters and editors are pressed for time, so invite them to meet for lunch or breakfast. Offer to pick up the tab but be aware that some larger media outlets, such as *The New York Times*, have a policy that prohibits their people from allowing a news source to pay for the meal. For smaller media outlets that usually isn't a problem. If they have no time for a meal, ask to meet at their offices. Corny as it sounds, bringing doughnuts or a fruit cup along can be a nice touch.

Regardless of whether you manage to arrange a face-to-face meeting, establish yourself as a source for expert information about your organization's area. If, for example, you work with mentally challenged adults, let the editor know you are available as a reliable resource for stories in that area. If the editor has a need for information, an expert's quote, or an interview with someone knowledgeable about the subject, she should be aware that she can turn to you. By making her job easier, you also help get your organization and its people into the news.

Building a Media List

In developing a list of media contacts, a nonprofit must first be clear about the target markets it is trying to reach. Once that has been established, it is a matter of determining which media outlets reach those target markets. Alicia Evans of the National

Black Public Relations Society recommends visiting the Web sites of local newspapers and radio and TV stations: "The names of who to send material to will be posted very clearly, right there on the Web site."

Cynthia Horner favors the "reverse engineering" method: seeing who in the media is reporting on competing organizations, and taking those names for her own. While doing PR for Community Outreach Health and Wellness Fairs at Harlem's North General Hospital, she faxed a press release to everyone on the hospital's contact list, which included many state and local political figures. The faxed press releases—she found faxes to be the politician's preferred mode of communication—brought a number of officials to the hospital's health and wellness fair, including New York Congressman Charles B. Rangel, who added a governmental imprimatur to the event.

At the Public Theater in New York, director of communications Arlene R. Kriv spends a lot of her time expanding her media list by developing media relationships. "It is very important to establish relationships with reporters who are covering the shows," she says. "We have a media database that is very current, we stay in touch, we know their work, we know their interests, and we often suggest an angle on a story that will help them 'sell' the story to their editor."

When Kriv first began at the Public Theater, a media list was already in place, and she immediately set about adding to it. Always on the lookout for new freelance writers and new publications to pitch the theater's shows to, she regularly uses *Bacon's New York Publicity Outlets*. Though it's not as up-to-date as the online version, she finds the printed version to be more cost effective.

"When I first started at the job, I called media people and took them for lunch and coffee meetings, and I still do. Two or three times a year, I meet with the media: once in the fall to tell them about the fall season, once in January or February to tell them about shows going up in March, and then again as opportunity allows."

The Public Theater has relationships with all the major newspapers as well as local TV and radio stations. The list is constantly expanding. Typical of most experienced PR practitioners, Kriv sees relationships with the media as an ongoing conversation.

"I try to understand what they're interested in. The more you know about them and their interests and what exactly each media outlet is looking for, the more readily you can come up with ideas that will appeal to them. I've developed the kinds of relationships that allow me to call and speak to a reporter and say, 'I have an idea—what do you think of it?' or 'I have an idea for a story—who should I speak to about it?' And they're happy to help."

In the performing arts, as in all areas of the nonprofit world, there is a lot of competition out there. The first step to getting your organization noticed is to get someone to take your phone call. To do that, you need to develop a reputation for reliability so that when you call, the other party knows that you have something to say.

A Tale of Two Seminaries

Nonprofits often compile several distinct and sometimes overlapping media lists to reflect different target markets. At Hebrew Union College–Jewish Institute of Religion (HUC-JIR) in New York (www.huc.edu), public relations is the responsibility of Jean Bloch Rosensaft, senior national director for public affairs and institutional planning. HUC-JIR is the seminary for Reform Judaism and trains rabbis, cantors, educators, and communal professionals on campuses in New York, Los Angeles, Cincinnati, and Jerusalem. Rosensaft has compiled an impressive media list that includes religion, education, and lifestyle editors and reporters at major newspapers in the cities where the campuses are located, including *The New York Times* and the *Los Angeles Times,* as well as in cities throughout North America where HUC-JIR's students and alumni serve. The list is drawn in part from the five-volume *Bacon's* directory on her shelf and in part from personal contacts she has established with journalists over the years.

Rosensaft has also compiled a media list that includes Jewish newspapers serving local Jewish communities throughout North America and editors of synagogue newsletters. Usually she sends her press releases out by e-mail as well as in conventional national mailings.

"We have relationships with religion editors and reporters at all the major papers in the country," she says. "But the Anglo-Jewish press is different from the mainstream press. These are small weeklies, biweeklies, and even monthlies, with limited budgets and staff, and some still prefer to receive the releases conventionally by mail."

The seminary for Reform Judaism, in New York, and the Episcopal Theological Seminary of the Southwest (ETSS), in Austin, deal with many similar PR issues, including the development of media lists. ETSS director of communications Bob Kinney sends stories about his seminary to a range of religious and secular publications. His standard media list includes the religious writers at major papers in Dallas and Houston and the editors of Episcopal diocesan newspapers of currently enrolled ETSS seminarians throughout the country. Like Rosensaft, however, he has another media list, comprised of a few small dioceses that do not have e-mail and to whom he sends releases by regular mail.

Kriv says her media contacts have complained about getting calls from publicists who don't know the publication, the beat, or the writer. From their side, publicists often say that they get no respect from the media. Kriv believes, "If you do your job well, you will get respect for what you do. And that translates into publicity for the organization."

Becoming a Source of Information

When you are pitching a story, it can be helpful to bolster the story's appeal by including statistics from sources other than your own organization. If you use the Web for research, it is a relatively simple matter for you to find a wealth of relevant material. By citing a national study that independently points up the scope of a problem, you give your pitch, and the journalist's subsequent story will have more credibility and will appeal to a wider audience. Alicia Evans employed this technique when she was pitching a story on problems involved in African American adoption: to give her story wider appeal, she incorporated relevant statistics about adoption in general.

When you approach a journalist with a good story, complete with supporting statistics from other sources, your efforts will be appreciated. Journalists will come back to you as a reliable source for future stories and will tend to be receptive to your pitches. By presenting yourself and your organization as a helpful source of research on a topic, you are helping journalists do their job, and that is something that busy journalists on deadline always appreciate.

Many public relations people have ongoing relationships with journalists whom they have never actually met in person. That is a result of the fact that most communication with the media today is by e-mail and phone. In some cases, PR people and journalists have never even spoken by phone, communicating only by e-mail. But that hasn't prevented them from establishing important relationships.

For example, Cathy Renna of Fenton Communications has relationships with many journalists, in cities all over the country, many of whom she has never actually met face to face. Because she has established her credibility as a helpful, reliable source, she often pitches stories for two or even three different clients in a single phone call to one journalist. "It works," she say, "because what I'm doing is making it easier for them to do their jobs. Journalists want good stories, and if you know how to present them, they will consider you a valuable resource."

Cause-Related Marketing

Cause-related marketing is a PR strategy that enables a for-profit company to do well by doing good. By linking its name to the right nonprofit organization, a company can enhance name recognition of its products while supporting a worthwhile cause. The process works best when there is a logical connection between the company and the cause, says Nancy Trent, principal of the New York–based PR firm Trent & Company.

Trent works with several clients, in the areas of jewelry, cosmetics, fashion, and spas, in a cause-related marketing campaign for Women Beyond Cancer, an organization that works to combat breast cancer. Because pink is the signature color of the campaign, Trent's clients give the campaign a portion of the proceeds from sales of pink versions of their products. The results are good publicity for Trent's clients and effective fundraising for a worthy cause.

The Power of Positive Public Relations

Public relations alone generally won't get people to write a check. But good public relations, good stories in the media, and general public awareness of your activities and programs will pave the way for effective fundraising. With that level of awareness, more phone calls from fundraisers will get returned, more direct-mail solicitations will get opened, and more people will show up at dinners and special events. Standing out from the crowd translates into more supporters and more money raised, and that in turn means a greater ability to accomplish the organization's mission.

Gary Perl, senior field director at American ORT, believes that good public relations is essential to effective fundraising. "PR makes you important," he says. "It enhances the organization's image and makes events seem special and appealing so that people want to be a part of the activities."

Public relations for nonprofit organizations has its own imperatives, and Pat Smith of Rubenstein Associates feels that this unique aspect of effective public relations was well expressed by one of his clients, a college president, who told him, "Publicity does not make my phone ring. But publicity does make people more ready to take my phone call." Publicity seriously affects a school's ability to attract the best teachers, the best students, the best coaches, and the best athletes and to appeal to alumni associations. It can have a similar impact for all nonprofits.

Publicity Begets Publicity

"Publicity begets publicity," says Howard Rubenstein. "Don't underestimate any hit. With the prevalence of the Internet, articles get posted and turn up when reporters begin looking for material or researching an issue. A piece in a local newspaper can result in a story that is picked up by the Associated Press and reprinted in hundreds of papers around the country and goes on to get national television coverage."

It can often be a good strategy to start small and then get bigger. A news item or article about your organization that is published in a small local publication can be parlayed into coverage in a large publication and can also generate radio and TV coverage. Once you begin to generate publicity, it can be like riding a wave and using its momentum to carry you forward into more publicity.

Local papers, as we have seen, offer advantages for nonprofits. They are read by people in the organization's target market who may be exactly the audience you are trying to reach. Local papers are also relatively easy to get into. If you provide a local story that affects local people, you have a good shot at getting it into print. A local story in a local publication is a good foundation for a portfolio of news clips that can be useful for promotional purposes. As an added benefit for someone relatively new to the field of public relations, placing stories in the local press builds confidence in the ability to generate good PR.

Just as publicity begets publicity, however, story pitches inevitably beget rejection. Not every pitch is going to succeed, nor does it have to. There are many media outlets and many opportunities to tell your story, and they are all there to be explored. Pitch your story to every outlet that is appropriate, but don't expect every story to get picked up everywhere.

Ken Sunshine, founder and president of Ken Sunshine Consultants, says, "Getting turned down is part of the job. Don't let it stop you from trying again."

"Nonprofits need to be persistent when it comes to pitching stories," says Rubenstein. "Not every pitch succeeds. But you should not let that stop you from practicing good public relations."

PART TWO

THE PR TOOLKIT

P art Two looks at the tools and techniques of the PR trade. There are a lot of them, which is why this is the biggest section of the book. Each chapter explains and illustrates the use of something from the toolkit. The sheer array of tools can be intimidating.

Whatever the tool, keep in mind that it is important to use it in the way the person at the other end of the communication wants and expects it to be used. That is why each chapter offers step-by-step guides. It's all pretty elementary.

When I became a father, circumstances dictated that I became a single father, raising my two daughters on my own. Every night after I made dinner and did the dishes, I would join the girls at our dining-room table to help them with their homework, which began to be assigned to each of them in the third grade.

Homework can be very confusing. The teacher writes an assignment on the board or maybe hands out a worksheet that you stuff into your book bag along with your pencils and sharpener and the books, all in a jumble, and when you open up the book bag at night, it's hard to keep straight exactly what it was the teacher wanted you to do. That can be very frustrating. It can lead to tears. Sometimes when I'd ask, "Got any homework?" it *did* lead to tears.

The solution to "no tears" homework, I taught my girls, was "See what they want and give it to 'em." Very simple. Be clear about what is wanted, and then prepare it. It is a rule that also works nicely for the practice of public relations.

In the case of homework, it meant that I bought each girl a little assignment pad that she was to use only—and I stressed the *only*—for writing down homework assignments. She was not to write down homework assignments anywhere but in the little assignment book. Period. That way, she would always know exactly what assignment her teacher expected her to do and where to find it, no matter how much of a mess her book bag was.

It was simple, and it worked. I found that it worked for me in my job as public relations director for a national nonprofit as well. I always made it a point to find out exactly how the various media outlets I dealt with wanted to receive materials. I would double-check who to send something to, when to get it there, and how to package it. In short, I followed the same advice that applied to my daughters' homework: "See what they want and give it to 'em."

Both daughters, all grown up now, tell me they still use that basic rule today. They sometimes modify the rule to "See what they want and give 'em *some* of it," but it has been a key to their success in their relationships and careers.

I also use the rule for the whole range of projects I'm involved in today. When dealing with the media, handling a client's account, planning an event, teaching a course, working with a video producer, or designing a training program, I begin by determining what it is that the people on the other side of the operation need from me to do the job I want them to do. Then I do my best to see that they get it. It all comes down to: "See what they want and give it to 'em."

As you go through the chapters in Part Two, keep the recipient of each news release, press kit, brochure, newsletter, or public service announcement firmly in mind. When you write a media advisory or news release, consider how it will look to the journalist who receives it. Is there a compelling hook that will get the journalist's attention? Is the most important information clearly indicated right up front? When you are crafting a pitch for a producer at a radio or TV station, imagine how you would react if you were in the producer's shoes and trying to juggle a million scheduling details under the remorseless pressure of deadlines in a world where the clock is always ticking. If you doubt that your pitch will immediately grab the producer's attention, go back and develop a new pitch that will.

PR does not exist in a vacuum. Everything is designed to have an impact on the people at the other end of your communications. Be sure you are clear about what they want and need. Then give it to 'em. The following chapters will show you how.

CHAPTER THREE

CHOOSING THE RIGHT SPOKESPERSON

Nonprofits are often involved in multiple complex projects, serving many different kinds of people and providing a range of services in a variety of ways. It can be difficult to effectively communicate the importance of what your organization does so that people come to know and appreciate you, but it is important to establish an identity in the mind of the public. How can an organization establish an identity that will help it stand out from the crowd? It can do what NASA did to put a man on the moon: it can acquire a human face.

One way to do that is to find photogenic, appealing people who have been helped by the organization and use their pictures in promotional materials so that they become the living embodiment of all that your organization does. This is the "poster child" strategy, and children suffering from muscular dystrophy, made famous as "Jerry's kids" by the Jerry Lewis–hosted telethons of the 1950s and 1960s, were an early and highly effective example of this approach. More recently, the Christian Children's Fund used a poster child for its TV spots, which featured a dark-eyed little girl in a bright red dress picking over scraps in a garbage dump; that image conveyed in strong, visual terms the children the organization helps, and it pointed up the urgency of the appeal.

But the "poster child" strategy doesn't literally have to use children. An adult who has been helped by a nonprofit's programs can also personify the organization. Still another way to link the organization with a human face is to use a spokesperson, preferably a celebrity spokesperson.

National Celebrities

The right celebrity spokesperson can work wonders for an organization's image, creating instant name recognition and helping it stand out from the crowd. The spokesperson must be someone who is a good fit with the organization—someone the target audience will recognize, admire, and trust. The celebrity comes to represent the organization in the minds of the target audience; and, thanks to the natural human tendency to identify with people we admire, admiration and trust for the celebrity are then transferred to the nonprofit organization.

The late Gregory Hines, the actor-dancer who was associated with the Harlem Renaissance of tap dancing, proved to be a highly effective spokesperson for New Alternatives for Children, Inc. (www.nac-inc.org), a New York City organization that works with inner-city kids with disabilities. After he died, his role was taken up by the actress Susan Sarandon, who has brought her own warmth and personality to representing the organization.

Other examples of good matches between spokespersons and good causes include former President Jimmy Carter's work as an on-air spokesperson combating pancreatic cancer, the actress Julia Roberts's testimony before Congress on behalf of funding to counter Rett syndrome, and *Today* cohost Katie Couric's efforts to raise millions of dollars for research on colon cancer after her husband died of the disease.

Sometimes a spokesperson chooses a nonprofit. The actor Gary Sinise is a big fan of the United Service Organizations (USO), which provides services to American men and woman in uniform. During an appearance on *The Oprah Winfrey Show,* Sinise made a point of telling Oprah and the audience about the work the USO was doing to keep U.S. troops in touch with their loved ones at home. As USO director of communications Donna St. John points out, millions of viewers whose only image of the USO, if they had one at all, was that of the Bob Hope specials of days gone by, learned that the organization is still very much alive and well and is doing an important job supporting young Americans far from home—great publicity for the USO and its mission, conveyed by someone who was obviously sincere in his feelings for the organization.

"It's wonderful when a spokesperson truly identifies with an organization," notes Alicia Evans of Total Image Communications. That was the case at Leading Ladies, Just for Teens, an inner-city community organization working to promote self-esteem among teenage girls. Evans reports that Brenda Braxton, a Broadway musical director, felt such strong affinity with the teens that the organization was able to use her as a very effective spokesperson.

As a spokesperson for the Gay and Lesbian Alliance Against Defamation, Cathy Renna has appeared on many major media outlets. "One day," she recalls, "I found myself battling it out on MSNBC with Joe Scarborough. I was glad I had done my homework and prepared for the interview so that I could fairly represent the organization.

The next day I got a ton of e-mails. Some said, 'You'll burn in hell.' Some others said, 'Thank God there's someone like you speaking on TV who sounds intelligent and normal.' Some said, 'I've never thought about it that way.' If you really believe in the cause you're a spokesperson for, it can be very gratifying to have such an impact."

Choosing the right spokesperson is essential. Elliott Gould, for example, was a good fit for American ORT, an organization whose supporters tended to be baby boomers and had grown up with Gould through his films, such as *M.A.S.H.* They liked him and identified with him, and his endorsement resonated with them. Until Gould came along, the impressive global scope of ORT's operations sometimes presented a problem for fundraisers: wanting to tell people what the organization did, they would begin listing all the fifty-plus countries that ORT serves, the myriad courses taught at ORT schools, and the proportion of the labor force in each country made up of ORT graduates. It was no surprise that people on the receiving end of this flood of details soon went blank. They might smile and nod politely, but they weren't hearing a word. (People in television have a term for this phenomenon: MEGO, which stands for "my eyes glaze over."). This is where Elliott Gould came in. People might not remember every detail of what he said in the American ORT video he made, but they would link him in their minds to the organization. In effect, Gould became the organization by becoming its representative. If people liked him, they would like ORT. If they trusted him, they would believe ORT worthy of their support—a somewhat illogical reaction, perhaps, but very human. Elliott Gould agreed to be a spokesperson for American ORT because he and a board member were buddies, so Gould did it as a favor for his friend. That is often how it works: somebody knows somebody. In the case of American ORT, Gould also believed in the work the organization was doing, but it was the personal connection that sealed the deal.

Local TV Celebrities

The community relations department of a local television station can be an excellent resource for a nonprofit seeking the right spokesperson. For example, Melvin Taylor, media specialist for the New York Urban League, approached the community relations department of New York's WPIX-TV, Channel 11, to request that Vanessa Tyler, a popular African American newscaster, serve as a spokesperson for the organization's outreach to New York's African American community. In another instance, he approached PBS station WNET, Channel 13, to request TV personality Rafael Pi Roman as an on-air spokesperson for a back-to-school initiative targeted at Latino high school students. In both cases, the stations and the on-air personalities were happy to lend their names, without charge, to positive efforts on behalf of the local community. This was excellent publicity for the Urban League and its work in the local community, and it was great exposure for the spokespersons and the stations. With smart PR, everybody wins.

The Consummate Professional

Working with a good spokesperson can be very gratifying. I was in Los Angeles directing a fundraising video I had written and was producing for American ORT. I was coaching the organization's new spokesperson, the actor Elliott Gould, for his on-camera endorsement. He had arrived at the Los Angles ORT Technical Institute promptly and proceeded to kid good-naturedly with the guys on the camera crew as they adjusted the lighting and did their sound checks.

I had sent him the script in advance, and while the technical people made their adjustments, he and I reviewed the pronunciation of words from several languages. Then, standing among a group of "extras"—students at their computers—he faced the TelePrompTer and read his first line: "Hello, my name is Elliott Gould, and I'd like to tell you about ORT."

The script that Gould went on to read told the story of ORT operations in more than fifty countries. It outlined the programs and talked about the important role ORT was playing in the lives of more than one hundred thousand people around the world. The final video, of course, was not going to feature Elliott Gould just standing there rattling on and on; no audience would pay attention very long to a "talking head." We would use Gould's reading of the script as a voice-over, a narration to be heard while images of the programs he was describing appeared on the screen.

After his opening line, we taped Gould saying a few more sentences as he stood among the students. We used some of that footage for the first scene of the video, and the rest for the closing. Because we knew that he would not be on camera for the remainder of the six-minute script, we were able to solve a problem—ambient noise—that comes with shooting on location.

The best way to get a really polished, professional look and sound to a video is to shoot in the controlled environment of a studio. You can control everything, and when the director asks for quiet on the set, you actually get quiet on the set. Unfortunately for production perfectionists, however, many celebrity endorsements need to be shot on the grounds of a nonprofit's facility.

The Los Angeles ORT Technical Institute was on the ground floor of a building on traffic-filled Wilshire Boulevard. Outside on the street, cars were speeding by, horns were blaring, brakes were squealing, and there was absolutely nothing we could do about any of it. Even getting those few on-camera lines was a matter of shooting take after take. Through it all, Gould remained pleasant and unruffled, but his patience was being sorely tried.

After we finished shooting Gould's on-camera footage and played it back on the monitor, just to be absolutely sure we really did have it, we grabbed a microphone and went looking for the least noisy place we could find in the school building. That turned out to be a storage closet. Soon Elliott Gould, the sound man with his headphones, and I were crammed together in the tiny closet. We left the TelePrompTer outside, and Gould, holding the mike close, read from a paper script while the sound man tracked the sound levels through his headphones. I concentrated on making sure that Gould placed the emphasis on the correct words and handled the tricky parts of the script, like correctly pronouncing the name of the capital of Albania.

When the sound man indicated that some particularly intrusive street noises were still getting through the closet door, we commandeered a heavy blanket from somewhere and draped it over Gould's head, to muffle the noise. Looking ridiculous, but sounding wonderful, he finished reading the script, did a second read-through as a backup, repeated a half-dozen problematic words, and then, still very pleasant and the consummate professional, left for a lunch meeting.

After I combined his voice-over with previously shot footage of ORT schools around the world, we had a powerful video that did a great job of telling the ORT story at chapter meetings and fundraising events throughout the country. The video became a very effective fundraising tool. It also established Elliott Gould as a highly effective spokesperson for ORT.

Finding Celebrity Spokespersons

How do you go about finding a celebrity spokesperson? You begin by asking everyone on the board, along with the lay and professional leadership, who knows a celebrity.

"That is how the North Shore Child and Family Guidance Center got Mary Tyler Moore to be a spokesperson," says Alicia Evans. "It was all personal connections. Someone on the board knew her and asked her, and she said yes. It was that simple."

It was equally simple getting the late Tony Randall to travel out to Long Island to be the guest speaker at the annual dinner dance I was working on for the Nassau County Mental Health Association. Someone on the board had a nephew who worked with Randall and asked him to lend his time and prestige to help the organization. Randall graciously obliged.

It has been said that there are only six degrees of separation between one person and any other person. Many people argue that the separation is really more like two degrees. To prove that point, the host at a meeting of an executive women's networking group asked one of the women in attendance who she needed to meet in order to advance her particular project. "Oprah Winfrey," the woman responded. The host then asked the thirty women in the room, "Who knows someone who knows Oprah?" Three of the women raised their hands. One of them knew Oprah personally. The other two were one degree removed. There was a similar result every time the host named a different celebrity. Some of the women in the room were amazed, but not the hostess. Networking experts know that no one is very far removed from anyone else.

Nevertheless, if you've run through your personal contacts and still haven't connected with a celebrity who is a good match for your organization, there is another way to go about it. You can hire someone to find the right spokesperson for you. Some speakers' bureaus provide spokespersons for organizations. You can find a host of speakers' bureaus online. Some specialize in athletes; others, in authors; still others, in political pundits. Some are "department stores" that strive to serve the need for every kind of speaker. Most, however, focus on providing one-time-only speakers for national conferences or annual events. Many prefer not to play "matchmaker" between a nonprofit and a person who will serve as the organization's regular spokesperson over the course of a year or more, but one bureau that does try to arrange the perfect match is American Speakers Bureau (www.speakersbureau.com), in Orlando, Florida. Frank J. Candy, founder and president, takes pride in finding just the right spokesperson for an organization. "It is important to be clear on exactly the image you want to project," he advises. "Organizations considering going the spokesperson route should realize that it can be like a marriage: you're in the relationship for the long term. And any relationship takes work."

Candy points out that a number of factors can influence the selection process. "You have to consider geographical locations, timing, travel, products, the budget, the client's needs and wants, and managing the expectations of everyone involved. In some cases, nonprofits have very unique situations, so there isn't a cookie-cutter solution to finding and working with celebrities, sports figures, and spokespersons. It is advisable to write down everything you want them to do so that when you start asking for it, it is in writing . . . because they will ask for it in writing."

Rita Tateel, founder and president of the Celebrity Source (www.celebrity source.com), in Los Angeles, has matched celebrity spokespersons with a range of nonprofits, including the American Heart Association, the Design Industry Foundation Fighting AIDS, and the Women's Sports Foundation. For Tateel, finding a spokesperson who is a good fit with a nonprofit means considering a range of celebrities, such as Cameron Diaz, Kelsey Grammer, John Travolta, Martin Sheen, Pierce Brosnan, Will Smith, Jennifer Love Hewitt, Patrick Stewart, George Clooney, and Danny Glover. She teaches a class at UCLA called "Recruiting and Working with Celebrities" and has been a featured speaker at the annual conference of the Public Relations Society of America. According to Tateel, the key in preparing to find a celebrity spokesperson for an organization "is to appreciate that time is the celebrity's most important commodity. So many people are clamoring for their time: their agent, manager, publicist, attorney, accountant, family, friends . . . so they have very little time left. It is best to ask for the least amount of time needed to accomplish the mission. Asking someone to lend their name—for example, by agreeing to be listed as an honorary member of the advisory board—takes no time beyond saying yes, so they are more likely to do it."

Other common requests that make minimal demands on celebrities' time include asking to use their names in press releases and quotes and asking to use their signatures on fundraising letters. These requests are often combined with others that are more time-intensive, such as asking celebrities to appear in public service announcements and to make personal appearances if scheduling permits.

Rita Tateel recommends that a nonprofit be creative in finding ways to use as little of a celebrity's time as possible. For example, if a celebrity is on the set of a TV show, ask her to shoot a thirty-second PSA as a talking head, reading your script from cue cards or a TelePrompTer on the set of the show, and perhaps using the equipment already there.

According to Tateel, celebrities usually get involved with charities for one of three reasons: because they or people close to them have been personally touched by an issue, because they have become emotionally involved with an issue after doing research for a movie or TV role, or because they have been asked to lend their names as a personal favor to people they know.

The first of these motivations is the most powerful. Denzel Washington, for example, spent a lot of time at the local Boys Club while he was growing up, and today he serves as the national spokesperson for the Boys and Girls Clubs of America. Michael J. Fox, who has Parkinson's disease, is associated with research on the condition, just as the late Christopher Reeve, paralyzed in 1995, was involved with research on spinal cord injuries, and Mary Tyler Moore, a diabetic, is involved with research on juvenile diabetes. The actor David Hyde Pierce, whose grandfather died of Alzheimer's disease, is involved with the Alzheimer's Foundation.

Bette Midler, who founded the New York Restoration Project to create parks throughout New York City, provides another example. "When I moved to New York City with my family, I was shocked and saddened to see vacant lots full of junk," writes Midler in her fundraising appeal. "So I decided to do something about it."

A classic example of the celebrity whose support for a cause evolves from research on a role is that of Tom Hanks, who got involved in advocating AIDS research after starring in the film *Philadelphia*. In the same way, he became involved with NASA after making *Apollo 13* and with veterans' organizations after *Saving Private Ryan*.

As for involvement as a personal favor, the cast of the TV show *Friends* all supported the Lili Claire Foundation for children with neurogenetic disorders, such as Down syndrome and Williams syndrome, because the show's casting director was involved with the organization, which holds an annual fundraising event emceed by Matthew Perry, one of the stars of the show.

The Cost of Celebrity

Tateel notes that if you don't ask for much of a celebrity spokesperson's time, there may not be a fee; at a minimum, however, the nonprofit should be prepared to cover all standard expenses. Standard expenses for an event featuring a celebrity typically include first-class round-trip airfare for two, a first class hotel (usually a suite), a limousine to and from the airport as well as to and from the event, and an allowance to cover meals ($100–$150 per day, depending on the city).

Many nonprofits can get all or most of these expenses donated. With the problems airlines have faced in recent years, they are less willing than they used to be to donate tickets, but a nonprofit should be able to get a supporter to pay for the airfare.

Limousine companies are often prepared to donate a car in exchange for the exposure because there is no cost to them for simply making the car available, but they typically ask the nonprofit to cover the gratuity to the driver, which ranges from 15 to 20 percent of what the fee would have been. A board member will often pick up that expense.

In addition, the nonprofit should plan on providing gifts to the celebrity. Like everyone else, celebrities enjoy receiving presents. Gifts provide a little extra incentive. Companies, in exchange for exposure, are generally happy to provide their products as gifts to celebrities. They like the public to see their products being used, worn, and carried by celebrities. In addition, they usually ask for exposure in program books for the event, in press releases, and so on. Arranging for the gifts is fairly straightforward. You ask a board member or local businesses to donate them, or you can contact the company directly by way of the PR department, which is most likely to appreciate the value of making the gift available to the celebrity.

It is always nice to enlist celebrity spokespersons who are willing to donate their time out of friendship or because of sympathy with a cause. When that is not the case, however, it may be necessary to pay an honorarium. Depending on the celebrity and the amount of time being requested, the honorarium typically ranges from $20,000 to $50,000; you should not plan to pay less than $10,000.

Celebrities, even "free" celebrities, usually do not come cheap. But the advantages of having the right celebrity identified with your organization can be well worth the costs.

CHAPTER FOUR

WRITING AND PLACING THE NEWS RELEASE

Rudyard Kipling, perhaps best known as the author of *The Jungle Book*, was also a journalist. He knew that to tell stories, whether about a boy raised by wolves or about the accomplishments of an organization, it is important to include certain basic elements. In his poem "Six Honest Serving Men," he named the same elements that are taught in journalism school, where they are usually presented in order of their importance: *who, what, where, when, why*, and *how*. Kipling's "six honest serving men" are the essential building blocks for telling a news story.

The beginning of a story is called the *lead* (sometimes the *lede*), and in a news release, that is where these basic elements of the story should appear. They are often in the first paragraph or even the first sentence. When a press release is written by committee, as it sometimes is at a nonprofit, the actual lead of the story may get buried in the third paragraph and be preceded by long, rambling statements about the organization's mission or history. Don't count on a journalist to have the patience to wade through all that to get to the meat of the release. The key material goes in the lead, and the lead, as its name suggests, belongs in the first paragraph.

When reporters or editors receive a news release, they do not read it over, pen in hand, deciding which parts to use and which to discard. When deciding how much of a release to use, they begin with the first paragraph and go on from there. To make it fit into the space available, they cut from the bottom up. This means that the last paragraph is the first to go.

If the story still does not fit, the next-to-last paragraph is also dropped, and so on. Sometimes when an editor is done trimming a story, the only thing left is the lead paragraph. That is why the really important parts of your story should be in the lead.

Deciding What Is Important

Lynn Diamond, former editor in chief of *National Jeweler*, the leading trade publication in the jewelry industry, is very firm in her advice to public relations people about sending send long releases to the press. "Three pages is usually way too long," she says. "It's an unrealistic way of trying to get a story into print. The publication typically only has room enough to give your story two or three brief paragraphs, if that. At many publications, the person who gets your story is relatively young, newly out of journalism school, and has little or no knowledge of the industry. Do you really want *them* to be the ones deciding which parts of your story are important enough to make it into the paper? Doesn't it make more sense to put the most important parts of your story right up front? That way, you are the one who decides what is important enough to make it into print. And the people at the publication don't have to play hide-and-seek, looking for a story lurking somewhere in those meandering pages. It's a win-win."

For those tempted to stuff a release with every possible tidbit, no matter how unimportant, Diamond further cautions, "Even if you tack on the trivial stuff at the end of the release, you run the risk of an editor thinking *that* is the really important material and running that instead of the information you wanted to get placed. Limit the release to the essentials, and you are in control."

Finding a Hook

Every press release needs a hook. A hook is something that grabs the reader's attention and compels him to read on. It is the most important part of your release because if you don't hook the journalist from the beginning, he will not go any further.

A hook can be something that links your story to a holiday or special occasion. People can be hooks. Try working a local celebrity into the story. A hook can also be a news event, a scientific breakthrough, a newly released study—anything that will cause a potential reader to look twice and actually read your story.

You cannot get your message across if no one is paying attention. Often the hook is in the headline.

Headline Hooks

Some PR people say that the headline is 100 percent of your release because if a journalist's attention isn't captured by the headline, she won't read any further. A good headline is one that compels a journalist to read the rest of your press release.

Always keep in mind that what the media want is a good story. Your hook should say loudly and clearly that you are offering a good story and that you are providing it in the way journalists want it and can use it.

Calendar Hooks

It is important to find appealing angles to a story. "Try to tie your story to something that will have appeal for the media," advises Alicia Evans of Total Image Communications. "Tried-and-true standbys include grandparents and kids. The media loves both, especially kids."

The calendar is a ready resource, too. "Calendar events, even relatively obscure ones, can also be a great source of hooks for a press release," says Evans. "When HUD [the U.S. Department of Housing and Urban Development] was breaking ground for affordable homes in Hempstead, on Long Island, it looked like it was going to be a pretty routine, ho-hum story. We've all seen lots of stories about groundbreaking ceremonies, and they're all pretty much the same. Different people with different shovels, but the same story."

So Evans went to a calendar and found that the event was happening during National Rose Month. "That gave me the idea I needed to make this groundbreaking ceremony different. In honor of the month, everybody who was going to be getting a house was given a bouquet of roses. It made the story more interesting and more visually appealing, with all those people holding their roses and smiling, and the story got some pickup."

The calendar offers many other possibilities as well. "The UN has declared June to be International Flag Month, so you can work in a photo of a line of children holding flags of many nations. All it takes is some imagination," Evans says, "and you can find a hook for almost any story in the calendar."

Local Hooks

Another good hook for a story is the local angle, notes Lynn Uhlfelder Berman, senior media relations manager at YAI/National Institute for People with Disabilities, New York. Berman sends out different versions of the same basic story to different regions, and in each region she focuses on a different local resident—for example, a Brooklyn family for the Brooklyn papers, or a Long Island family for the Long Island papers.

The Local Angle: The American Airpower Museum

The local angle is key to publicity for the nonprofit American Airpower Museum (www.americanairpowermuseum.com) at Republic Airport in Farmingdale, Long Island. Gary Lewi, executive vice president at Rubenstein Associates, Inc., heads the museum in his time off. According to Lewi, the story is never just about the museum's vintage aircraft but always about the people whose lives the aircraft have affected.

"Just because I love the sound of a P-47 engine roaring in at five hundred feet doesn't mean I expect every newspaper editor to be moved by it also," says Lewi. "What editors are looking for is a story that will interest readers. They want a story about people."

To commemorate the anniversary of D-Day, the museum hosted a visit from *Fifi*, the last World War II–era B-29 Superfortress still flying today. To give the story local appeal, the museum invited two Long Island residents to the event, both veterans of the war in the Pacific. The story focused on the two men's personal connections to the giant airplane.

One of the men had served as a bombardier aboard a B-29 as part of the 20th U.S. Army Air Force. The other had survived the fall of the Philippines, the Bataan Death March, and three and half years of inhumane treatment in a Japanese POW camp. The first time he had seen a B-29 was in 1945, as he looked up from inside the barbed wire while the huge bomber dropped food packages down to the starving American soldiers in the camp. If the plane had not made its lifesaving food run, many of the Americans in the camp would not have survived the war. Powerful stuff—and all delivered with a local slant, to provide the all-important hook.

"This works especially well for the neighborhood weeklies," Berman says. "A good story, with solid information and featuring a local resident, is gold to them. They will usually run the story word for word as we send it to them. It gives us a chance to get our message out and to include a quote from the chief executive officer or president, but we are always careful to keep the focus on the local person."

Exclusive

When you pitch an exclusive story to someone in the media, you should contact only one person at a time. No journalist likes to find out that you've pitched the same "exclusive" story to the competition. If you do it and are found out, it can seriously impair your credibility.

Writer's Block

Dorothy Parker is credited with having said that no one likes to write but people do like having written. Before the age of computers, the great terror writers faced was a blank sheet of paper in the typewriter. That has been replaced today by the terror of the blank computer screen. Even professional writers have a quiet terror of that empty screen, so if preparing a news release seems a daunting task, you are in good company. The trick, as with so many things, is to "just do it." Write down something, anything, just to get past that first awful blank page or screen.

Don't worry about style, grammar, or spelling in your first draft. You'll deal with all that later, when you rewrite. For now, just get the story down as plainly as you can. Pretend you are writing a letter to a friend, and answer the question, "What's new?" Begin with "who," go on to "what," deal with "where," and then take care of "when." If "why" is not clearly implied, put that in, too, and then, if appropriate, "how." Get that opening sentence down, and you've started your news release.

Most stories, however, are not sent out on an exclusive basis. They go out to as broad a reach as possible, in the hope that they will be widely picked up and printed and aired.

The Format of the News Release

Editors and reporters get hundreds of news releases every day. If your release does not look professional it will not be read (see Exhibits 4.1 and 4.2). There is a right way to prepare a news release. The following guidelines explore the elements of a news release in detail.

Length

Brevity is always a good idea. If you are sending your release by e-mail, try to limit it to no more than half a dozen short paragraphs, and fewer whenever possible. A release that is faxed or mailed should ideally be limited to one page, and it should not be longer than two pages. This is a rule sometimes observed more in the breach than in the observance, but it is nonetheless sound. Journalists have neither the time nor the inclination to read longer releases.

For an e-mail, keep everything in the main message, and do not send attachments unless they are specifically requested. For a hard copy, use only one side of the paper,

EXHIBIT 4.1. PRESS RELEASE FROM ST. HUBERT'S ANIMAL SHELTER.

Contact: Kelly G. Vanasse
908-707-8101 or kgvanasse@kellycommunication.com

CANINE COTILLION: DOGS ON THE CATWALK
St. Hubert's New Breed of Charity Dinner for Dogs
and Their People Aids Homeless Pets

Madison, New Jersey, April 5, 2004—It will be *Fashion Unleashed* when St. Hubert's Animal Welfare Center celebrates its 4th annual **Canine Cotillion** on April 18. The gala benefit will spotlight fashion as dogs and their people dress to the "K-9's" for this society event of the spring season.

Dogs and dog lovers are invited to attend this elegant affair on **Sunday, April 18, 2004 at a new venue: the Birchwood Manor located at 111 North Jefferson Road in Whippany, New Jersey.**

The Canine Cotillion will help raise much-needed funds to feed, shelter and provide care for the nearly 4,500 animals that find safe refuge at St. Hubert's animal shelters each year.

In addition to fine dining and wines, the Canine Cotillion will feature "Dogs on the Catwalk"—St. Hubert's version of a fashion show with "real dogs." Four-legged guests will have the opportunity to strut their stuff on the runway for a spectacle of high canine couture. Entertainment will include live music and auctions.

This year's live auction, a model search for the 2004 "Runway Rovers," will give guests the opportunity to bid on their dogs to earn the coveted titles of "Gucci Poochi" and "Ruff Lauren." These lucky dogs will enjoy a professional photo shoot with the Image Maker Studios and their photos will appear in *New Jersey Life Magazine*. Winning dogs and their owners will also win fashion and indulgent prizes that will make them feel like models for a day.

The formal dining event will begin at 4:30 p.m. with a Cocktail Reception and Silent Auction.

Seating is limited. Tickets are $225 per person and $25 per dog; sponsorship opportunities are available. For more information or to make reservations, call 973-377-4962. Visit www.sthuberts.org for more information and photos from last year's Cotillion.

Editor's Note: High resolution photos available upon request.

ABOUT ST. HUBERT'S ANIMAL WELFARE CENTER
Founded in 1939, St. Hubert's Animal Welfare Center is a nonprofit organization dedicated to the humane treatment of companion animals. Its services to the community include pet adoption and animal rescue, animal-assisted therapy, humane education, dog training and pet loss support. St. Hubert's animal shelters in Madison and North Branch, NJ, provide care for approximately 4,500 animals every year. For more information about St. Hubert's call 973-377-7094, or visit St. Hubert's on the Web at: www.sthuberts.org.

Source: Courtesy of St. Hubert's Animal Welfare Center.

EXHIBIT 4.2. PRESS RELEASE FROM THE AMERICAN RED CROSS.

American Red Cross

in Greater New York

FOR IMMEDIATE RELEASE

Contact: Annie Lazar
212-875-2133 (w)
lazara@arcgny.org
www.nyredcross.org/pressroom

RED CROSS RESPONDS TO INCREASED NUMBER OF INCIDENTS IN LAST 24 HOURS—COLD SNAP A FACTOR

Residents of Building Collapse Expected to Be Housed Through Monday

New York, NY, November 11, 2004—Responding to 15 incidents in the past 24 hours, the American Red Cross in Greater New York was on the scene at a building collapse in East Harlem, a fatal fire in Staten Island, and additional fires in the city's other boroughs.

During the day and evening hours, 42 Red Cross staff and volunteers assisted 107 people with temporary housing, food, clothing, and government agency referrals and fed nearly 100 firefighters and other first responders and city personnel at the various incidents.

According to Rosemary Calderalo, disaster services administrator at the American Red Cross in Greater New York, "The cold weather was certainly a factor in the high number of incidents. Usually we respond, along with the city's Office of Emergency Management, the Fire Department, and other agencies, to about eight fires and emergencies a day, and last night it was up to fifteen."

The major response yesterday was to the building collapse at 1723 Lexington Avenue, in Manhattan. The Red Cross set up a reception center at the Julia de Burgos Cultural Center to provide immediate shelter for the 65 clients who were evacuated from the five buildings directly affected by the collapse. The Red Cross also registered them for additional assistance, including temporary housing for 62 people (51 adults and 11 children in 9 families), food, clothing, psychological support, and referrals to other agencies for additional assistance.

"We comforted many people who were shocked when they came home to find out they had no place to go," stated Lauren Ginsberg, director of health and mental health in Disaster Services. The Department of Buildings is expected to make a determination about the safety of the structures by Monday. Until that time, the Red Cross will continue to support these families and other residents who need assistance.

"This was a particularly complicated response and involved a close degree of cooperation and coordination between the Red Cross, Office of Emergency Management, NYPD, FDNY, MTA, and Department of Housing Preservation and Development," added Calderalo.

Be Prepared . . . Families and individuals can learn simple safety steps to take before a disaster strikes by attending a Red Cross *Preparing for the Unexpected* class. The one-hour presentation teaches participants how to create an emergency communications plan, how to assemble a disaster supplies kit, what to do if disaster strikes and basic First Aid. The class begins at 6:15 P.M. every Thursday at 150 Amsterdam Avenue (between 66th and 67th Streets). To register, call 1-877-REDCROSS or visit *www.nyredcross.org* <*http://www.nyredcross.org*>.

The American Red Cross helps people avoid, prepare for, and respond to emergencies. We also help them rebuild their lives after an emergency. In addition to responding to major disasters like the events of September 11, the American Red Cross in Greater New York responds to an average of eight emergencies a day, such as fires, water-main breaks, and building collapses. The Red Cross also offers a variety of health and safety courses on such subjects as first aid and adult and child CPR. To schedule a safety course, call 1-800-514-5103 or visit *www.nyredcross.org* <*http://www.nyredcross.org*>. For general inquiries, call 1-877-REDCROSS.

Source: Courtesy of the American Red Cross in Greater New York.

Release on a Survey Report

A release announcing the results of a report or survey may defy many of the rules of length simply because so much information is being made available from which journalists are invited to pick and choose. When Ken Brown, public relations director for New York University's School of Continuing and Professional Studies (www.scps.nyu.edu), issued a release reporting on a university study of patterns of philanthropy in New York City, it ran to three full pages of small type. Had a more standard point size been used, the release would have run to four or even five pages.

The headline read "NYU Philanthropy Survey: More Than Half of New Yorkers Gave to Charity Last Year" and was followed by four subheads citing different aspects of the report's findings. Each area was covered in detail in the release. The format allowed reporters to quickly focus on specific areas of interest.

Brown structured each of the first three paragraphs as single long sentences and reserved the fourth paragraph for a quote about the changing nature of fundraising from Naomi Levine, executive director of New York University's George H. Heyman, Jr. Center for Philanthropy and Fundraising (www.scps.nyu.edu/phil). Levine is quoted throughout the long release, offering insights into the survey that put the results in perspective. Brown notes that although Levine's comments contribute to the length of the release, they also make the story more usable for journalists because the comments clarify the significance of the study's findings.

---

and allow a one-inch margin on both sides and at the top and bottom. Copy—that is, the text—should be double-spaced. The last paragraph on a page should end on the page; a paragraph should not be carried over to the following page.

Paper

When you send a news release by fax, use 8½-by-11-inch white paper. If you're sending it by mail, make sure the paper is 20-pound weight. Your organization's letterhead will usually work well for the first page of the press release. Subsequent pages should be on blank sheets. While it seems obvious, you might be surprised at how many people miss this one: make sure the paper is clean. Coffee-stained pages will not endear your release to an editor.

Identification of the Organization

If you are not using letterhead for the first page of the release, then place the name of your organization and its address and telephone number, as well as the Web site and e-mail address, in the upper left-hand corner of the first page. You don't want a journalist to have to guess where the story came from or be unclear about how to contact the organization for follow-up information.

Release Time

Begin flush left, about an inch down from the organizational information at the top of the page, and indicate the timing for release of the information with the words FOR IMMEDIATE RELEASE, all in caps. This tells editors that they have your permission to print the story as soon as possible. Unless there is a specific, time-sensitive reason to hold your story until a certain date, "immediate" is what you want.

Sometimes a news release is issued with a time qualifier—an indication that the story is not to be released until after a specific time. For example, if your story is tied to the results of a survey that will not be officially released until later in the week, the release might be sent out early, with the stipulation that the information not appear until the date indicated. In that case, the following words will appear in caps, flush left and directly under the date: FOR RELEASE ON [DATE].

Release Date

Begin flush left, just under the release information, and enter the date that the release is being sent, which is not necessarily the date it was written.

There is an alternative format for dating a news release. After the headline (see "Headline," below), skip a line and, starting flush left, spell out, all in caps, the name of the city followed by the two-letter U.S. Postal Service abbreviation for the state (for example, CHICAGO, IL). If you haven't already indicated the date at the top of the page, it goes here, typed in upper- and lowercase: May 13, 2005. The story begins on the same line. Again, when you date the release, use the date it is being sent, which is not necessarily the date it was written.

Contact Person

On the right side of the page, flush with the right-hand margin, and on the same line as FOR IMMEDIATE RELEASE, give the name of an organizational contact person and his or her title. Make sure that the person whose name is listed is well informed and prepared to answer questions about the release.

Directly under this person's name, and also flush right, give his or her contact information. In addition to an office phone number, it is usually a good idea to provide a cell phone number and an e-mail address as well. It may make sense to give the names of two contact persons and accompanying contact numbers, to ensure that someone will always be available. If a journalist has questions about your story and can't get the answers quickly, a story from some other organization may make it into the news instead of yours. If a journalist does call with questions, it is acceptable to answer by saying, "I don't know the answer to that question, but I will find out and get right back to you." Obviously, you should get back to the journalist promptly. In all cases, you need to deliver the information quickly and, above all, accurately.

Headline

Skip down a space, and position your headline in the center of the page. A headline should be in all caps. It should be brief, clear, and "punchy" and may contain the hook for the story. The headline should grab the reader's attention. If it doesn't capture a journalist's attention, he may not read any further.

Since all journalists are pressed for time, they tend to look kindly on a story that comes in with a good, ready-made headline. If you can't be punchy, a good alternative is to be clear. Right from the start, let the journalist, and the reader, know what your story is about and why it is of interest. Aim for impact.

Sari Botton (www.saribotton.com), a veteran journalist who writes for *The New York Times*, the *New York Daily News*, and *Time Out*, is also a regular panelist at the National Publicity Summit, where she advises PR people on the best ways to get through to the press. She says, "Press releases need compelling headlines that tell us what we're going to be reading about in a nutshell. They shouldn't be too dense—short and sweet works best."

Botton's advice is sound. When I worked with a nonprofit that sponsored a kids' concert to raise money for children with disabilities, the headline of the press release read "Rockin' the Day Away for a Very Special Cause." Some papers ran the full headline; others shortened it to "Rockin' the Day Away," and one cut it to the single word "Rockin.'" All worked to grab readers' attention. Partly because of all the advance publicity, the concert was a sellout.

Subtitle

A short subtitle can appear under the headline. It should be in upper and lower case and in the same font as the headline. The purpose of a subhead is to flesh out the headline with a little more information, to further intrigue the reader without lessening the impact of the headline.

Bottom of the First and Subsequent Pages

At the bottom of every page—except the last page of the release—place the word *more* in lower case, centered between two dashes. It should look like this:—more—.

Top of Subsequent Pages

It is a convention to "slug" the second and all subsequent pages of the release so that the continuation of the story can be located if the pages are separated. A slug repeats the first few words of the headline in the upper right-hand corner, flush right. It indicates that the page is the continuation of the story. The slug is followed by a forward slash and the page number: Rockin' / 2. Alternatively, on the line immediately under the slug line, and flush right, you can indicate the page number along with the total page count of the release: Page 2 of 3.

Gathering of Pages

Clip or staple the news release's pages together in the upper left-hand corner.

Sentence Length

Keep sentences simple and short, ideally under twenty words. People will get the message faster in a shorter sentence. Your goal is to communicate, and you do that best by being brief. If you must include a long list of names and titles that extends a sentence to awkward lengths, try not to put it in the first paragraph.

Paragraph Size and Spacing

Paragraphs should be short. Paragraphs in the body of the release should usually be no more than three or four sentences. Use a new paragraph for each separate point in your story. Big blocks of type on the page are a turn-off to anyone who has to read them.

A paragraph, referred to as a *graf*, should finish on the same page it begins. This can take some juggling and shifting up and down on the page and may mean leaving a little extra room at the bottom of the page, but it makes for a neat, professional appearance.

Looking professional sends the message that the organization is to be taken seriously. In the realm of the weary journalist, the neatly presented press release is king.

Paragraph Structure

Like a sonnet or a haiku, a press release has its own definite structure. It is a structure composed of paragraphs, with each successive paragraph serving its own function. This is writing to a formula for purposes of clarity. The instructions that follow do not represent the only way to write a press release, but they describe a way that will provide clarity and increase the chance of your news release becoming news.

First Paragraph. Skip down a space after the headline, indent, and begin your news release. The first paragraph of your release is vital. It should convey all the main points of your release. Keep Kipling's "six honest serving men" in mind. If the journalist reads no more than the headline and the lead paragraph, she should know all the basic information of the story.

The lead paragraph should have no more than three or four sentences and often runs only one or two sentences long. Again, be sure the key information is there in your first paragraph, just in case one paragraph is all the space the editor decides to allot to your story.

Second Paragraph. The second paragraph is a good place for a quote from an organizational leader. Be sure to include the leader's full name and title. You stand a better chance of getting her name into the news if you give her something substantive and newsworthy to say rather than just empty platitudes. Numbers are good. If your leader is quoted about the number of people attending an event, the total raised, the scope of the need, or the dimensions of the expected crisis, her words read like expert commentary and present her as a knowledgeable authority.

Third and Fourth Paragraphs. The story is fleshed out in the third and fourth paragraphs. Details are given that explain, supplement, and "put meat" on the bare-bones facts stated in the first paragraph. If there is a call to action, this is where it usually goes.

Final Paragraph. The last paragraph of your release should feature the "boilerplate" (that is, standard) information about your organization that you hope will make it into print but know probably won't. The paragraph typically includes information about the organization's founding, its scope, its key statistics, and its mission statement.

As pointed out earlier, editors don't pick and choose which parts of your release to print and which to leave out. They cut from the bottom up, whittling away paragraph after paragraph until the story fits the available space, so the first thing to hit the editing room floor is that last paragraph. Still, sometimes you get lucky, and the editor has some extra space, so that final paragraph makes it into print, too.

Ending the Release

On the last page, after the last paragraph of the release, skip several spaces, and then center three pound signs in the middle of the page: ###.

News Releases by E-Mail

E-mail has become the standard delivery system for news releases, media alerts, AFI (available for interview) notices, usually simply called *AFIs*), features, and basically all other communications with the media. With the exception of some media outlets that prefer getting their news by fax, assume that news releases will travel by e-mail.

George DeTorres, account manager at PR Newswire (www.prnewswire.com), a public relations research and distribution source, says that many nonprofits use large-scale electronic news releases to disseminate stories. An eight-hundred-word news release going out nationwide to 4,200 media outlets and posted to 3,600 online Web sites and databases will typically cost about $1,100. According to DeTorres, "E-mailing a news release allows you to directly penetrate media newsrooms and the newsrooms of your target audience."

E-Mail Subject Lines as Headlines and Hooks

Because most press releases are sent by e-mail, the subject line serves as a de facto headline. A good subject line will often include a hook.

New York public relations professional Julie Farin, who has worked with a range of nonprofits, including the Leukemia Society of America, has relationships with many journalists to whom she has never spoken on the telephone, let alone met face to face. The majority of her communication with them has been by e-mail.

"Many times the way you deal with journalists today is by e-mail, and not by phone," she says. "The most important element in your e-mail is the subject heading. The subject line must be short and engaging, even provocative, to get them to open it. Journalists receive way too much information every day, and they are overwhelmed by it all. You must make your e-mail stand out. I usually type subject lines in all caps, just like a traditional headline. Once they open your e-mail, you want them to get the point right away. To make it easy, I like to make the first four lines very short items, with bullet points."

Cathy Renna of Fenton Communications notes that many journalists prefer not to get phone calls at all. "They leave a recorded message on their voice mail saying, 'Please do *not* leave a message, send me an e-mail.'" Renna says the majority of her communication with journalists is by e-mail. She always sends releases by e-mail except in the case of local TV stations, which usually prefer to have releases faxed to the assignment desk. She finds that instant messaging (IM) is also becoming a popular mode of e-mail communication.

It is not uncommon for a journalist to have an official e-mail address, which is posted in his or her newspaper or magazine, and also to have a private e-mail address that is not generally known or available to the public. Renna has the personal e-mail addresses of a number of journalists at *The New York Times* as well as at other papers, but she uses them sparingly. Although she is careful not to abuse them, when an organization she is representing has a really important story, she will use those private e-mail addresses to connect with the journalists she needs to reach.

"Establishing that kind of relationship of trust is not easy," Renna says. "Like all relationships, they take effort and develop over time."

Alicia Evans of Total Image Communications has not sent out a press release by "snail mail" for years. "With the anthrax scare after 9/11, many journalists no longer trusted the mail as they had," she explains. "And anyway, there's really no point in sending out a release by mail and then waiting two or three days for it to arrive."

Evans says she e-mails or faxes everything. "When I send an e-mail, I never send anything as an attachment unless someone specifically asks me to. People won't open attachments because they are afraid of downloading a virus. I put the entire release in the body of the e-mail."

Evans e-mails her release first, and then she faxes and often also calls. "I leave messages on the journalist's voice mail in the evening, so they will find it on their machines when they come to work in the morning. I leave very brief messages, nice and direct, saying, 'If you would like additional information for the story, you can reach me at . . . ' I'm always courteous, always try to convey that I'm offering to be a resource to help them do their job."

Lynn Uhlfelder Berman of YAI/National Institute for People with Disabilities uses e-mail to send one-page media alerts.

"I'll sometimes send an e-mail and cut and paste elements of a news release directly into that," she says. "But I keep it short. No one has time to read a lot of copy." Like Evans, she advises never sending a release as an attachment because of the pervading concern at media outlets about viruses.

In an e-mail release about her organization's annual Central Park Challenge event, Berman focused on Bill Ritter, a local and national TV news personality, and shaped the release more as a personality profile or news "item" than as a straight news story. For New York–area media outlets, Berman highlighted Ritter's role as co-anchor of the local WABC/Channel 7 news program because that was the strongest local appeal of the story. "When sending it to national outlets, I played up his role as a correspondent for *20/20* on ABC, since they wouldn't be interested in his job at the local station," Berman explains. Exhibit 4.3 shows the e-mail as Berman sent it to Richard Huff, TV columnist for the *New York Daily News*. Note the phrase "Time sensitive TV column item" in the subject line. It indicates that the e-mail is coming from someone who knows what is important to the journalist on the receiving end and helps ensure that the e-mail gets opened and read. The story appeared as the lead item in Huff's column "Inner Tube" the following day, under the headline "Ch. 7 Anchor's Personal Tribute to the Disabled" and featured a head-shot photo of Ritter, supplied by the station. The item, placed at the cost of an e-mail and a follow-up phone call, garnered great publicity for YAI and its Central Park Challenge.

E-Mail Overload

Berman has also encountered problems of what can best be described as "journalist e-mail overload."

"I had sent an e-mail to a journalist at a major daily and then followed up with a phone call. When we spoke, he told me hadn't seen the story. He said his work mailbox was so inundated with releases that he usually didn't even bother looking at it. He gave me his personal e-mail address and asked me to resend the release to it. He had just stopped looking at his work e-mail because he was overwhelmed."

Once the story reached him, the journalist liked it enough to run it in his column. But the placement might not have happened if Berman hadn't followed up and found another way to get the story to him.

For many journalists, e-mail can be too much of a good thing. Connecting on a personal basis can be the best way to cut through the problem of information overload. As with all media relations, establishing a relationship can be key to getting stories into the news.

Follow-Up E-Mails

Not all journalists have given up on their e-mail. It is a fact, however, that many journalists often do not return phone calls. This means that the best way to follow up an initial e-mail is with another e-mail. The usual rule is that if you haven't sparked enough interest for a journalist to get back to you after three contacts, take it as a "no" and move on.

It is relatively simple to find the e-mail addresses of media people by going to the Web sites of their news organizations. Generally, the names and e-mail addresses are listed under the "Contact Us" link or in the "Editorial Information" section. Some Web sites provide direct links to reporters' e-mail addresses. Their e-mail addresses also often appear at the end of bylined articles or columns.

It cannot be repeated too often that you should not even consider sending a release or press kit as an attachment unless you are specifically requested to do so. With the proliferation of viruses, no journalist is going to open an attachment from you unless he knows you personally, nor should you open attachments unless you are absolutely sure of the senders.

Anatomy of an E-Mail Release

As has been pointed out, the most important part of the e-mail is the subject line. Media people receive literally hundreds of e-mails every day, which means that the few words in the subject line must be compelling if they are to be noticed. If you don't catch the recipient's attention and whet his appetite for more information right from

EXHIBIT 4.3. SAMPLE E-MAIL RELEASE.

From: Lynn U. Berman/YAI
Date: Tuesday, June 1, 2004, 1:45 PM
To:
Cc:
Subject: Time sensitive TV column item

Hi Richard:

I thought this might be of interest for your TV column. If you have any questions, please let me know.

Thank you for your consideration.

Lynn U. Berman
YAI/National Institute for People with Disabilities
212-273-1234 W
212-981-4567 Cell
212-123-4567 H

PEOPLE WITH DISABILITIES HOLD A SPECIAL PLACE IN BILL RITTER'S HEART

WABC-TV's Co-Anchor to Support YAI/National Institute for People with Disabilities' Central Park Challenge

NEW YORK (June 1, 2004)--When WABC-TV's Bill Ritter joins YAI/National Institute for People with Disabilities' Central Park Challenge on Saturday, June 5th, he will be thinking of his younger brother Alex, who was born in 1957 with Down syndrome. "He was back then known as a retarded child," said Ritter, who supports YAI/NIPD's programs to help people with developmental and learning disabilities and their families throughout the New York metropolitan area. "If he had been born today, he would have been just a child with special needs. It is not just a semantic difference, not just political correctness . . . but a difference in approach and attitude.

"Today Alex would have been a child--first and foremost. Had Alex been born now, instead of the 1950s, he likely would have survived and even thrived with the support of programs like YAI/National Institute for People with Disabilities. I think my parents knew that. Until the day they died, my mom and dad couldn't speak about Alex without breaking down."

Ritter, who also is a correspondent for ABC's "20/20," will join Dominic Chianese (Uncle Junior from "The Sopranos"), David Eigenberg (Steve Brady from "Sex and the City"), Miss Teen USA Tami Farrel, Zach Leibowitz of ESPN2's "Cold Pizza," and other celebrities to support people with disabilities. YAI's Central Park Challenge features a competitive 5K run, a 3K fundraising walk, Junior All-American races for children 12 and under, a children's activity area, and fun for the whole family. The event will run from 8:30 A.M. to 1 P.M., at the 72nd Street entrance to Central Park at the bandshell. The day is a celebration of the abilities of all individuals and promotes inclusion of people with disabilities in the community.

"On Saturday, June 5th, I'll be doing more than just helping an organization raise consciousness about people with special needs--it's about giving them equal opportunities to reach their individual potential," Ritter said. "I'm also paying tribute to my brother Alex, and to my parents. And for me, what a great honor indeed that is."

To support YAI's Central Park Challenge, call 212-273-6526, or log on to www.yai.org/cpc.

Established in 1957, YAI/National Institute for People with Disabilities is a not-for-profit health and human services organization dedicated to building brighter futures for people with developmental and learning disabilities and their families. Among YAI's more than 400 community-based programs are early intervention, preschools, counseling, day services, employment training and placement, health care, residential services, and recreation. For more information about YAI, log on to www.yai.org or call toll-free 1-866-2-YAI-LINK.

Source: Courtesy of YAI/National Institute for People with Disabilities.

the beginning, he is likely to delete your e-mail instead of opening it. But if you do manage to pique his interest, you've managed to get a foot in the door.

Once your attention-grabbing subject line has prompted him to open your e-mail, a brief, well-conceived pitch should be the follow-up. Put the most important information in the first two sentences of the first paragraph, and assume that this is all he is going to read. That is the "two" in your "one-two punch." Convince the journalist that the story will be of compelling interest to his readers, and he will read on.

E-Mail and Professional Etiquette

If someone from the media calls to get more information, be sensitive to the fact that he is working on deadline. A quick response is essential and appreciated. If you don't have at your fingertips the information he is seeking, offer to get it to him quickly, and be sure to follow through. Such demonstrations of professionalism and respect are part of building relationships with the media.

How do you establish such relationships? You may not be able to physically meet the people you are sending your stories to, but you can establish a kind of "pen pal" relationship. If you read something a journalist wrote, or if you see or hear a story he did on TV or radio and think it noteworthy, take the time to send off an e-mail to him, praising a job well done. It is rare for journalists to get that kind of positive feedback. Sincere appreciation is appreciated in turn. Similarly, if you come across a bit of information that augments a story he has done, forward it with a note. Again, it lets him know someone is paying attention to his work.

Although relationships are nice, be careful not to lose professional perspective. Remember that communications with journalists are on the record. If you put something in an e-mail, even in a casual, personal note, you may see it in print, so be careful with what you send.

Plain Text or HTML? There are two ways to send an e-mail release. Plain text is the simplest. In the body of the e-mail, you simply type your release in the same format you would use for a release traveling by regular mail.

The alternative to plain text is HTML (hypertext markup language), which is available with most e-mail programs. It enables you to format your release to look like a Web page, complete with your logo and other graphics. It looks much more impressive than plain text.

But that elaborate look comes at a price. The extra file size means that a release in HTML will take longer to download at the other end than a release in plain text—as much as two or three times longer. Since most people won't wait eight seconds for a Web page to download, you can be fairly sure that an e-mail that takes too long to open is likely to be deleted unread. With competition already so fierce for media attention, why stack the odds against yourself?

Also, after it has been received, a release in plain text can be read offline. HTML often cannot be read offline, and if the recipient has signed off, he may have to go online again and download the release a second time in order to read it. And, one more negative, not every e-mail system can read HTML, so you run the risk of sending something that will not be readable when it gets to the address to which it has been sent. Because you are reaching out to media people whose prime concern is to get information, the no-frills, plain-text option is typically the best choice.

However you send your release, be sure to proofread it carefully before you send it. Mistakes in grammar, spelling, and punctuation detract from the professionalism of the release, the organization, and the sender of the release—you. Also be sure that your contact information includes the organization's Internet address so that a click can take the recipient of the e-mail directly to your Web site and to the wealth of information in its virtual press room.

CC or BCC? If your media list of newspapers, magazines, and radio and TV stations contains up to a few hundred e-mail addresses, the favored technique for sending out your e-mail is to address it to yourself and copy your list of e-mail addresses into the "BCC" (blind carbon copy) line. Don't make the mistake of pasting all those addresses into the "To" line or into the "CC" (carbon copy) line. If you do, the first thing all the recipients will see is the e-mail address of everyone else on your list. Each recipient will know that his address is being shared with everyone else on the list. People tend to get very annoyed when that happens. It is worth taking care to avoid placing your contact list in the wrong line.

If a journalist replies to your e-mail and you in turn reply to him, be sure that you remove all the names from the BCC line. You don't want to inadvertently send your reply, meant perhaps for his eyes only, to other people.

After the Placement. As with all stories that appear in newspapers and magazines or on radio and TV, make a point of thanking the media person responsible. Thank him or her with an e-mail, certainly, but also with a handwritten note. Because such old-fashioned courtesies are rare, they are all the more appreciated.

Mailing Lists on CD and Online

You can expand your reach by purchasing a mailing list on CD. Companies like Bacon's (www.bacons.com) and Gebbie Press (www.gebbie.com) sell CDs that can be used to find the specific media outlets that relate to your areas of interest.

If your budget allows, you can also arrange for an online service to e-mail your press release. A number of companies, such as Business Wire (www.businesswire.com), Internet Wire (www.internetwire.com), Online Press Releases (www.onlinepressreleases.com), PR Newswire (www.prnewswire.com) and Xpress Press (www.expresspress.com) will not only distribute your release but, for an added fee, will also write it for you. Business Wire and PR Newswire offer broadcast faxing services as well.

Sending Logos, Mastheads, and Other Graphics

When Jean Bloch Rosensaft, senior national director for public affairs and institutional planning at Hebrew Union College–Jewish Institute of Religion, sends a release by e-mail, she does not include the school's logo, masthead or other graphics. She just sends plain text. "The graphics take a long time to download, and so the e-mail will be slow, especially at smaller papers and for independent journalists who may not have broadband service." However, as more subscribers have shifted to faster Internet connections, she has begun to experiment using a simple masthead with the institution's identity branding on the e-mails. When she faxes a news release, however, she typically does include the organization's distinctive masthead and logo at the top of the page. "Our logo, an open Torah scroll surrounded by our motto in Hebrew lettering, is very much part of our identity and appears on all our literature. Identity branding reinforces the school's recognition, impact, and outreach to the media."

When PR consultant Ronni Faust sends out complex graphics, such as magazine covers, she usually sends them as an attachment accompanying her text e-mail. In rare instances, she will send the actual artwork by messenger or will send the link to the client's Web site, where the graphic can be accessed. "It depends on how the publication prefers to receive material," she says. "Most are very computer-friendly. In fact, I don't know of any publications these days that don't prefer digital pictures. My job is to make it easier for journalists to do their job." In either case, Faust likes to make a follow-up call a couple of hours later, to be sure the reporter got what he or she needed.

When Faxes Are Preferred

New York publicist Cynthia Horner, while working on the health and wellness fair at Harlem's North General Hospital, an event briefly described in Chapter Two, accessed the hospital's contact list and found a wealth of information. "The hospital had contact information for all the offices of every local political leader, including the mayor, the governor, both U.S. senators, and all the congressional representatives."

Horner set to work calling each office to find out who to send invitations to. In most cases, she was advised to fax a one-page release on the event, with a cover sheet addressed to the specific person she had spoken to and a note indicating that the release was being forwarded on the basis of that conversation, and at that person's request. She included her own contact information, being sure to clearly indicate her cell phone number, and asked recipients to get back to her if there was any interest.

"Virtually every office said they preferred faxes to e-mails," says Horner. "Several people told me they are totally inundated with e-mails. And they like faxes because with a fax, all the information is right there in front of them." Horner notes that radio and TV program directors as well as editors at some smaller weeklies often prefer faxes to e-mails for the same reason.

She was also told to include a detailed schedule, with the timing of the various parts of the event. "The person may want to arrive at the same time as a specific speaker, or they may want to avoid being there at the same time as someone else, or they want to be there when certain things are happening, or when certain people will be there for a photo op."

As mentioned in Chapter Two, among the notables her efforts netted was Congressman Charles B. Rangel, who was a big hit with the crowd gathered for the event. Horner made sure that his staff had her cell phone number so they could let her know when the congressman was on his way. She alerted her own staff to look out for him, and when he arrived, she was ready to greet him and introduce him to people at the hospital.

Horner advises people who have not done this kind of thing before not to be intimidated by the prospect. "It's not that complicated and is largely a matter of some common sense and planning and knowing what you are trying to accomplish."

When the Local Development Corporation of East New York (LDCENY) (www.ldceny.org), a nonprofit that encourages entrepreneurship, held its Women's

Entrepreneur Business Conference in Brooklyn, the featured speaker was Congress-woman Nydia M. Velázquez, the ranking Democrat on the House Small Business Committee. The congresswoman's office worked with Ojeda Hall-Phillips, director of the Women's Business Center at LDCENY, to create a news release on the event. The media advisory issued by Congresswoman Velázquez's office was sent by both e-mail and fax and featured the very impressive heading "NEWS FROM CONGRESS-WOMAN NYDIA M. VELAZQUEZ" all in caps at the top of the one-page release.

Writing the News Release

Avoid the All-Purpose Release

Whenever possible, avoid using a "shotgun" release, an all-purpose release sent to every publication. The slant of a release going to a metropolitan daily will be different for one written for a suburban weekly or a trade or association publication. Preparing in-dividual releases for each type of outlet requires more effort but can be well worth the time spent.

Before starting to prepare the release, you should be familiar with the various media outlets to which it is being sent. Become familiar with their interests and style requirements, and then craft your release to fit in with each publication. Major cor-porations often send out "shotgun" releases, but they have the advertising clout that gets editors to assign someone to rewrite as needed. Nonprofits generally have to make it easy for an editor to use their releases.

Keep Your Audience in Mind

If you are reaching out to a community TV or radio station or publication, you will usually concentrate on the local angle, emphasizing things that are of interest to that community. Human interest pieces are popular for just that reason. People enjoy read-ing about their neighbors.

A professional association is a different kind of community. The members may be widely separated geographically but have common interests. To communicate with this audience, you will probably want to concentrate on things that are of professional interest to the group. Dentists, for example, would find stories about how other den-tists overcome patients' fear of the drill useful in their own practices.

If you are reaching out to a bird-watching society, for example, a story highlighting a discovery made by a local club about the migratory habits of Canada geese may be the best way to get your group some attention. Similarly, a piece that offers useful tips for teachers may be a good vehicle to garner publicity in the journal of a teach-ers' association. Every market has its own concerns and interests. Once you identify and understand those interests, you can play to them.

Have Something to Say

Your preparation does not end with identifying your market and determining its concerns. You need to shape your news release in a way that makes it worth reading. You must ask and be able to answer the question "Who cares?"

If a journalist reads your headline and lead and reacts with a shrug, you've wasted an opportunity. Your release has to contain something she believes will interest her readers. You don't have to be offering the key to world peace, but your information does have to be significant to the market you are attempting to reach.

A news release that conveys information about an upcoming bake sale or blood drive is presenting news that is of value to local readers. By contrast, a long, rambling statement from an organization's president about its goals or long-term mission will not be perceived as news.

If your president is determined to orate in print, you will need to find a newsworthy angle to his message. Identify an issue in which your organization has an interest. Quote your organization's president or spokesperson offering a solution, suggesting an alternative, or providing helpful information on the issue. Your release then becomes a vehicle for disseminating valuable information to the public from someone who is knowledgeable on the subject. Make the spokesperson's comments a news story, and you can put them in a news release.

Alternative vehicles that provide a good platform for organizational leaders are letters to newspaper and magazine editors and op-ed pieces.

Write Clearly

Use familiar words. Think of your press release as a conversation with a reasonably intelligent person. Pitch the level of your language to that level. Don't try to impress the reader with your extensive vocabulary and complex sentence structure. Just be clear and straightforward, as you presumably would be in a conversation.

Unless you are writing for a trade publication whose readers can be assumed to be familiar with the special technical terms of their industry, avoid using jargon. If you do use specialty words—and they can add a note of color to the piece—explain what they mean, or be sure their meaning is made clear in the context in which they are used.

Proofread Carefully

It is very easy in the heat of the moment to make mistakes involving grammar, spelling, names and titles, and numbers, but even a minor mistake can undermine your credibility. Carelessness in spelling suggests carelessness in getting your facts right. Relying on your word-processing program's automatic spell-check function may not be enough, because it will OK a wrong word as long as it is spelled correctly.

Read over your release slowly and carefully, and then read it over again. Ask someone else to read it over as well, looking carefully for errors. It is worth taking that extra time to calmly review and reflect before you send out the release. The devil is in the details, and accuracy counts.

Get the Name Right

"Say what you want to about me, just spell my name right," goes an old saying. Getting the names right is as crucial in the nonprofit world as it is in the commercial sector, sometimes more crucial. In the for-profit world, people get paid for jobs well done. In the nonprofit world, often the only reward supporters receive is recognition. Making sure they get that recognition is an important part of the PR function.

To be sure that the name of the organization's president or a particular chairperson gets into the story, make a point of placing the person's name early in the release. The second paragraph is usually a good place for a quote or a statement attributed to a leader. Choose a significant statistic or important fact and attribute it to that person by using the words "according to" or "announced" or "noted": "The organization's goal is to plant 2,500 shrubs in city parks within the next six months," according to Green Parks president Jane Smith.

Be sure not only to spell names correctly but also to get middle initials and titles right. Take the time to be sure. Getting someone's name or title wrong is a sure way to create unnecessary ill will.

Mistakes will happen. Just try not to let them happen in print. Double-check everything in your news release, and pay special attention to the names.

Do the Work for Them

Reporters and editors are always strapped for time. You can help get your story into print by doing the bulk of the legwork yourself. Write the headline, develop the angles, do the research, suggest people to interview, and include their contact information. Make it as easy as possible for the journalist to do the story.

Local publications are wonderful sources of publicity for nonprofits. Many are small weekly publications with very limited resources. They are always searching for ideas and stories with a local slant and will often print your complete story, exactly as you send it to them.

After receiving a press release, many journalists prefer getting the supporting materials they need online rather than in a traditional press kit. Your press release should clearly indicate the address of your organization's Web site so that a journalist can download background information, bios, photos, maps, suggested questions, and anything else that may be needed for the story.

A Photo Is Worth a Thousand Words—Sometimes

When you send a release about an event that has already taken place, it is often a good idea to include a photo with the story. A captioned photo to accompany a story is usually welcome and can increase your chance of getting the story into a publication. Steve Friedman, who runs Steve Friedman Photography and Video in New York City (www.stevefriedmanphoto.com), advises asking the publication exactly how it wants to receive the photos. Find out whether it prefers black-and-white or color; otherwise, consider sending both. Although color photos can be printed in black-and-white, they sometimes look washed out or too "contrasty".

Photos are generally sent via e-mail, as attached JPEG files. It is a good idea to find out what size and resolution the publication prefers. Newspapers and magazines typically want to receive photos that measure 5 by 7 inches and have a resolution of 300 dpi (dots per inch). The exception is when the photo will be printed larger than 5 by 7, in which case you'll need to send the photo in a larger size that is at least as big as the print size. When e-mailing photos it is usually a good idea not to send more than one or two at a time in order to keep the message size down. The usual comfortable limit to send in one e-mail is two megabytes.

When there are many photos involved, it may be easier to send them to the publication on a CD. Alternatively, you can post the photos on your Web site, using FTP (file transfer protocol) software, and include a direct link to them in the e-mail you send to publications. Keep in mind that a small weekly paper or church bulletin may not be able to handle digital photographs and may prefer hard copies of photos. Again, asking what the editor wants is always a good idea.

There are some basics to follow in taking photos to accompany a press release. Newspapers and magazines are about people. You want to limit the number of people in the frame so that everyone can be easily identified. With some exceptions, like graduation photos, photos of a group of fifty people taken from thirty feet away do not get used. It is too hard to make out who everybody is.

The photo should be something an editor will want to use and will be able to use. Get the people in the photo to do something other than stand stiffly, staring at the camera. For example, if your group is repairing a house, get everyone painting and hammering and hauling. Have something that identifies the organization in the frame. T-shirts, with the name of the organization clearly visible, can be good. A hat, sign, or banner works too. Make sure the name of the organization is clearly visible in the photo since you can't always rely on people to read the accompanying caption when it is published.

Each photo should be accompanied by a caption. When you caption the photo, explain the action and identify each person in the picture, from left to right: "The Harbor View Committee is hard at work repairing homes damaged in the winter storms. Shown, left to right, are Sally Smith, president; Harry Jones, treasurer; and Jane Brown, volunteer coordinator."

If you are sending a hard copy of the photo, the caption should be typed, beginning halfway down the page of a standard 8½-by-11-inch sheet of paper. Using clear tape, attach the blank top half of the page to the back of the photo so that the caption is positioned under the photo, making it possible for the editor to read the caption while looking at the photo. Fold that bottom half of the paper up over the photo to protect it in transit. Never write on the back of the photo or use glue to affix the caption to the back.

If you can't afford to hire a professional photographer to cover your event, someone on staff can take photos. The quality and ease of use of digital cameras are such that as long as you don't cut off anyone's head in the picture, chances are you'll be able to take a good photo of the event. Prepare a caption for each photo, and you're ready to send the photo digitally to local publications. If your photo is good, chances are they'll run it.

Note that it is never a good idea to send poor-quality photos. They will not be used by the publication and will be taken as an indication that you are an amateur and not to be taken seriously.

As a media specialist for the New York Urban League, Melvin Taylor has worked a lot with community papers. He advises sending photos with accompanying captions along with a post-event release to local newspapers. "They often don't have the staff to cover an event themselves," Taylor observes, "but they like to run pictures of local people, so they're fairly likely to print the photo and the release."

Experience has taught Taylor another lesson as well. "It's always a good idea to position the important people in the center of the group, just in case the editor has to crop the photo to make it fit the page. You don't want the guest of honor, or the president of the organization, to be the person being cropped out of the photo."

Local publications welcome good photos of local-area residents and activities. A post-event press release on a special event, accompanied by a selection of good photos, can result in an attractive photo spread that gains visibility for the organization and is a nice way to provide some well-earned recognition for the people involved.

A good example is provided by the post-event coverage of the annual February luncheon and fashion show held by the Richard David Kann Melanoma Foundation of West Palm Beach, Florida. The week after the event, the society page of the *Palm Beach Daily News* featured half a dozen photos, each capturing two or three well-dressed people smiling happily at the camera. The organization's annual golf tournament, held six months later, generated a single large photo of eighteen members of the tournament committee sitting and standing as they, too, smiled at the camera. In both cases, the photo was accompanied by a four-paragraph story about the organization and the event. The names of the people pictured in each photo appeared in captions beneath each photo. The photos were not particularly creative or dramatic—nothing about them was going to advance the art of photography—but for a community-based, people-centered organization, they were very effective indeed.

"Sometimes the paper sends a photographer, and sometimes we take the photos ourselves," says Emily Painter, the foundation's special events/community liaison, who handles public relations. "We always shoot digitally and then either e-mail the photos to the paper or deliver them on a disc." When the stories and photos appear in the paper, Painter makes photocopies of the articles for inclusion in press kits and mailing to the organization's supporters. Coverage in the press adds to the organization's credibility and hence to its effectiveness in carrying out its mission.

The United Service Organizations (USO), which provides support services for U.S. service personnel, sometimes acts as a kind of matchmaker between photojournalists in the field and publications seeking good photos. Donna St. John, the USO's director of communications, explains how the system works. "We provide the e-mail address of publications that need photos to photographers in the field," she says. "For example, if *People* is doing a piece that they need photos for, and they have a tight deadline, we'll contact the photographer in the field, and instead of sending the photo to us, so that we can forward it to the publication, he or she will send the photo directly to *People*. We work with people who have a long background as photojournalists, and they know the kind of photos the magazine needs."

Digital photos, as already described, travel via e-mail. If you are sending a hard copy of a photo, it should go into a sturdy manila envelope. The pages of the release, the caption page, and the envelope itself will usually be enough to protect the photo. You may want to write or stamp "Photographs—do not bend" on the envelope to discourage a letter carrier from cramming it into tight corners. New York photographer Steve Friedman stamps his envelopes with the distinctive: "Photo! No Bendo!"

Sending the Release

Timing

Timing is everything. Afternoon newspapers, called *PMs,* generally go to press from 11:00 A.M. to 3:00 P.M. Your release should get to the editor or reporter you want to reach no later than 9:00 A.M. Morning papers usually go to press in the evening, between 6:00 P.M. and 11:00 P.M. Get your story in by noon.

Sundays and Mondays are good days for placing stories. Sunday papers have more space, and Mondays tend to be slow news days. Try to avoid days that coincide with major local or national events that will take up space and leave less for you.

Weekly papers that come out on Thursday generally go to press on Tuesday. It is usually best to get them the material by the previous Thursday.

Who Gets It?

Send your release to the right media, and address it to reporters and editors by name. More releases are discarded because they were sent to inappropriate media than for any other reason. A little time spent identifying the best outlet for your release can save a lot of wasted effort.

Identify the specific reporter or editor you want to send your release to at each publication. A school or an educational organization, for example, would usually send stories to the education editor. Send your release to the appropriate person by name and title. If you don't know the name of the reporter or editor, make a point of finding out.

Review the publication, and go to its Web site to find out who at the paper covers what kinds of stories. You can also just call the publication and ask. Tell the person who answers the phone what section you think your story best fits into, and ask for the name and title and e-mail address of the person you should send your release to.

Again, be careful to get the spelling of the name right. No one likes to get mail with his or her name misspelled. Also, if you are careless about accuracy when it comes to names, it suggests that you will be careless about getting other details right. That is not a good way to begin a relationship with someone in the media.

"Check out various media outlets, and decide which are likely to publish your story," advises Deborah Sturm Rausch, director of public affairs for the New York State Office of Mental Retardation and Developmental Disabilities in Albany. "Then identify reporters and editors who are likely to be interested in your story and who will either write about it themselves or assign someone to cover it. Each media outlet, producer, editor, and reporter has their own area of interest. Seek out those whose interests match up well with what your organization does."

Rausch emphasizes that "knowing the media outlet is vitally important." Be sure that you are current on stories that different outlets have done on your subject, especially recently. The last thing you want to do is pitch a story to someone who just recently wrote about it. Propose something you know will interest the editor's or reporter's public.

Where to Send It?

How do you decide where to send your news release? Chances are you are already familiar with a number of publications in your geographical or professional area. Reviewing the selection of periodicals at a good newsstand can suggest an additional range of placement options. The Internet is an excellent source of research on media. Start with www.newspaperlinks.com, which offers free links to every newspaper by city and state and by specific name. Other free sites include www.benton.org and www. iwantmedia.com.

To put together a really comprehensive media list, you need media directories. Directories are available in both printed and online versions; a list of media directories appears at the end of the chapter.

Of the media directories available, Bacon's (www.bacons.com) and BurrellesLuce (www.burrellesluce.com) are the main players. Some directories focus on just one medium; others combine TV, radio, Internet, and print opportunities among their specialties. Bacon's, for example, offers a selection that includes *Newspaper/Magazine Directory*, *Radio/TV/Cable Directory*, *Media Calendar Directory*, *Internet Media Directory*, *NY Publicity Outlets Directory*, and *Metro California Media Directory.*

Specialized directories are available that are geared to various industries, such as LexisNexis (www.lexisnexis.com), which serves the medical and legal fields. There are also geographical directories, organized by city, state, and region. If your organization has offices in different regions of the country, you should get the names of key media outlets from staff people in each location.

A useful resource for reaching specific ethnic groups is *The NCM Directory of Ethnic Media* (www.ncmonline.directory.com), which describes itself as a bridge to America's ethnic media and communities. Available in both print and online versions, it provides comprehensive listings of over eighteen hundred ethnic media organizations in the United States, including print, online, radio, and TV outlets. It features media serving African, Asian, European, Middle Eastern, and Native American populations and operating in virtually every language on the planet, from Arabic to Yiddish. A sampling of the NCM site includes a listing of 51 Jewish media outlets nationwide, from the *Algemeiner Journal* to the *Yiddischer Kemfer*; 355 African American media outlets, ranging from *About Time* magazine to radio station XHRM/92.5 FM; and 683 Hispanic/Latin American outlets, ranging from *Acción Latina* to Z Spanish Radio Network/KZSF 1370 AM.

The sheer number of directories makes it impossible for most nonprofits with multiple target markets and audiences to purchase every one they might need. In any case, printed directories are usually outdated upon arrival. For this reason, Internet-based media guides have become very popular. They are constantly updated, and the user can download choices into Microsoft Excel and then use mail/merge to print out letters and envelopes. Online guides also offer the ability to sort through lists instantly, combining and targeting various lists at will. The user receives a password that allows use of the service at any time, from any computer.

For large companies, organizations, and agencies, the cost of online directories can be money well spent because their releases are usually going out on a weekly or daily basis. In addition, the "pitching information" given for follow-up can be helpful, featuring things like how various editors prefer to be contacted (e-mail, telephone, fax, letter), which days not to call, and so on. The lists are constantly updated, so every time you retrieve a list, there is a message noting how many changes have been made since the last time you visited. This allows more time for pitching and sending out releases, which can mean more productivity for PR staff.

For many nonprofits, however, especially smaller ones, it may not make sense to buy directories unless there is one that suits an organization's specific needs. For a small nonprofit with limited resources, a good source of directories is the reference section of the public library. Another way to get around the high cost of printed directories is to approach local public relations or advertising firms and ask them for the last editions of their directories after they have replaced them with newer editions. Some of the names and contact information will have changed, but most of the listings will be fairly current. These "lightly used" directories can be a valuable resource for a non-profit building a targeted media list.

Following Up

Follow-up is essential. Track the stories you pitch. After you have sent your release, wait a day or two, and then follow up with a call. Many people are reluctant to make follow-up calls, not wanting to annoy the media. Be polite, be respectful of their time and professionalism, but be persistent. Make that follow-up call.

Journalist Sari Botton advises, "Send materials with plenty of lead time. Send reminders as dates get closer—an email, a letter. Don't overuse the phone, but don't rule it out completely."

When you call, it is a good idea to have some additional information to convey, something that makes the story even more newsworthy. Point out how your story ties into events in the news. Consider possible links to an upcoming holiday, special event, or anniversary. Think about how your story relates to a special supplement the paper will soon be running.

Your goal is to be thought of as a valuable resource, not a pest. If you send out releases every week, for example, it is not a good idea to call about each one.

If a journalist calls you to follow up, remember to be flexible. She is on a deadline and has plenty of other stories she can do if you are not available. Make the time to speak with her at her convenience. Earning a reputation as a helpful professional who is efficient, reliable, and readily available can count for a lot, especially the next time you want to get a story placed.

Distribution Services and Media Directories

Distribution Services

If you want to send your release out for nationwide distribution, you can consider using one of the large commercial wire services, such as PR Newswire (www.prnewswire.com) or Business Wire (www.businesswire.com). The cost of sending an eight-hundred-word

---

Managing Expectations

PR professionals like Ronni Faust know you can never be 100 percent sure about whether a release will be picked up by the press. In addition, she notes, many reporters will want to speak with the key executive or spokesperson to get original quotes and anecdotes to make the story more original. "I've sent out stories I didn't expect to be picked up and because of a slow news day, they got great play. It sometimes works the other way as well. If you're a strategic planner, you're most likely going to meet your expectations. But you can't control other news that might be breaking the same day, so sometimes, it goes beyond planning. The client deserves to understand the entire picture, which will go a long way to managing expectations."

---

release to every print and electronic news organization in the country is approximately $1,000. Shortening the release to four hundred words and limiting the distribution to a single geographical region can cut that cost to a few hundred dollars.

Should a nonprofit incur the added expense of a distribution service? Donna St. John of the USO feels the expense is justified by the results. She says the fax system that USO previously used to distribute its releases did not work very well. Since switching to PR Newswire, she says, "we've seen an increase in PR contacts and coverage. We can see that far more of our articles get picked up in the print media and electronic media and on Web-based publications. And we are getting more calls from the media about our releases."

Media Directories

Bacon's MediaSource
Bacon's Media Directories
New York Publicity Outlets
Metro California Media Directory
Bacon's Information, Inc.
332 S. Michigan Avenue
Chicago, IL 60604
(312) 922-2400
(800) 621-0561
www.bacons.com

BurrellesLuce MediaConnect
BurrellesLuce Online Media Directory
BurrellesLuce
75 E. Northfield Road
Livingston, NJ 07039
(973) 992-6600
(800) 631-1160
www.burrellesluce.com

Editor and Publisher
International Yearbook
P.O. Box 16689
North Hollywood, CA 91615-6689
(800) 562-2706
www.editorandpublisher.com

Gale Directory of Publications
and Broadcast Media
Thomson Gale
27500 Drake Road
Farmington Hills, MI 48331
(248) 699-4253
www.galegroup.com

Gebbie Press All-in-One Directory
P.O. Box 1000
New Paltz, NY 12561
(845) 255-7560
www.gebbieinc.com

Standard Periodical Directory
National Directory of Magazines
Oxbridge Directory of
Newsletters
Oxbridge Communications Inc.
186 Fifth Avenue
New York, NY 10010
(212) 741-0231
(800) 955-0231
www.mediafinder.com

NCM Directory of Ethnic
Media
275 9th Street
San Francisco, CA 94103
(415) 503-4170
(415) 503-0970 (fax)
www.ncmonline.com

News Media Yellow Book
Leadership Directories Inc.
104 Fifth Avenue
New York, NY 10011
(212) 627-4140
www.leadershipdirectories.com

Senior Media Directory
Mature Market Resource
Center
1850 W. Winchester Road,
Ste. 213
Libertyville, IL 60048-5335
(800) 828-8225
www.seniorprograms.com

Standard Rate and Data Service
1700 Higgins Road
Des Plains, IL 60018-5605
(847) 375-5000
(800) 851-SRDS
www.srds.com

CHAPTER FIVE

MAXIMIZING ALTERNATIVE PRESS TOOLS

Some nonprofit organizations seem to have the attitude that because their cause is so worthy and their work so compelling, publicity should be a matter of the media just naturally beating a path to their door. That attitude tends to get in the way of mounting an effective public relations campaign.

At the other extreme, and perhaps more common in the nonprofit world, is the conviction that only large organizations with huge PR budgets can afford to play the PR game and get into the news. That attitude can shut down an organization's PR campaign before it ever gets started.

Like anything else, effective public relations is a matter of mastering some basic techniques. Among those techniques, according to Pat Smith, executive vice president at Rubenstein Associates, Inc., is "learning who gets the material you're sending out, how they want to receive it, and when they want to receive it. Then it's a matter of filling in the blanks. Unfortunately, many nonprofits are not very good at doing that."

Experienced public relations professionals stress that the key to getting publicity is giving journalists what they need to do their jobs. Lynn Uhlfelder Berman, senior media relations manager at YAI/National Institute for People with Disabilities, regularly places stories in the press and on radio and television by understanding what the media needs. It was that win-win synergy that led to WABC-TV meteorologist Bill Evans doing live remotes from the finish line of YAI's 5K Run and Family Fun Day fundraiser. YAI provided a staff member to help with logistics as well as a board member and a person with a disability served by the agency to fill the two-minute segment that appeared with the weather forecast. The coverage gave Evans what he needed—great visuals for his remote—while also providing excellent publicity for YAI. Everybody won. Good PR can be that simple.

Calendar Listings

Perhaps the most basic kind of publicity an organization can get is the calendar listing. All newspapers and most other publications print listings of upcoming events of interest to their readers. The key to getting your organization listed can serve as a good rule of thumb for all public relations outreach to the media. It is essentially a matter of seeing what they want and giving it to them.

"The best way to get an organization's activities into a newspaper's calendar listings," advises Alicia Evans of Total Image Communications, "is simply to know the paper's rules and follow them. That's really all there is to it."

Get a copy of the publication you are submitting your material to, and note how it presents its calendar listings. Different papers use different styles. Some begin with the date, others with the name of the organization, and still others with the kind of event that is being listed. Copy the style that the paper uses. Note, too, what is all in caps or abbreviated. Follow the format scrupulously.

If a contact person is listed, address your material to him by name and title. Find out how he prefers to receive the information, and then mail, fax, or e-mail your calendar listing by the deadline indicated.

The same process should be followed in preparing all materials for the media. There are many PR vehicles that provide an opportunity for an organization to present itself. This chapter presents a range of good examples.

AFI: Available for Interview

A good vehicle for publicity, both print and electronic, is the "available for interview" notice, known simply as an AFI. Tied to an event in the news, an AFI tells an editor or producer that someone from your organization is available to comment on something in the news. Your spokesperson is presented as a qualified expert who is prepared to be interviewed in conjunction with the event. That can be an invaluable asset to a journalist preparing a story on a tight deadline—and journalists are always on deadline.

It can be helpful to pitch the AFI before sending it in. Call the paper, and ask whoever answers the phone for the name of the person who covers the area you are dealing with. Then ask to be connected to that person. When she answers the phone, always begin by asking, "Are you on deadline or is this a good time for you?" Just asking that question will mark you as a savvy professional. You will have scored points before you even begin to pitch. If she is on deadline, ask when would be a good time to call back. Make an appointment. Call back promptly, as scheduled, and don't be too surprised if she is unavailable when you do. The time of a reporter or editor is not hers to control. Call back again later; be polite, but be persistent.

Once you do connect, make your pitch in a sentence or two, highlighting the "juicy" or "sexy" aspects of the story that will appeal to the publication's readers. It's usually a good idea to write your pitch as a script so you can be as brief as possible without leaving out anything important. When you have made your pitch, stop talking.

Answer any questions. If you sense the journalist is especially interested in a certain aspect of the story, shift your focus, and concentrate on that aspect. Keep your conversation brief, and keep it interesting. Then ask, "How can I send you material? Fax, e-mail, snail mail?" And then follow her instructions.

An AFI should be prepared on letterhead, or with the organization's contact information at the top of the page, and should be only one page long. It should have the words AVAILABLE FOR INTERVIEW centered, all in caps, above the headline. The headline itself should tell the story.

The body of the AFI should give the name of the spokesperson and very briefly state why he and the organization are qualified to comment on the issue. It should contain no more than two or three brief paragraphs and should include some statistics to show that you know the issues and to assure journalists that you can provide them with the data they need for their story.

The last line, all in bold, should be a one-line sentence: "To arrange an interview with so and so, contact . . . ," and be sure to give a phone number that will be answered by someone who can respond, or who will at least take a message.

At the bottom of the page, type ###, the ubiquitous three-pound-sign ending, to indicate that there is no more copy to follow.

If a reporter or producer calls the number on your AFI, be friendly and helpful, and arrange for the interview to take place in person or on the phone, as soon as it's convenient for the reporter. By being friendly, cooperative, and professional, you are taking the first steps in establishing a relationship. The next time this reporter or producer is doing a story on a related issue, he will know who to call for expert comment, and when you want to get a feature piece done or a press release picked up, you will have the ear of a friend who can help pave the way for you.

A caution about AFIs: they are easy to do and are often well received by journalists, who count on outside sources for their expert information, but be selective. You may want to think twice before you have someone comment on an issue that involves unsavory characters or controversial issues. If the public links your organization with negative personalities, it can be hard to overcome that link later on. Are you sure, for example, that you want a spokesperson from your organization offering commentary on the latest shenanigans of a celebrity involved in drug abuse, domestic violence, and criminal activity? Those might be just the issues your organization is involved with, and putting a spotlight on your organization could be ideal. But it might also send a confusing message to your supporters that your organization is somehow connected to the celebrity. Take a moment to consider before you announce that that someone is available for an interview.

Media Advisories

A close relative of the AFI is the media advisory, also called a *media alert*. This is essentially an invitation to the media to attend an event that will feature your organization in the news. It is often used to herald the release to the public of the results of a study or a poll and so is a favored tool of organizations that conduct studies, such as schools and universities, although it lends itself well to studies released by virtually any other type of nonprofit organization.

A media advisory is typically sent to daily newspapers and the electronic media the day before the event; weeklies and monthlies need more lead time. Prepared on one page of letterhead, with all the relevant contact information at the top, it is headed all in caps with the words MEDIA ADVISORY followed by the headline, which might read, generically, "XYZ University Releases Poll Results on Public's Attitude Toward the Issue in the News." The body copy is typically a two- or three-sentence paragraph, offering just enough information to tease the media into sending someone to cover the story. This is followed by bold headings, all in caps, reading DATE, TIME, and PLACE and giving that specific information.

To maintain suspense and timeliness, details of the study are not released until the date indicated. A variation on this theme entails sending out a media advisory announcing that the results of a poll or study will be released to the media by phone or fax on a specific day, at a specific time. Clearly indicated on the page are the name, title, and phone number of a person from the organization who will be available to comment on the results in a telephone interview. Phone interviews are kept short so if more than one journalist calls, it is a matter of speaking to one and arranging to get back to the others promptly.

As in all dealings with the media, being considerate of the time pressures at their end is appreciated and can be the foundation of a continuing relationship that yields more stories and more coverage of the organization. Exhibit 5.1 shows a sample media advisory that was mailed, faxed, and e-mailed to the media by YAI's Lynn Uhlfelder Berman, who favors one-page media alerts: "I come to things from the perspective of having worked in the media, and I know that no one has the patience to read a three-page press release. And never send an advisory as an attachment, since most outlets are worried about viruses."

EXHIBIT 5.1. SAMPLE MEDIA ADVISORY (YAI).

From: Lynn Uhlfelder Berman/YAI
Date: Tuesday, June 1, 2004, 11:32 AM
To:
Cc:
Subject: Event on Sat., June 5th

Hi [Reporter's Name],

I thought this might be of interest to you and the Sun's readers. If you have any questions, please call me.

Lynn U. Berman, Media Relations Manager
YAI/National Institute for People with Disabilities
Contact: Lynn U. Berman
212-123-4567 (w)
917-123-4567 (cell)

Susan Wilson
212-123-5678 (w)
917-123-5678 (cell)

YAI'S CENTRAL PARK CHALLENGE ON SATURDAY, JUNE 5TH, 2004, CELEBRATES PEOPLE WITH DISABILITIES' SUCCESSES IN THE COMMUNITY

WHO: Until the early 1970s, people with mental retardation and developmental disabilities were hidden away in institutions like the Willowbrook State School. Now, more than 30 years later, many of these same individuals are leading dignified lives in the community. On Saturday, June 5, 2004, thousands of people with and without disabilities, their families, friends, and celebrities will gather to support YAI/National Institute for People with Disabilities.

Among the celebrities stepping up for YAI are:

Dominic Chianese, "Uncle Junior" from "The Sopranos"
David Eigenberg, "Steve Brady" from "Sex and the City"
Bill Ritter, WABC-TV anchor
Tami Farrell, Miss Teen USA 2003
Keith Hernandez, former New York Met and current Mets broadcaster
Zach Leibowitz, from ESPN2's "Cold Pizza"
Richard Kind, from "Spin City"
Marc Coppola, Q104.3 disc jockey

WHAT: YAI/National Institute for People with Disabilities' Central Park Challenge

5K run (9 A.M.), $20
3K fundraising walk (9:45 A.M.), $10 suggested contribution (pledges can be applied)

Junior All-American races for children 12 and under (11 A.M.), $10
Children's activity area (8:30 A.M.-1 P.M.), $10
Children's package, $15 for Activity Area and Junior All-American Races

WHEN: Saturday, June 5th, from 8:30 A.M. to 1 P.M.

WHERE: Central Park, 72nd Street entrance, by the Bandshell.

SUPPORT: YAI's Central Park Challenge is cosponsored by the **New York City Parks Dept.** The event would not be possible without the support of **ABM Engineering Services, Update Legal, Empire BlueCross/BlueShield, Oxford Health Plans, WABC-TV, Time Warner Cable, Hoy, SBLI and Q104.3 FM.**

For more information, call 212-273-6100 or log on to www.yai.org/cpc.

WHY: Proceeds from this event will support YAI's more than 400 community-based programs, which serve more than 20,000 people with developmental and learning disabilities and their families. Established in 1957, YAI/National Institute for People with Disabilities is a not-for-profit network of health and services agencies serving people with disabilities--from birth through all stages of life--throughout the New York metropolitan area and Puerto Rico.

Source: Courtesy of YAI/National Institute for People with Disabilities.

News Conferences

There are times when the best way to reach out to the media is with a press conference. Also called a *news conference*, it entails bringing the media to the organization and is often used when a problem arises and getting a message out to the media quickly is essential.

Deborah Sturm Rausch, director of public affairs for the New York State Office of Mental Retardation and Developmental Disabilities, has considerable experience with news conferences. She advises approaching the news conference as a collegial undertaking rather than an adversarial encounter.

"Everyone is there for the story," she says. "Your job is to make sure the media gets the story right, and that your message is clear."

To that end, she recommends some basic guidelines for maximizing the effectiveness of a news conference, from the point of view of the media as well as that of the organization.

Guidelines for News Conferences

1. When you notify the media of a news conference or of someone's availability to the press for an interview, be sure to define what kind of event you are having. A news conference is held to announce something for the first time. A press availability is held simply to make someone available to answer questions or demonstrate something.
2. Don't call unnecessary news conferences or availabilities. If it's not worth their time, the media will only be angered.

3. When scheduling a news conference, tell the media in advance some details of what you will be announcing.
4. Gauge the size of your crowd carefully when reserving a room. It is better to have too much space than too little. Make sure microphones, chairs, lighting, and water are in place at least thirty minutes prior to the event.
5. Decide on the format in advance. Be clear about who will introduce speakers, who decides when the question-and-answer period ends, and other details.
6. Decide in advance whether handouts are needed. If a speaker is giving a talk for which there is a text, you may want to wait and hand out the material after the talk so the media will stay and listen to the whole presentation. Be sure to let the media know in advance that you will be providing a text of the speech so that they are not irritated by having to take unnecessary notes.
7. In order to avoid scheduling conflicts, check to see what else is going on in the community before scheduling a press conference.
8. Consider whether you need to let other organizations and agencies know that you are having a news conference. You may want to invite some of them to attend or even participate in your event.
9. Decide who will maintain control at the news conference—for example, who will decide where the cameras are to be set up, who will sit where, and so on.
10. Schedule the length of the news conference, but be flexible.
11. Consider the time of the news conference. If you want to make the noon, 6:00 P.M., or 11:00 P.M. TV and radio news, you need to allow time for crews to travel and edit tape.
12. If you are going to set restrictions on an event, such as limited photo access, try to put the restrictions in writing, and communicate them to the media at least twenty-four hours in advance.

Online Press Conferences

Technology has transformed all aspects of communications, providing an ever-expanding range of options for public relations. One such option is the online press conference.

While still conducted in the traditional face-to-face way, press conferences are increasingly conducted online., When she was public relations director for the Leukemia Society of America (www.leukemia.org), Julie Farin arranged a live, on-air Webcast from a press conference that the organization held in Washington, D.C. More than three hundred fifty people listened in during the press conference, which featured three blood cancer specialists. Farin followed up by posting a link on the organization's Web site to the audio archive of the press conference stored on Broadcast.com, which gets more than half a million hits each day. "It's basically opening up your local press conference to the entire world," Farin says.

Letters to the Editor

Many newspaper readers turn first to the section containing letters to the editor, and surveys show that these sections tend to have a high readership. Readers want to see what their neighbors and fellow citizens think about the issues of the day. There is an intimacy about letters to the editor that appeals to our native curiosity, and this fact makes a letter to the editor an effective vehicle for getting your organization's message out. Newspapers usually publish several letters in every issue, providing several opportunities for you to get your letter into print.

A letter to the editor offers visibility for your organization. It is a helpful building block in establishing you as "the" source for expert opinion on an issue. When readers see the name of your organization and read what its president or spokesperson has to say about an issue in a letter to the editor, your organization's commitment to the issues is underscored, and its credibility and authority are enhanced.

Surprisingly, however, many nonprofits do not take advantage of this very effective tool for getting their messages out to a receptive audience. Kathryn Kimmel, vice president of marketing and communications at the Gemological Institute of America, believes they are missing a valuable opportunity. "Nonprofit organizations can make effective use of free communications to reach wide audiences," she says. "A simple letter to the editor, when well written, can be of great use in supporting a campaign or providing public awareness of a problem or phenomenon that your organization helps with as part of its mission."

How do you do it? You begin, obviously, with knowing the publications that serve your target market. Make a point of studying their letters to the editor, to get a sense of what kinds of letters they like to publish. Then look for opportunities. Favorite occasions for writing a letter to the editor include correcting a mistake, adding new facts to an article that the paper ran in an earlier issue, offering a "sidebar" look at how an issue may affect the local community, and presenting a reasoned disagreement with a previously published position or conclusion.

For the best chance of getting published, the letter should be brief—less than one page and, ideally, no more than two hundred words. The writing style should be clear and direct, getting quickly to the point. Letters that wander around before making their point are unlikely to be printed. The letter should be written in a respectful, thoughtful tone. You want to present your organization as a concerned and responsible partner in the community.

A letter that appeared in the *Washington Post* from Julia A. Erickson, executive director of the nonprofit City Harvest, New York (www.cityharvest.org), struck just that note. Headed "Obese—and Hungry," Erickson's letter was written in response to an op-ed column that had appeared in the paper the previous week. Erickson, taking issue with that column, pointed out that "low-income people and families in the United

States may lack access to healthy food or to stores with good produce, leading them to consume more high-calorie, cheaper foods." Written in a serious, conversational style, Erickson's brief letter made her case and presented City Harvest as a knowledgeable, concerned partner in the community and as an organization worthy of support (see Exhibit 5.2).

You can target local, regional, trade association, and national publications that deal with your organization's area of concern. If your organization has chapters throughout the country, consider having each chapter contact its own local publication with a letter modeled on one prepared at national headquarters. You can also send out a letter from central headquarters to a nationwide list, but, given the intimate nature of letters to the editor, locally written letters tend to have a better chance of being published.

Determine the most appropriate issues on which the organization can provide commentary. Develop the general outlines of response in advance, and be prepared to fine-tune them when related events develop in the news. Know the deadlines of the publications you are targeting, and be sure to get your letters in with plenty of time to meet those deadlines. If you have developed a cordial relationship with an editor, you can give her a call and ask if she would be interested in seeing a letter from your organization. Or you can just send it in.

The assumption is that you are writing a single letter to the editor of a single publication, and some publications, such as *The New York Times*, do demand exclusivity. You should check the policy of the publication to which you are considering sending a letter. If you want to convey your message to several publications, it is a good idea to

---

EXHIBIT 5.2. LETTER TO THE EDITOR OF *THE WASHINGTON POST* FROM CITY HARVEST.

Obese—and Hungry

In response to Robert J. Samuelson's March 17 op-ed column, "The Afflictions of Affluence": Obesity can co-exist with hunger. Low-income people and families in the United States may lack access to healthy food or to stores with good produce, leading them to consume more high-calorie foods. And many suffer from a time crunch because they work more than one job.

City Harvest, the world's oldest food-rescue organization, in partnership with Share Our Strength, is teaching New York City's low-income men, women and children the cooking, nutrition and food-budgeting skills they need to make healthy and economic food choices.

Julia A. Erickson
Executive Director
City Harvest
New York

Source: Courtesy of City Harvest.

significantly change the wording and structure so that you are not sending the same letter to all of them. This is less of a problem in the case of publications whose readerships do not overlap, such as those serving different geographical or interest areas.

Use organizational letterhead, and be sure that contact information accompanies the letter. Typically, the president of the organization or the chairperson of the local chapter will sign the letter. If he is the person to be contacted for clarification and fact checking, be sure that his contact information appears with the letter. If someone else is to be contacted—the public relations person, for example—then his contact information should be clearly displayed.

Be sure that the person whose name appears on the letter knows that the letter has gone out, and to which publications, and see that he has a copy for himself. This avoids possible embarrassment should someone approach him with a comment about his letter. If he doesn't know what the person is talking about, then he, and you, will feel very foolish.

When the letter is published, pick up several copies of the publication, and prepare a one-page photocopy of the letter on an 8½-by-11-inch sheet of white paper that includes the masthead of the publication at the top, the words "Letter to the Editor," the date, and the letter itself. You many want to enlarge the letter to make it easier to read. Add your own contact information at the bottom of the page. You now have a new addition to your press kit (see Chapter Six, "Crafting Press Kits").

You also have an instant mailing piece. The photocopy of the letter to the editor, combined with a letter from the president on a sheet of organizational letterhead, can be mailed to board members, supporters, potential supporters, government agencies, foundations, and anyone else who may be favorably impressed with a published statement from your organization. The letter to the editor can also be reprinted in the organization's newsletter and posted on the organizational Web site. Note that the masthead and the published letter are the property of the publication, and you need permission to use them.

Op-Ed Pieces

In a newspaper, the page opposite the editorial page is called the op-ed page. It serves as a kind of community bulletin board where readers can post short articles, essays, and opinion pieces on subjects of interest to the publication's readers. Like letters to the editor, they are written in the first person and express the writer's opinion on a current topic. The credit note at the end of an op-ed ensures that readers know the source of the piece—for example, someone from your organization. Like letters to the editor, op-ed pieces demonstrate that the organization is proactive on issues that relate to its area of concern.

Op-eds run from five hundred to eight hundred words; the typical length is about seven hundred fifty words. Check with the publications you are targeting to determine more precisely what they prefer.

Because the purpose of an op-ed piece is to provide knowledgeable, thought-provoking commentary on an issue of interest to readers, op-eds represent an excellent opportunity for nonprofits. A well-written op-ed piece positions your organization as a good citizen with special expertise that is being made available to the community at large. The publication of a thoughtful piece that looks at the broader scope of an issue or breaks new ground allows you to highlight your nonprofit as a thoughtful, progressive organization that has something to say that matters. That is very appealing to potential supporters.

The space taken up in a newspaper by an op-ed is usually preferable to the same amount of space devoted to a paid ad. Because the organization has not paid for the space, the message is perceived as having more credibility.

Op-eds for national magazines deal with topics of interest to a national audience. Those appearing in trade publications focus on issues of interest to a particular trade or profession. Many mass-market magazines feature op-eds that concentrate on topics of interest to their readers. Local newspapers tend to address local topics of interest.

One reason why newspapers and magazines like to publish op-ed pieces is that they provide a sampling of expert opinion from outside sources. Your goal is to enhance your organization's visibility and credibility, and so it is important to be very thorough in your research and accurate with all your data.

The piece should be written in simple, accessible prose. A clear conversational style works well. Unless you are certain that readers will be familiar with specialized terms, slang and jargon should be avoided. Sentences and paragraphs should be short.

Imagine your prospective readers flipping through the newspaper with their morning coffee and coming across your op-ed piece. A full block of unbroken type is likely to send the eye skimming down the page, seeking something less intimidating to read, so keep everything short and easily digestible.

Space is limited, so you need to be very focused in your op-ed. Address one issue only. Be clear about exactly what your message is, what you are "selling," and what effect you want the piece to have.

Outline your op-ed first. Traditionally, opinion pieces are constructed in three sections: a statement of the subject, a comment on it, and a conclusion or proposed solution. Grab the reader's attention right at the beginning. One way to do that is with an anecdote about people who have been affected by the issue you are addressing.

For example, if you are writing in support of a bill extending the hours of city parks, tell a quick story about someone who benefited from such an extension, or about someone who suffered because a park closed too early. You want to make it clear to readers that the issue you are writing about affects them and the people they care about.

Once you've narrowed the focus, you can widen it by giving the big picture. Statistics can effectively convey the large number of people affected or the many hours of use involved or the total dollars expended. Some background on the issue should come next—an explanation of why a problem exists, along with some history of the problem.

Now that you've outlined the problem, it is the time to offer a solution. Having proposed a solution, suggest the action necessary to implement that solution. Repeat the urgency of the problem, and urge the reader to take the action you have suggested.

Your tone throughout should be one of reasoned concern. You are not on a soapbox, haranguing the masses. You are speaking up in a town meeting, sharing your informed viewpoint with your neighbors. Be wary of sounding strident, abusive, or harshly critical.

When preparing your op-ed, use organizational letterhead for the first page, with your contact information—name, title, phone number, and e-mail address—clearly displayed. If you are not using letterhead, be sure to include all that information on the first page. The piece should be typed, double-spaced, and the first page should include a title and your name as the author. At the end of the piece, skip a couple of lines, and briefly note, in a sentence or two, why you are qualified to be commenting on the issue. Keep this in the third person so that the editor can simply print it as is.

Some publications, such as *The New York Times*, require exclusivity for op-eds, as they do for letters to the editor, so you should check the publication's policy. In cases where exclusivity is not an issue, you can send your op-ed to many different publications as long as the readerships of those publications do not overlap. Newspapers in different locations, magazines catering to different interests, and journals serving different trades can all receive the same op-ed piece. Be aware that you may need to change the wording somewhat for different publications, to be sure that the piece works for their readers.

It is usually a good idea to contact the publication's editor to ask if there is any interest in the piece before doing the work of writing and submitting an op-ed. This is also a good time to check on the publication's policy regarding exclusivity. Get the name and title of the correct person to send your piece to, and be sure to spell his name correctly. At daily and weekly newspapers, send your piece to the editorial page editor. At smaller local publications, often the right person is simply "the editor." For trade publications, send it to the editor. Include a brief cover note with your submission.

Find out how the editor prefers to receive your op-ed piece—by e-mail, fax, or regular mail. Most editors prefer electronic submissions because they do not have to be retyped.

When you send your op-ed by e-mail, you can attach the file, but you should also paste the text into the body of your e-mail, after the few lines of your cover note. Because of the pervasive concern about viruses, editors at many publications are reluctant to open attachments. There are sometimes problems of incompatibility between systems, too. By sending your piece both ways, you ensure that it will get through to the editor.

When you submit your piece via regular mail or fax, it may be a good idea to indicate that you are prepared to resubmit it via e-mail upon request, if it is accepted for publication. Most editors will appreciate the option.

If the issue you are writing about is urgent and time-sensitive, follow up with a call or an e-mail to the editor after a few days. Usually two weeks is an appropriate time to wait for a response. If you haven't heard back from the editor in that time, follow up with a phone call or a brief e-mail.

Columns

A regular column in a newspaper or magazine gets your message out to a highly targeted group of readers. By regularly appearing in print or online, the column presents your organization as a concerned partner with expertise to share. It is an excellent device for getting name recognition and standing out from the crowd.

Because a column also establishes its author as an expert in the field, it also nicely positions organizational leaders as potential speakers, in demand for interviews in the print and electronic media and on the meeting and seminar circuit. There's a lot to be said for doing a column.

The length of a column varies with the publication, but five hundred to seven hundred fifty words is fairly typical. Newspaper columns usually top out at six hundred fifty words.

Although a column for a nonprofit organization is often staff-written, it typically carries the byline of the organization's president, the chairperson of a chapter, or the head of a specific committee. That person's photo is typically featured as well. Readers like to see pictures of the people whose columns they follow.

Writing a column is like writing a letter to the editor, an op-ed piece, or an article, but you do it on a regular basis. It gets you exposure with your target audience upon publication, and it can then be photocopied and recycled. A regular column, whether it appears weekly, monthly, or quarterly, suggests that your expertise runs deep. Because so much effort goes into creating a worthwhile column, you may want to consider making it a monthly rather than a weekly effort.

The purpose of a column is to educate and entertain. If your organization deals with health care issues, you might consider offering to provide a regular column to a local daily or weekly newspaper or magazine, offering information, advice, and insights on health issues affecting its readers.

A note of caution: any information provided in a column must be checked and double-checked for accuracy. It is essential to establish and preserve your credibility.

Once it has been compromised, even if it is not your fault, you may never be completely trusted again.

Like local daily and weekly newspapers, trade and business publications also feature columns offering information and advice to readers. Columns can also appear on the organization's Web site and in its newsletter and online mailings to supporters.

Like a news release, a column should be typed, double-spaced, and the first page should include the title of the column and the name and title of the author. The standard format for news releases can be followed for columns as well. At the end of the column, skip a couple of lines and briefly note, in a sentence or two, why the author is qualified to write the column. Keep this in the third person so that the editor can simply print it as is.

Feature Articles

Getting a feature article into a publication that reaches the right target audience can give instant credibility to an organization or a project. The process begins with identification of potential publications.

A good source of information on publications to which you might want to submit an article is the *Standard Periodical Directory* published by Oxbridge Communications. This massive one-volume directory weighs in at seven pounds and is the largest directory of U.S. and Canadian magazines, newsletters, journals, and college student newspapers, with more than 63,000 listings.

Oxbridge also publishes the *National Directory of Magazines,* which lists 15,800 U.S. and Canadian business and consumer magazines organized by publisher, title, and geographical area. Both publications are available in printed format as well as on CD-ROM. You can look for them in the reference section of the library, or you can request them from a sympathetic PR firm, advertising agency, or direct-mail house that is replacing its old editions with this year's edition. You can also contact the publisher, Oxbridge Communications, Inc., at 186 Fifth Avenue, 6th Floor, New York, NY 10010 (www.mediafinder.com).

Learn about the publications to which you want to submit a feature article. Inform yourself about their readers and about the kind of material these publications are looking for. Reviewing several back issues is always a good idea. A lot of information can be found online, at a publication's Web site. The Web site is also a good place to find the publication's editorial calendar, which outlines the topics that will be the focus of upcoming issues. Information about the editorial calendars of publications nationwide is also available at the subscription Web site www.edcals.com.

"Articles are much better than ads or press releases," says Lori J. Greene of the American Cancer Society. As director of special events for the organization's Eastern Division, Greene oversees the organization's highly successful annual Relay for

Life. "Committees often want to take out an ad," she says, "but an ad costs money, and it can get lost on the page with all the other ads. And press releases don't always get in. But a great feature article, complete with pictures, about a seventeen-year old cancer survivor—that really gets the story across."

Greene cites a series of articles in the local *Montclair Times* as a good example of the power of articles to have an impact on a nonprofit's campaign. The articles, written by staff writer Ken Thorbourne, appeared under such headings as "Lighting a Path in the Battle Against Cancer" and "High School Students Walking the Walk for Cancer Cure," and they included photos of local residents.

"When the articles appeared, we received a flood of phone calls," says Greene, who credits the articles with boosting participation in the Relay for Life.

Placing an article typically requires an understanding of the publication and its readership. It also helps to develop a rapport with journalists.

"You have to be persistent," Greene advises. "You have to call the reporter personally, get to know them, and establish a relationship."

After an article about your organization appears in print, it has additional potential as a public relations tool. Reprints and copies can be included in press kits and fundraising mailings. The article can be republished on the organization's Web site or reprinted in its newsletter. Copies can be displayed on literature tables at conferences and placed in the reception area of the organization's offices. The published article and the masthead are legally the property of the publication, so be sure to obtain permission before you start mass-producing and distributing copies.

Copyright

When it comes to letters to the editor, op-ed pieces, and articles submitted for publication, who owns the copyright? According to Neil A. Burstein (www.neilburstein.com), a New York attorney specializing in publishing and intellectual property, "As the creator of an original work, you are generally considered the owner of the copyright at the time of creation. This would be the case for most freelance writers unless you have signed a written agreement to the contrary. There are certain instances, however, when copyright ownership does not initially vest in the creator. For example, works created by employees within the scope of the employment relationship are considered 'works for hire' owned by the employer. In either case, the party submitting an original work—you or the organization (employer)—owns the work unless and until the publication asks—and you agree in writing—to grant the publication exclusive rights to it, a practice that is not uncommon. If you agree, it becomes the publication's property, and you may be restricted from submitting it elsewhere or reproducing it later without the publication's permission (unless you have the negotiating clout to reserve certain rights)."

Burstein notes that as long as the piece is your property—that is, until you sign over the exclusive rights to it—you have every right to submit it simultaneously to as many publications as you like. It is not generally a good idea, however, to submit the same material to competing publications. Editors tend to frown on printing the same things their rivals do. No one likes to be perceived as a copycat. It is acceptable, however, to submit the piece to newspapers in different locations, to magazines catering to different interests, or to journals serving different trades.

Once the piece has been published, you will want to make photocopies for circulation to supporters, inclusion in press kits, posting on your Web site, and so on. If the piece has become the property of the publication, you will need to ask permission, which is granted pretty routinely. It usually adds to the effect of a reproduced piece if the publication's masthead is featured at the top of the page, sometimes at reduced size, to allow more room for the piece itself.

"Keep in mind," Burstein says, "that no matter who owns the letter to the editor, the op-ed piece, or the article, the masthead always remains the property of the publication. To reproduce the masthead, you need to get the publication's permission. This, too, is routinely granted.

"I think it is fair to say," notes Burstein, "that most publications would be more inclined to grant permissions to nonprofits, so the nonprofit status should be indicated when asking for permission." He adds that when articles are reproduced, many publications stipulate the inclusion of a statement that the article has been reprinted with the publisher's permission.

Pitching the Article

The Query Letter. When you have identified a publication in which you want an article to appear, look for a connection between the publication's area of concentration and your organization.

Many publications' Web sites provide detailed guidelines for pitching story ideas to those publications. Following those guidelines increases the chance that your pitch will find a welcome reception. You can also call publications to request writers' guidelines, or you can find them on line or in *Writer's Market.* Once you know what your targeted publications are looking for, you can more readily adapt your material to suit their requirements.

In making your pitch, it can help to refer to an upcoming issue that you know will be concentrating on a certain topic. This shows the editor that you have done your homework by learning about the publication and its readers, something that always impresses editors favorably. Indicate in your pitch that you are aware of the publication's lead time. It shows a lack of savvy to send an article for the Christmas issue in November, for example, because magazines prepare their Christmas issues in July.

Show that you are familiar with the readership and understand its needs by suggesting a distinct benefit readers will derive from reading your article (for example, an appreciation of local historic sites, or an awareness of warning signs for a health care problem). Most initial inquiries are by phone or e-mail. When you are asked to send backup material, keep it minimal. Consider including a news release, news clips, published articles, photos, a brochure, and the like. If you have a good Web site, and you should, include the address prominently in your initial contact material as well as in the follow-up. You don't want to overwhelm the editor, but you do want to show that you are familiar with the publication's readership and are offering a story that will interest readers.

The Telephone Pitch. Pat Smith of Rubenstein Associates, Inc., recommends using the phone to make a preliminary story pitch: "Say, for example, that you work with an environmental group, and you want to pitch a story to a newspaper in another city. If you have access to a current issue of the publication or a current media directory, or their Web site, identify the name of the editor or reporter who covers your kind of story. If you can't get their name that way, call up the paper. When someone answers, say, 'Good morning, can you tell me who handles stories on the environment at the paper?' Ask to be connected to them. When the person comes on the line, always begin by asking, 'Have you got a minute, or are you on deadline?' If they can't speak to you at the moment, ask when would be a good time to call back. When you do call back, plan on making a very brief, very intriguing, pitch. Remember that you have to hook them in the first ten seconds, so work at crafting that pitch to make it clear and compelling. You will probably be asked to send material. Be prepared to invite the editor or producer to your Web site. Send information, if they request it, but don't bury them in material. Make it easy for them to do the article you want them to do. If the reporter or editor isn't interested, pitch another publication."

When it comes to verbal pitches, it can help to begin with the smaller, less important publications and work your way up, polishing your presentation with each call. An added benefit of this approach is that if you don't succeed with your first few calls, you can decide to consider them "small potatoes" as you go on to bigger media outlets. If you do it the other way, an early rejection is liable to batter your morale.

You can use the same basic material, but be careful to reshape it appropriately. Make it clear that you understand the publication's audience and why your story will appeal to it.

Writing the Article

The basic rules for queries also apply when it comes to complete articles prepared and distributed by the organization. Identify the publications that reach your target audience, and then identify the editors who deal with your area. Contact them by phone, query letter, or e-mail, offering them your article, and indicate why readers will find it fascinating.

Before you send the article, find out how the editor prefers to receive it—by mail, fax, or e-mail—and observe the requirements for length and format. You can submit the same article to more than one publication as long as they do not compete with each other in the same geographical area or publish for the same professional or trade group. It can be helpful to modify the basic article to make it more specifically relevant to different audiences.

If writing is not the strong suit of anyone on staff, consider hiring a freelancer. Ask for referrals from people working in communications. Consider asking a local editor to recommend a good writer who will do the job for hire. You can also find freelance writers online (try elanceonline.com and www.wordsmitten.com).

Using a Distribution Service

Another way to get the article out to targeted publications is through a distribution service. Stephan Schiffman, president of D.E.I. Management Group Inc. (www.dei-sales.com), a leading sales training company and the author of a dozen books on sales techniques, regularly uses PR Newswire (www.prnewswire.com).

"When I write a brief article on sales skills and release it through PR Newswire," he says, "the article will typically appear in seventy-five to eighty publications."

The same approach can work equally well for a nonprofit that wants to distribute an article offering clear benefits to a well-defined target market of readers.

Obtaining Reprints

When the article has been published, some editors will automatically send you a copy of the publication with your article in it. Some may just not remember to get around to it. It's a good idea to keep an eye out for the appearance of your articles in all the publications you send them to.

While your published article will be seen by some people in your target market, many are probably going to miss it. But you can arrange to get it to them directly, hugely magnifying its effectiveness as part of your public relations campaign. Many publications are happy to prepare reprints of your article for a fee. The reprints feature the publication's masthead at the top of the page, with your article nicely displayed below. Printed on glossy paper, reprints make very impressive inserts into a press kit and excellent pieces for a direct mailing.

You can make your own reprints, of course. Cut and paste the publication's masthead at the top of the page, along with the date. Don't be shy about cutting and pasting your article to reposition an important photo toward the top of the page. One major use of the reprinted article is for inclusion in press kits, and an impressive photo does you no good if it is positioned at the bottom of the page, where no one will see it because it is below the level of the press kit's pocket (see Chapter Six, "Crafting Press Kits"). If you have an electronic copy of the article, the same homemade cut-and-paste job can be done digitally, with a basic software package. Again, remember that the published article and the masthead are legally the property of the publication, so be sure to obtain permission before producing and distributing copies.

The reprinted article, perhaps accompanied by a note from the president of the organization, can be sent to the organization's other leaders and to the board and to major contributors as well as to government agencies with which your organization works. It can also be included in pitches to other, noncompetitive publications, and it can be used in the organization's newsletter, reprinted in the annual report, placed on the Web site, and distributed at expositions and conferences. In all these ways, you can continue to use the article for months and years beyond its initial publication date.

Saying Thanks

When the article appears, send an e-mail or, better yet, a note of thanks to the reporter or editor who wrote or published it. Just a brief note on a card or on organizational letterhead, saying that you appreciate the time and effort put into the piece, and that you think the reporter or editor did a good job, will be very much appreciated.

CHAPTER SIX

CRAFTING PRESS KITS

A press kit, also called a *media kit*, is a basic promotional tool. Writers, rock stars, and motivational speakers all have press kits, and so should a nonprofit organization.

The main purpose of a press kit is to provide information about your organization that can be used by the media in preparing stories. It includes informational material that presents your organization in a positive, newsworthy light.

The big public relations agency Ruder Finn, Inc., typically charges $10,000 to produce a top-of-the-line press kit. Smaller agencies will do it for less but still typically charge $2,000 to $5,000. Before you start worrying about what that kind of expense will do to your budget, you should know that you can create a professional-quality, highly effective press kit basically for free.

Why a Press Kit?

In this digital age, does it still make sense to go through the time, effort, and expense of creating a customized press kit? Isn't it easier to send a basic two-pocket folder, with a one-page news release in one pocket and a photo in the other, and direct journalists to the organization's Web site by simply listing its Web site address? Opinions vary.

Some people feel that traditional press kits are an awkward holdover from an earlier day, something that gets in the way.

"You have those glossy folders full of glossy photos and glossy pieces of paper sliding all over your desk," says Pat Smith of Rubenstein Associates, Inc. "Nobody looks at those things any more. Editors of national magazines get 150 press kits a day. They're inundated. It's much better to just send a postcard with your Web site address. Let them go your site and see everything there." For pitching interview subjects, Smith advises using e-mail to send a photo in JPG format and a link to the organization's Web site.

Rick Frishman, president of Planned Television Arts, an independent division of Ruder-Finn, says the deluge is even greater at TV stations.

"TV producers get three to four hundred press kits a day," says Frishman. "You should never send a press kit without calling or e-mailing first. If the producer asks you to send information, that's when you send the press kit. And even when it's been requested, at best the producer is only going to glance at it for a few seconds. So you generally only want to put a few things into a press kit: a bio, a photo, a list of questions for an interview, and something to establish credibility, like a page of endorsements."

Nancy Trent, principal of the New York–based PR firm Trent & Company, disagrees.

"People want to see what the story looks like while they're considering your pitch," she says. "Pictures and well-written copy help them do that. But do not overstuff the press kit. People don't have patience for bulging folders. When it comes to information, lean is better."

George DeTorres, account manager at the public relations research and distribution source PR Newswire, notes that the CD-ROM, with its huge storage capacity, was once seen as the next-generation press kit. A newer variation is a version with the size and shape of a business card. It has a high-capacity CD implanted in its center, and it can be inserted into a computer for easy viewing. It is capable of carrying a great deal of information, photos, and other graphics as well as text, and can include a link to your Web site. Small and lightweight, it is easy to mail.

Some people feel that CD-ROM technology has already been superseded by the ability to download information directly from the Web. One advantage of downloading from an organization's Web site is that the information tends to be the most current. DeTorres notes that widespread fear of computer viruses has made people reluctant to put CDs into their computers, and this is one factor that has contributed to growth in the popularity of online press kits.

PR Newswire offers an online hosting service for press kits. It provides this service to a range of nonprofit clients, including the March of Dimes, AARP (the former American Association of Retired Persons), the American Jewish Committee, and the New York Foundation for the Arts. A typical fee is $500 for a ninety-day hosting cycle. Online press kits may eventually replace more traditional press kits, but most nonprofits are likely to continue using the standard two-pocket folder for some time to come.

Whether the press kit is digital or print-based, it remains a standard tool for journalists preparing stories about an organization. Some journalists consider traditional print-based press kits fodder for trash cans, but others still prefer them to online versions. It may be a good idea to check with a journalist in advance to find out which version she prefers to receive.

A not-for-profit organization may want to consider avoiding a "too slick" look for its press kit. A fancy folder and glossy printed sheets may lead some recipients to conclude that the organization is wasting its money on impressive presentations instead of putting it to more direct use on behalf of its mission. You do want to look polished and professional, but it may be a good idea to opt for simple rather than fancy.

Once you have created your basic press kit, you can add and subtract items from the kit to suit a specific recipient. Keep the press kit's news stories updated, and always try to connect the kit's contents to the specific interests of your target market.

Traditional press kits continue to be commonly used as selling tools. They tell the organization's story to prospective supporters, government agencies, other organizations, and foundations considering funding, and they can be distributed at meetings and conferences. Because a press kit can easily be tailored to suit each of those uses, it is worth taking a look at what goes into putting the press kit together.

Elements of the Press Kit

Folder

The folder gives the first impression of your organization. Inexpensive two-pocket 9¼-by-11½-inch cardboard folders are available at any stationery or office supply store. Available in a range of colors, these folders can be fine for use by a small community organization. They come with a cutout on the left inside pocket for inserting a business card. Information goes into the two facing pockets. The organization's printed mailing label can be placed on the front. It's not fancy, but it does the job. For a small nonprofit that is not concerned with presenting a slick image, these can be a good choice.

One notch up is a laminated, slightly larger two-pocket folder that also comes in a selection of colors. More expensive, it conveys a sharper, more professional image. Putting an organization's mailing label on the front transforms it into a press kit folder. If looking polished matters, and it usually does, spend a little more, and go with the laminated version.

There are, of course, many variations on the theme. Instead of a mailing label on the front of the folder, you can attach a flyer for an upcoming event, a colorful ad for your organization, or an attractive page from your newsletter or brochure. You can also have your organization's name and logo printed on the folder. If you do, be sure that the printing is dark enough, and the folder light enough, for the logo to be easily readable.

Envelope

You may want to send the press kit by overnight mail so that it stands out somewhat from the crowd, although there is no guarantee that doing so will actually give it any added impact. Or you may choose to send it by first-class mail in a 10-by-13-inch envelope. For added strength and a professional appearance, it may be worth spending a little more and mailing it in one of the tough white plasticized envelopes that can be purchased at most office supply stores.

When you send the press kit to a journalist you have spoken to, consider marking the envelope with the words "Requested Material." That will flag the package as something that has not simply dropped in unsolicited, out of the blue.

Cover Letter

A press kit should not be sent without an accompanying cover letter. A personal letter on organizational letterhead to the journalist receiving the press kit is usually clipped to the front cover of the kit. The letter should be brief and remind the recipient about any earlier phone conversations or other contacts. If the press kit is going to a board member or potential supporter, you may want to single out an element of the kit that relates to one of her personal interests.

Press Release, Media Advisory, or AFI

The primary goal of a press kit is media coverage, which is why your press release is the most important element in the kit. In some cases, instead of a press release you may want to include a media advisory or AFI notice. Whichever you choose, it should convey the basic information that the journalist needs to do the story.

Studies done to determine the most productive placement for advertising have identified the right-hand side of any visual presentation as more important than the left-hand side. Because the right-hand pocket is the more important pocket of your press kit folder, you should make sure the top sheet in that pocket is the piece you consider the most important. Typically, that is the press release, media advisory, or AFI.

Fact Sheet

The pages inside the press kit should all be printed on white 8½-by-11-inch 20-pound paper. An essential element of the press kit is a fact sheet, often presented in bulleted format. Typical information includes the size and location of branches of the organization, the number of members, the scope of operations, and the like. The organization's mission statement should be included as well. A well-prepared fact sheet makes it easy for journalists to include key facts about your organization in their stories.

Cheat Sheets

As a journalist who writes for *The New York Times,* the *New York Daily News,* and *Time Out,* Sari Botton is regularly inundated with press kits. She says that journalists appreciate press kits that present key information in an easily accessible format.

"In general," she says, "cheat sheets in press kits are great—very short, bulleted, encapsulating the main points and maybe a couple of angles. They can be in addition to a letter or press release. If you're pitching a profile of someone, offer a few choice quotes from that person on the cheat sheet."

Backgrounders

Backgrounders provide more in-depth information about the organization. Typical backgrounders include a history of the organization, an outline of its structure, a breakdown of funding sources, and membership demographics.

Another type of backgrounder you may want to use in your press kit is a one-page brief on a specific issue your organization is dealing with. Charts and graphs are useful for providing statistical information and are much to be preferred to pages full of dry statistics. Additional possibilities include a list of current projects, biographies of organizational leaders and spokespersons (sometimes with photos), profiles of people served, and case histories underscoring how the organization makes a major difference in people's lives.

Interview History

When the person who will be appearing has had previous experience with on-air interviews or even print interviews, be sure to make a note of that fact in your pitch letter, and include a list of his or her appearances. Producers are more inclined to invite someone to appear on a show if they know the guest has a record of successful appearances.

When you can, include several letters from the hosts of other interview shows, stating that the subject was a wonderful, articulate, and fascinating guest. Enclosing a sample audiotape or videotape may also be a good idea.

Question List

When the press kit is being submitted as part of a pitch for a radio or TV interview, it is standard practice to provide a list of suggested questions that the spokesperson is qualified to answer. With the rush of deadline pressure at radio and TV stations, that list will often become the script for the person conducting the interview.

The questions should be worded simply and lend themselves to short, easy-to-understand answers. Questions should direct attention to the scope of the problem and to the importance of the organization's work in dealing with the problem.

A question list is not appropriate for a print-based publication, because print journalists frown on question lists and see suggested questions as attempts to control the interview.

Brochure

Your organization's brochure, often the most colorful item among the mostly black-and-white pages of your press kit, should be prominently featured. It is the standard vehicle for conveying key information about your organization succinctly and effectively, and it shows the media how your organization has chosen to present itself to the public.

Newsletter

The latest issue of the organization's newsletter should be included in the press kit. The purpose of a newsletter is to maintain communication with supporters. Including a copy of the newsletter in the press kit shows the media that you have a significant body of supporters who care about what the organization is doing.

Because your newsletter will feature photos of your members, projects, and activities, along with news stories about the organization, it can give the reader a feel for the character of your organization. If your organization has opted for an online newsletter instead of the printed kind, you can print out a copy for inclusion in the press kit.

Photos

If you are submitting the press kit to a smaller community publication, you may also want to include captioned photos to accompany the story. Check to find out if the publication prefers to receive photos digitally or in hard copy. A small publication may be more likely to run your story if you package it with a usable photo. Photos should be 5-by-7s or 8-by-10s. Don't send snapshots—they look amateurish. Color has become standard, but black-and-white is acceptable. When it is reproduced, the quality of a black-and-white photo is often sharper and "crisper" than a color photo, especially when the color photo is reproduced in black-and-white.

You can make a photo even more appealing if you offer it as an exclusive. You can do that by very clearly including words to that effect in the caption: "Exclusive to *The New York Times*." A good, eye-catching photo can spark up a page layout and be a welcome addition. It can be what decides the editor on running the story. If you are pitching an interview to a TV station, including a current photo of the proposed interview subject is essential.

Press Clips and Articles

Including articles about your organization that have appeared in outside publications is a good idea. These serve as third-party endorsements, showing that the organization is important enough to have been featured in the press for what it does. Articles by and about your leaders and supporters, and profiles of people served by the organization, can also be considered.

The top of the first page of each clip should feature the publication's masthead, but be sure to get permission before you use it. A publication's masthead is its property, as is your published article. If you intend to photocopy the masthead and article for use in your press kit, you are required to obtain permission from the publication for reproduction and distribution of its article. You may also have to pay a fee, although as a nonprofit organization, this requirement may be waived. You can contact the publication directly or contact the Copyright Clearance Center (www.copyright.com). (See Chapter Five to review copyright issues and the need to obtain permission for the use of previously published pieces.)

Three or four clips are generally enough. If you include more than that, the press kit begins to look like a scrapbook. So give some careful thought to which clips go into the kits you send to journalists. If a story that has already appeared in a newspaper is too close to the story you are pitching, some journalists may not want to do it, especially if the previous placement was with their competition. If you are pitching a publication with a completely different readership, or a radio or TV station, this is usually less of a problem.

Sometimes you may want to consider not including clips of previous stories in the press kit, thereby creating the impression that the media outlet you are pitching will be the first one to cover the story. It's a judgment call. You need to know who you are pitching and then assemble the press kit accordingly.

The Kitchen Sink and Other Elements

The media tend to prefer simple, lean-and-mean press kits. Depending on the use to which a press kit will be put, however, sometimes including additional material may be a good idea. A journalist doing an in-depth story on the organization may want all the documentation he or she can get.

If the kit is being used as part of a solicitation of a major donor, key fundraising materials may be included as well. If the kit will be distributed as general information at an exposition, fair, or conference, you may want to include lots of souvenirs and give-away items. The possibilities are virtually endless, but the following items are popular:

- Testimonial letters from important people
- Testimonials from people the organization has helped
- An invitation to an upcoming event
- Issue briefs
- Biographies of organizational spokespersons, leaders, and guest speakers
- Quotes from experts or leaders on the issues your organization deals with
- Speeches by organizational leaders
- Reports and studies for public release
- Campaign information, including the case for the campaign, a pledge card, and a response envelope
- A response card, to facilitate requesting additional information or personal contact
- Selected visuals, such as charts, graphs, maps, and photographs of your organization's accomplishments

Although such items are not included with every press kit, because of the expense of producing them, the organization's annual report may merit inclusion for people to whom you want to convey more in-depth information about the organization's finances, membership, and operations.

Other things that can be and sometimes are included in a press kit are audiotapes and CDs, videos and DVDs, and items bearing the organization's logo, such as calendars, posters, decals, bumper stickers and other types of stickers, magnets, flags, banners, pads, pens, pencils, key chains, flashlights, T-shirts, and hats.

Electronic Press Kits (EPKs)

While some journalists still prefer print-based press kits, the trend toward online press kits is growing. Many journalists prefer electronic press kits (EPKs). Organizations are increasingly sending them by e-mail and posting them on their Web sites. Before sending out your press kit, you may want to contact the journalist in question and ask how he or she prefers to receive it, as hard copy or online.

Like the more traditional press kit, the EPK features relevant press releases, articles, biographies, and interviews with organizational leaders, as well as downloadable images that are made available to journalists doing stories about the organization. The press kit should be downloadable from your Web site as a PDF file or as a word-processed file (that is, a file created in Microsoft Word, Corel WordPerfect, or other such programs). Photos should be in JPG files, 300 dpi, and standard five-by-seven-inch size. This will also make your press kit available in a format that you can e-mail.

Because journalists are almost always working under deadline pressure, they may balk at visiting your Web site for the information they need. To make it as easy as possible for journalists to do the story you want them to do, try sending e-mail with an embedded link not to your Web site's home page but directly to the EPK or to another specific page on your site that you want the journalists to see. As one harried journalist responding to a PR person's invitation to look at an online EPK once said indignantly, "What makes you think I have the time to wander around your Web site?!"

CHAPTER SEVEN

CREATING BROCHURES

A brochure represents an organization to the public. Often the first line of communication, the first thing encountered, it functions as a kind of ambassador from the organization to the world at large.

A brochure should, of course, convey key information about an organization. But, ideally, it should also do more than that. It should also capture the organization's *spirit.* Someone looking at the brochure should get a sense of the organization's heart. A brochure should tell the world not only what the organization does but also why it matters so much. To do that effectively, a brochure should draw on the things that make an organization unique. Often those things can best be communicated visually.

Effective Brochures: Two Examples

The Yellowstone National Art Trust

As founder and board president of Yellowstone National Art Trust (www.ynat.org), Bozeman, Montana, Laurie Simms had no shortage of strong visual elements to use in her brochure. She founded the nonprofit in 2001 in order to "preserve awareness of the cultural legacy of Yellowstone National Park," as she told the *Bozeman Daily Chronicle*; she wanted to help people visiting Yellowstone National Park "learn about art and appreciate the park through the arts."

Simms combines her love for Yellowstone, the world's first national park, with a passion for the arts. In preparing to do a brochure, she reviewed the park's collection of artwork, which included twenty-one priceless watercolor sketches by Thomas Moran, an English artist who accompanied the 1871 survey of Yellowstone. Those magnificent plein-air sketches, three of which Simms finally chose for her brochure, helped convince a skeptical Congress to designate Yellowstone as a national park in 1872—a unique concept at the time. Adding to the visual impact of the brochure is a fourth piece of art, a beautiful rendering of the park's famous geyser, Old Faithful, painted by a contemporary local artist expressly for installation in the historic Old Faithful Inn.

In the brochure, the paintings are framed by black panels that set off their beauty. The artwork is accompanied by explanatory copy printed on a white background. The result is a brochure that is itself virtually a work of art. The brochure's appeal rests in large measure on its strong visual impact. Simms achieved that impact by drawing on the basic elements of what makes the art trust itself unique: its collection of paintings.

Conveying the spirit of an organization is often a matter of getting down to the basics of what the organization is all about. To continue the theme of strong visual impact, and to underscore the centrality of Yellowstone to its work, the plasticized envelopes in which the Yellowstone National Art Trust mails its press kits are always a very bright, eye-catching yellow.

Gilda's Club

Linda Gordon, president of Linda Gordon Communications in New York, was able to make use of a powerful graphic (sometimes also called a *graphic identifier*) when she produced the operating manual and other print materials for the nonprofit Gilda's Club Worldwide (www.gildasclub.org). Named in honor of the late *Saturday Night Live* comedian Gilda Radner, Gilda's Club is an international network of communities where men, women, and children living with cancer come together for free emotional and social support in local "clubhouses" as an adjunct to medical care.

The organization's logo features a charming caricature of Gilda, adapted with permission from an original Al Hirschfeld drawing, laughing broadly as she leans around an open red door, offering a hearty welcome into a place of sanctuary. It is a powerful image and one that is particularly well suited to the organization's mission.

"What sets the organization apart is the legacy of Gilda's spirit and humor, and the graphic does a great job of capturing that," Gordon says. "The logo is featured prominently whenever the Gilda's Club name is used and can be customized for each clubhouse."

The logo is prominently featured on Gilda's Club brochures, heightening their impact and appeal (see Exhibit 7.1). By drawing on its own "natural resources," the organization has been able to create a unique and dynamic tool that very effectively conveys its message.

EXHIBIT 7.1. GILDA'S CLUB GRAPHIC LOGO AND BROCHURE.

Source: Courtesy of Gilda's Club Worldwide.

Why a Brochure?

As with every other PR tool, before starting to create a brochure, you need to ask why you are creating it in the first place.

Why a brochure? Why are you going through all the time, effort, and expense involved? In the nonprofit world, as in the business world, there is a sense that a brochure gives credibility. You are not "real" unless you have a brochure.

But it makes no sense to create a brochure until you have answered some basic questions. Who is the target audience for the brochure? What do you want the audience to know? What do you want the audience to do?

Who Is the Audience?

A child service agency may be trying to raise money within the community to help provide snacks for schoolchildren in grades K–12. Its target market may be local community members who need to be convinced that the children involved are worthy of their support. An appeal to the heart—brief profiles of children, accompanied by appealing photos—will be much more effective with the target audience than just presenting a long list of statistics and pie charts analyzing the scope of the problem. That information might well be included, but it would be wise to keep the focus on the appealing children.

An environmental group may want to rally support for the preservation of local wetlands. A map showing the location of imperiled wetlands could be useful, especially when augmented by a photo of mallards coming in to land on an open lake. Such an appeal reaches out to both the head and the heart. Consider your audience. Will that mix be appealing? Do you need more appeal to the head? One solution could be to include a chart illustrating the scope of the problem, with projections of what will happen to the wetlands if no steps are taken. More appeal to the heart? A photo of ducklings paddling along behind their mother could strike just the right chord.

Make it a point to know the people in your target market and what resonates with them. Know your purpose and what you are trying to accomplish, and only then begin to create your brochure.

What Do You Want the Audience to Know?

The easy answer is often something along the lines of "information about the organization." But what information, exactly? Are you going to list every one of your projects? Are you going to go into detail about specific programs? Are you going to list the names of major supporters? Will you present the history of the organization, its founding, and evolution? What about a listing of funding opportunities, with a detailed listing of specific giving options?

You may want to include a pie chart illustrating the proportion of the funds that go to various kinds of projects, or showing how little of the money raised goes to overhead. You might consider a chart showing the scope of the problem you are dealing with, and maybe something to illustrate the impressive success you have had in dealing with it.

Often included are lists of major accomplishments, profiles and photos of the people the organization serves, and, of course, the organization's mission statement.

With such an exhaustive menu of possibilities, it is no wonder that some organizations seem to pick just a few items at random or, even worse, try to cram everything into a brochure. The end result is predictable: an unreadable document that no one ever looks at. But, hey, it's a brochure.

What Do You Want the Audience to Do?

What do you want your brochure to accomplish? What do you want the members of your targeted audience to do after they've read it? Write a check? Come to a rally? Be moved to learn more about the organization and its activities? Volunteer their time? The answers to these questions will dictate the design of the brochure and help decide which elements will be included in that design.

Everything begins with your goal. If the purpose of the brochure is to raise money, then everything about it should be targeted to that end. The design, graphics, and copy should all lead the reader to the actual request for action or support, and that request must be a strong element of the brochure. It must contain a strong solicitation and answer the question "Why should I give?" It is essential that the appeal itself be appealing.

How Will the Brochure Be Used?

Too often, organizations print thousands of brochures and then try to think of ways to use them. Before creating a brochure, you should be clear not only about who is going to receive it but how it is going to get to its audience.

Is the brochure designed for the general public? Current supporters? Potential donors? The media? Every organization has several target markets, and you may want to reach out to those different markets in different ways.

How is the brochure going to reach its intended audience? Will it be mailed as part of a fundraising package? Distributed at meetings and conferences? Sent with press kits to the media? A single, well-thought-out brochure may be able to work for a variety of audiences, or you may find that it makes sense to create separate brochures to serve different needs.

Design Considerations

Size

The most common style of brochure is an $8\frac{1}{2}$-by-11-inch sheet of paper folded into three sections so that it fits neatly into a pocket, purse, briefcase, or standard #10 business envelope. Because such brochures are so common, they are relatively inexpensive to design and print. That is the plus. The negative is that such a brochure doesn't automatically stand out and make a strong impression.

You may want to opt for something different. There are many choices available, complete with matching, ready-made envelopes. Ask your designer or printer to show you samples. When a brochure from another organization or business catches your eye, hold on to it. Consider what elements appeal to you and how you might adapt them for your own purposes. You may find something that suits your needs perfectly.

You can also have something designed from scratch and have envelopes specially made to go with it. But that boosts costs, and many recipients of the brochure may not even notice or be particularly impressed by your creativity. Be wary of reinventing the wheel; it is often easier and less expensive to use the wheel that has already been invented.

Overall Appearance

Popular desktop publishing software offers templates for a range of basic brochure designs. If you have the talent to design the brochure yourself, or if you know someone who can do a serviceable job, then that may be the way to go. You may also want to consider working with a professional. A good graphic designer can often take your basic concept and make it sing, or the designer can suggest a different concept that effectively helps to "sell" your organization.

Look online or in the Yellow Pages, or ask your printer to recommend a graphic designer. Check out the designer's work on his or her Web site, or ask to meet with the designer in person to review his or her portfolio. After a few minutes of leafing through the samples in a designer's portfolio or looking at his or her work on a Web site, you may decide that design expertise is worth the expense.

According to David Grupper, president of David Grupper Design, a Brooklyn-based graphic design firm, "When it comes to design, there are a few basics. Don't crowd the page. The eye likes space—what printers and designers call white space, no matter the actual color of the page. Avoid big blocks of type. Keep it simple. Less is definitely more."

Up is more impressive than down. Consider the front page of your favorite newspaper. A story that appears above the fold seems to have more significance than a story that appears below the fold. Put the things you really want the reader to see up, and place the less important elements lower down.

Right is better than left. In a two-page spread for a magazine or newspaper, it is usually best to put the things you really want to highlight on the right-hand page. Publications that sell advertising charge more for a right-hand page, and they get the added rate because advertisers regularly ask for that placement. Right is the stronger side of a two-page spread. It is interesting to note that the same relative right-left balance holds true for the television screen. When you watch two commentators on the screen together, notice which one you look at most and which one seems to be more important. TV producers, well aware that the right side of the screen is the stronger side, will sometimes balance out a "weaker" announcer by putting him on the right-hand side of the screen, to boost his strength and strike a more even balance with a stronger announcer. Whatever the psychological reasons for the eye's perception that up and right are more important than down and left, you should take note of the fact and use it in deciding which elements of your brochure to highlight.

Grupper believes a brochure has to accomplish four basic goals: get the reader's attention, hold the reader's interest throughout, convey key information, and make it easy for the reader to take action. He advises using a design in which one main element dominates. When the reader looks at a single brochure panel, or at an open brochure that reveals several panels at once, his or her eye should be drawn to the key element that conveys the most important part of the message.

Typeface

To make the brochure easy to read, it is usually best to use no more than two or three different typefaces in one brochure. Typefaces come in two basic styles: serif and sans serif. Serifs are the little "feet" and other flourishes on letters that add style and serve the function of carrying the reader's eye along the line of type. For body copy, a serif typeface is easier to read than a sans serif face. Times Roman and Courier are both very serviceable favorites. Sans serif simply means without a serif. Typefaces without the little flourishes tend to look more stark and bare than serif faces. They are not ideal for long passages, because there is nothing to carry the eye along the line, but the same no-frills aspect of sans serif faces makes them ideal for headlines and subheads containing only a few words. Arial and Helvetica are popular sans serif typefaces for headlines.

Elements of the Brochure

In a brochure, space is limited. That means everything in a brochure must serve a purpose. If you don't know why something is in a brochure, it probably doesn't belong there.

Mailing Panel

A question to ask early in the design process is how the brochure will be mailed. If the brochure is usually going to be mailed on its own, without any accompanying literature, then you may be able to save the expense of an envelope, and the cost of stuffing the brochure into an envelope, by designing the brochure with a mailing panel.

A mailing panel is a back panel that carries the organization's return address in the upper left-hand corner, perhaps a box in the upper right-hand corner indicating where first-class postage needs to be placed, and an empty space in the center for the mailing address. An organizational message can appear at the bottom of the mailing panel as long as enough space for the address is left to meet the requirements of the U.S. Postal Service.

The advantage of allocating a portion of your brochure to a mailing panel is that it saves on the cost of envelopes and stuffing. The disadvantage is that you are giving up one section of a piece that has limited space to begin with. If you are sure that the brochure will never be mailed alone, and that it will always travel inside an envelope along with a cover letter or other literature, then there may be no need to allocate space for the mailing panel. In that case, you can use the space on the back panel for other elements.

In designing any mailing piece, it is always a good idea to check with the post office early in the process, to be sure that the piece meets postal requirements. Similarly, all packages to be mailed should be carefully checked for weight. Even a little over the line is still over the line, and you could find that your mailing is costing you a lot more than you planned.

Copy

Few people actually read brochures. Usually they just flip through the pages. They have learned from experience that brochures usually make pretty dull reading. The wording is often clumsy and obtuse, as though produced by a committee—which, all too often, it has been. With some thoughtful planning, however, it is possible to create a brochure that people actually will read.

Keep the copy sharp and punchy. Whenever possible, opt for small words rather than big ones, and for short sentences rather than long ones. Make your points in as few words as possible. Your copy should be clear, succinct, and easy to read.

Heads

Heads, or headlines, serve to break the brochure's copy into subject areas. Like headlines in a newspaper, they catch the reader's eye. Heads can be very helpful as organizing tools in the initial planning stages.

Decide what information you want the brochure to convey, and then assign each piece of that information a specific area of the brochure, giving it a title, such as "Projects," "History," or "Mission Statement." You may decide to leave the heads in place as guideposts for the reader, or you may eliminate them as unnecessary. If you do keep them in, they should help by leading the reader's eye from point to point to point throughout the brochure.

Graphics

To make the brochure visually interesting and appealing, appropriate photos, illustrations, and other graphics should be used throughout. Used tastefully, graphics can enhance the overall look of your brochure and help guide the reader's eye in the direction you want it to go. Graphics can make the entire piece more effective and enhance its impact, contributing to the likelihood that people will actually read your brochure.

A word of caution, however, about graphic designers: sometimes a designer will produce something that is visually stunning but that just doesn't work for your purposes. One designer favorite is using large blocks of "dropped-out" type: instead of black type on a light background, the designer uses a technique that makes the type appear white on a colored background. That white type is very pretty to look at and almost impossible to read, especially when the background is a light color. Adding insult to injury, the type is often very small, which makes the copy even more difficult to read, especially for readers who are over forty.

The best way to test a potential design for a brochure is to run off a test copy and show it to people who know absolutely nothing about your organization. Watch how they react to the brochure, what they look at first, where their eyes linger, how much they seem to squint when reading it, and how quickly they tire of looking at it and put it down. After they've looked over the brochure, you can ask them a few quick questions about the organization, to see if they've actually learned anything from reading the brochure. At least ask them what overall impression they may have gleaned. If you get nothing but blank stares, you may want to take the brochure back to the drawing board.

Name of the Organization

The name of the organization should appear prominently on the front panel of the brochure—perhaps in a distinctive, stylized typeface, linked to your logo—and it should be repeated throughout the brochure's pages. The name is part of your organization's "brand." You want people to remember the visual image of your organization's name in the same way that the distinctive logos of Coca-Cola or FedEx are remembered and associated with those brands. The name of your organization may not yet be a household word, but you are aiming at name recognition, and that means putting your name on everything, including your brochures.

Logo

A logo can be an effective visual tool for enhancing your organization's name recognition. Some logos are interestingly archaic, evoking the earlier history of an organization. For example, the logo of the International Brotherhood of Teamsters features the heads of two horses, recalling the days when a teamster was someone who drove a wagon pulled by teams of horses. The logo for the U.S. Army infantry is a pair of crossed muskets, weapons dating back to the Revolutionary War, when the Continental Army was first created. Other organizations use symbols in their logos that seem fairly obvious. The American Heart Association uses a red heart. It is also possible to make creative use of type, using the initials of the organization's name to create a graphic that is visually pleasing.

Your logo should be linked in the mind of your audience with the name of your organization. The logo should enhance the organization's image and make it stand out from the crowd. If your logo is attractive and does justice to your organization, you should include it on the front panel of your brochure along with the name of your organization. The logo should also appear with your contact information and, if you have a mailing panel, it should appear there as well. Proper exposure of your logo can help to heighten the impact of the name of your organization in the minds of the people you want to reach.

Tag Line

It is important for an organization to have a strong tag line. A tag line is a short, high-impact phrase that conveys what the organization does and why it matters. The tag line should also appear prominently on the brochure, linked to the organization's name and logo, on the front panel.

Stacey Kratz is communications coordinator for Girls Incorporated, a national nonprofit organization that works to help girls confront "antigirl" messages about their value and potential. Kratz says the organization's tag line—"Inspiring all girls to be strong, smart, and bold"—is an excellent tool for conveying the organization's message. As such, the tag line appears on all the organization's promotional materials and is prominently featured on its brochures.

"It works very well as an elevator-pitch way of summing up what Girls Incorporated is all about, in just a few seconds," says Kratz. "People ask, 'What does Girls Inc. do?' and when they hear 'Inspiring all girls to be strong, smart, and bold,' they'll often pause for a moment and then say, 'Oh, really? I have a daughter' or 'I have a niece.' And they'll want to know more about the organization."

A tag line should be visually linked with the name of the organization so that the reader links the two in her mind. Think of a tag line as the second punch of a one-two punch: "Girls Incorporated? Oh yes, that's the organization that inspires all girls to be strong, smart, and bold."

Mission Statement

A good tag line is short, but an organization's mission statement tends to run long. Unless it has punch, the mission statement probably does not belong on the front panel.

The front panel serves the same function for a brochure as a headline does for an ad: to draw readers in and keep them reading. If a long, wordy statement appears on the front panel, most people won't bother opening the brochure to read what is inside. A long, thoughtfully worded mission statement may work best if it is tucked away on an inside panel.

Statement of Goals

The statement of goals is an extension of the mission statement. The mission statement outlines the organization's purpose and raison d'être; a statement of specific goals tells the reader exactly how the organization intends to carry out that purpose.

The advantage of listing a statement of goals is that it tells the world specifically what you intend to do. Supporters know exactly what they are signing on for. The disadvantage is that you run the risk of turning off potential supporters. Someone who dislikes even one of your goals may hesitate to support you. Moreover, if you make your goals too specific, your brochure may become dated. If some of those goals are accomplished, or if situations change to make them irrelevant, your brochure—and by inference, your organization—may appear out of date or out of touch with current realities. One suggestion for keeping the brochure timely is to keep the goals general and consider using inserts to list current goals.

Contact Information

Essential contact information is obviously a key element. It is important, but this does not mean that it has to occupy a prime spot on the front panel of the brochure. It must be clearly presented and readily accessible to the reader so he can easily contact the organization, but it can be positioned out of the way, perhaps on the back panel.

You want to include the name of the organization along with the address, phone number, fax number, e-mail address, and Web site address. You may also want to list relevant departments. It usually is not necessary to include the name of an individual contact, and, because people tend to change jobs, it may be a good idea not to list individuals by name. Unless there is a good reason to include names, leave them out.

Be sure to double-check for accuracy. Every printer has stories to tell about clients who OK'd big jobs, only to realize, after printing, that they carried the wrong address or phone number.

Lists of Projects, Services, and Awards

Lists of projects sponsored, services provided, and awards won by the organization can be impressive, but they can also be tedious. The tendency is to list everything, in the hope that something on the list will impress the reader. But a long list presents the eye with a formidable block of type and may simply be ignored. Consider placing lists on an inside page, perhaps down and on the left.

Photos of Projects and of People Served

Photos can be the one of the strongest elements of your brochure. A picture truly can be worth a thousand words, and one powerful image is worth a dozen run-of-the-mill photographs.

There is an understandable temptation to include a selection of photos, especially on the front panel, to show off a wide range of projects. There may be a photo of a senior citizen juxtaposed with a photo of a young child, and perhaps one of a family sitting under some trees, and maybe a photo of a cute puppy, for good measure. So many disparate images are confusing. There is just too much information to absorb.

Choose one strong image that represents what your organization does, and make that the centerpiece. Use other photos throughout the brochure to show the range, but not too many. Photos convey information, but, more important, they convey emotion. Keep the emotion strong, simple, and focused. Too many emotions tend to cancel each other out.

Avoid using photos that are crowded with many people or objects. Printed small, as they will be in a brochure, photos often lose their impact. Close-ups of faces are usually good. If the photo captures action, make sure the nature of the action is conveyed. You can caption photos, but the most effective images are those that need no captions. Also, many people will not read captions. Ideally, your photos should be able to tell the story on their own. If you don't have a selection of good photos to choose from, it may be wise to hire a photographer to take the photos you need for the brochure.

Photos of Leaders and Spokespersons

It may be useful to include a photo of an organizational leader or a celebrity spokesperson in order to add a literal "human face." The photo links that person to the organization in the mind of the person reading the brochure. If the person is a fitting representative of your organization, does not get voted out of office, and does not become the focus of a media scandal, it may be a good idea to include his photo along with a brief quote from him about why he is proud to be associated with the organization.

Quotes

Quotes are often a nice addition to a brochure. Whether spaced throughout the brochure or gathered together on one panel, the actual words of real people always have a certain impact.

The quotes can be from people served, civic leaders, or celebrities attesting to the importance of the work, or they can come from past and present leaders enthusiastically explaining why they are proud to support the organization. Adding a photo of the person being quoted can add to the impact of the quote itself.

You should always get permission from the people you are intending to quote in your brochure. The easiest way for all concerned is to send them an e-mail or letter indicating the quote you intend to use and asking for their OK. If you use a quote from a politician, be aware that after the next election, if that politician is no longer in office, your brochure is going to look dated. The same can be true for entertainment and sports figures, whose celebrity may come and go. Either print a limited number of brochures or consider using more "timeless" sources for your quotes.

Testimonials

Like quotes, testimonials are a nice way to allow others to sing your praises. They tend to be long and often involve telling a story about just how your organization helped, so there probably won't be space for a full-blown testimonial in your brochure. Choose a pithy quote that gets to the heart of the matter, and use that. Save the full testimonial for use elsewhere.

Biographies of Important People

Biographies of founders, leaders, and beneficiaries of the organization's work are all potentially interesting and may even be the stuff of legends, but the fact is that most people don't like to read long blocks of copy in a brochure. Brochures are generally designed to be glanced at, not studied. If you do decide to include a biography, keep it short, and avoid complex phrasings, jargon, or any assumption that the reader is familiar with terms or events not known to the general public. You may want to include a photo of the person being profiled so readers can see who they are reading about.

History

The history of the organization—why it was created, and how its role has evolved over the years—is often an important part of its identity. This may make for fascinating reading, but if you're going to include it in your brochure, keep it brief and straight-forward. If you include a time line featuring significant dates in the organization's history, make it an attractive graphic element, perhaps running along the length of the open brochure, to tie the panels together. Limit the number of events highlighted. If you provide too much information, readers may feel overwhelmed.

Statistics

The famous line "There are three kinds of lies—lies, damn lies, and statistics" has been attributed to any number of sources. Statistics can be very helpful in presenting the scope of a problem or the range of a solution, but it is wise to use them sparingly, and be sure to cite the source. A few pointed statistics can be very useful for emphasis; too many, and you risk boring your reader. A bored reader is one who stops reading your brochure.

Response Card

To make it easy for readers to take action, you must be clear about just what action you want them to take. Do you want them to write a check? Include a payment vehicle. Do you want them to go to your Web site or call for more information? Make your contact information clear and easy to follow.

Sometimes the purpose of a brochure is to get a response from the reader. Incorporating a response panel into the design facilitates that goal. Because people tend to be reluctant to cut up a brochure in the middle, the response card should be an end panel, not a center panel. Because readers will be mailing the response panel back to you, make sure that whatever information is on the other side of it is not something you want them to hold on to or that they will need for their records.

If the response panel is designed to be mailed back on its own, you will want to print it, and therefore the entire brochure, on heavyweight card stock. If it is to travel on its own, you'll want to indicate where first-class postage is to be placed, and have your return address in the upper left-hand corner as well as in the center. If it will be traveling back to you in an envelope, it can be printed on lightweight text stock. You may want to have the edge of the response-card panel perforated, to make it easier for the reader to tear off neatly.

In either case, the response card should clearly indicate the information you want. Leave enough room between the lines for the person responding to provide any information that is requested. If you are asking for a pledge or a contribution, you will want to have spaces indicating the categories of giving that are available. Make it easy for the responder to respond the way you want him to.

It is always a good idea to double-check that the response card meets postal regulations before you do a large print run. To track the results of your own mailings, add codes to the response card. (This topic is dealt with in more detail in Chapter Ten, "Making Direct Mail Work.")

CHAPTER EIGHT

COMMUNICATING THROUGH NEWSLETTERS

Organizations strive to maintain an ongoing flow of communication with their members. A *newsletter*, as the name indicates, can be an ideal vehicle for doing that. Online newsletters are gaining in popularity, but many people still prefer the old-fashioned paper-and-ink variety. This chapter looks at print-based newsletters; online newsletters are covered in Chapter Fifteen, "Using the Internet."

Why a Newsletter?

Newsletters are popular. By some estimates, more than ten thousand are published in the United States. Approximately 20 percent are subscription newsletters published as moneymaking vehicles. The rest are free newsletters published by businesses and organizations for marketing and public relations purposes. The popularity of newsletters attests to their perceived effectiveness.

A newsletter gives an organization consistent exposure, keeping members current on what is going on and striving to keep their level of interest and commitment high. Because it arrives on a regular and predictable basis, it comes to be welcomed as part of an ongoing routine, part of members' lives. One intended by-product is the enhancement of the organization's fundraising efforts.

An all too common complaint from supporters of virtually any organization is "The only time I hear from you people is when you ask me for money." One function of a newsletter is to provide a buffer against such complaints.

Although the request for support is always implicit, a newsletter tends to be more of a soft sell than a direct fundraising pitch. A newsletter is a neighborly communication, a way of sharing information about things of common interest to members of a like-minded community. A knowledgeable supporter is more likely to be a committed supporter, and the committed supporters are the ones who keep the organization vibrant and able to carry out its mission.

Standing Out from the Crowd

By making a personal connection with supporters, and by highlighting the things that make an organization special, a newsletter can help the organization stand out from the competition. But if your newsletter comes across as boring or irrelevant, it will go unread into the circular file, perhaps to be replaced by a newsletter from another organization that did the job better. The stakes are high, and getting it right matters. Sometimes getting it right takes some out-of-the-box thinking.

Offering a Look Inside

Because a newsletter provides a look inside your organization, the current issue can be a good addition to your press kit. It can also be distributed at conferences, conventions, and expositions where your organization is represented, with copies of the most recent issues made available to the public.

A recent issue of the newsletter can also be included in mailings to media contacts. Similarly, when the organization sends out a speaker or seminar leader, she should bring along copies of the current issue and make them freely available.

Enhancing Customer Relations

Because newsletters are a fairly basic means of communication, they can be an excellent way of keeping in touch with customers. As a cornerstone of its customer relations program, the Metropolitan Transit Authority's Metro-North Railroad (www.mta.info), which serves New York and Connecticut, publishes a series of monthly newsletters designed to keep passengers apprised of the latest developments on the railroad's lines. The newsletters are distributed on trains and in stations, and each is targeted at a specific line and passenger base. In keeping with the railroad theme, the main newsletter is called *Mileposts* (see Exhibit 8.1). Distributed to passengers traveling to and from Grand Central Terminal, its masthead describes it as "a publication for MTA Metro-North Railroad customers." A spinoff series of newsletters includes *Outposts* (also in Exhibit 8.1), for "reverse-peak customers," targeted specifically at commuters traveling to work outside

An Award-Winning Newsletter

Morris Ardoin, director of communications at the Hebrew Immigrant Aid Society (HIAS) (www.hias.org), believed that a nonprofit's newsletter could be used to increase the organization's membership. In 2000, he set out to prove it.

The HIAS mission is an exciting one. HIAS, founded to help Jews who were escaping persecution in Europe, today assists a wide range of refugees fleeing from persecution and poverty. Heroic tales of rescue are the organization's daily fare.

But the low-key, conservatively designed eight-page newsletter that Ardoin inherited when he joined the organization was far less exciting than the organization's mission. Titled *Headlines & Highlights,* it was printed in reflex blue and black ink, but Ardoin was convinced that he could do better. He believed that if he could transform it into a full-color, thirty-two-page magazine with the capacity to cover the organization's stories in more depth, and if he could significantly expand its distribution, then the organization's active membership rolls would increase. A by-product of the transformation, he said, would be "the opportunity to produce more and better content about HIAS, the benefit we PR people like the best."

His proposal to spend more money producing the newsletter was initially rejected. When he finally did manage to make the changes he wanted, the new publication, now renamed *Passages,* went out to an expanded distribution list, with seventy thousand copies printed and distributed quarterly. It immediately met with enthusiastic response. Ardoin's hunch turned out to be right.

Transforming the newsletter into a magazine, and using it to reach more people, did help increase active membership—by 250 percent over three years. The magazine also brought in a number of nonmembership contributions. The HIAS fundraising department credits *Passages* with generating more than $25,000 in unsolicited gifts to date.

Ardoin obviously knows his business. In 2004, *Passages* was the winning entry in an annual competition held by the International Association of Business Communicators (IABC). With thirteen thousand members in more than sixty countries, IABC receives a flood of entries to the contest every year. Only 13 percent of the IABC's members work at nonprofits. Most (47 percent) work in corporate communications. The award signaled that *Passages* can hold its own with publications produced by much larger, better-funded corporate communications departments. Nonprofits definitely can produce first-class communication tools on a limited budget. Just ask HIAS—and Morris Ardoin.

EXHIBIT 8.1. MTA'S METRO-NORTH NEWSLETTERS: *MILEPOSTS* AND *OUTPOSTS*.

Mileposts

A Publication for MTA Metro-North Railroad Customers   *November 2004*

For All Of You Bird Lovers Out There

Forget about the black-capped chickadee or the rose-breasted grosbeak. . . . The only bird worth watching this time of year is the turkey. (And that's when it's in the oven, where you can baste it regularly!)

So for all you "bird lovers" out there, we offer a special Thanksgiving Holiday timetable that will get you to your "turkey sightings" on time—without suffering from the headaches associated with traffic or the high price of gasoline.

Starting on Wednesday, November 24, we will have 13 additional trains leaving Grand Central between 1 PM and 4 PM.

On Thanksgiving Day, Thursday, November 25, nothing works up an appetite like watching the Macy's Parade. (Those balloon wranglers do work hard!) We have special early morning inbound service to get you there bright and early. First trains arrive at 6:20 AM, and the parade is a short walk from Grand Central. We also have plenty of outbound service—from late morning to mid-afternoon—to get you or your guests to the holiday feast.

Feel free to enjoy that other great Thanksgiving tradition—the after-dinner nap. Lie on the couch, pretend to watch football, and drift off into a

tryptophan-induced trance. Thanks to our expanded evening service back to Manhattan, you can always catch the next train home.

For those of you who must work the Friday after Thanksgiving, we will run a Saturday schedule with extra trains in the AM and PM peak periods. Remember: The early bird gets the best gifts. So for those of you spending the money of those going to work, we offer "Shoppers' Specials"—express trains arriving in Grand Central after 10 AM and departing in the late afternoon. (In fact, on Saturdays from November 6 to December 18, extra "Shoppers' Specials" will run on the Hudson and New Haven lines. Harlem Line customers can use the already frequent weekend service we provide.)

In the holiday spirit, all trains will have off-peak fares throughout the holiday weekend! And you can take advantage of unrestricted parking (no permits, no meters) at many stations. (Check for signs at your station, or call **800-METRO-INFO**; in New York City call **212-532-4900**.)

You will be so thankful if you buy your train tickets in advance and avoid those long holiday lines. Use WebTicket (**www.mta.info**) or one of our "Tickets" machines. Remember: On Thanksgiving Day, between 10 AM and

Prest-o, Change-o . . .

Just like magic, our new timetables will go into effect on Sunday, October 31. And thanks to those wizards of the right-of-way, also known as our schedule planners, we have some treats in store for you.

On the **Hudson Line**, reverse-peak ridership has grown 28% during the past five years. That's why we're adding two new trains to the schedule.

A new upper Hudson Line train will depart Grand Central at 7:16 AM and arrive in Poughkeepsie at 9:04 AM. This train will make stops at Harlem-125th Street, Marble Hill, Yonkers, Tarrytown, and Ossining as well as all stops from Croton-Harmon to Poughkeepsie.

A new lower Hudson Line local train will depart Grand Central at 6:50 AM and arrive in Croton-Harmon at 7:56 AM. This train will stop at Harlem-125th Street and then make all stops between Marble Hill and Croton-Harmon.

In conjunction with this change, the 6:51 AM train to Poughkeepsie will now depart at 6:41 AM.

Also, the 7:44 AM train out of Grand Central will now make all stops between Marble Hill and Croton-Harmon, where it will now arrive at 8:50 AM.

On the **New Haven Line**, the 6:02 AM train from Grand Central, currently making all stops to Harrison, will now also stop at Rye, Port Chester, and Greenwich before running express to Stamford.

Adding these stops to the 6:02 AM train allows us to eliminate them on the 6:17 AM train to New Haven, which will now depart Grand Central six minutes later at 6:23 AM. It will stop at Harlem-125th Street, Fordham, and Greenwich as well as all stops from Stamford to New Haven. Those of you traveling to Stamford and destinations east will benefit from this change.

On the **Harlem Line**, the schedules of most AM and PM peak Lower Harlem Line trains are being changed to include new stops, different arrival and departure times, and revised running times. These changes will also provide a one-seat ride for lower Westchester customers traveling to the Bronx in the AM peak and from the Bronx in the PM peak.

In the AM, three inbound Lower Harlem trains that used to begin their run in Fleetwood or Mount Vernon West will now originate in North White Plains and make all stops from North White Plains to Grand Central. This change will provide a one-seat ride for customers traveling between stations on the Mid-Harlem Line or in the Bronx.

In the PM, four Lower Harlem Line trains

Source: Outposts (in English and Spanish) and *Making Tracks,* courtesy of MTA Metro-North Railroad, Department of Corporate & Media Relations.

New York City, the railroad's fastest-growing market; *Mileposts West*, designed for riders traveling to and from Hoboken and Secaucus, New Jersey; and *Making Tracks*, Metro North's "third-track project newsletter," designed to keep passengers informed about a major project to add a third track on the busy Harlem line.

Most newsletters in the series are simple, attractive one-page 5½-by-11-inch sheets printed in black ink on beige or gray heavyweight text paper. Simple and attractive in design, some are printed in a dual-language version, with English on one side and Spanish on the other, to accommodate Metro North's diverse ridership.

Graphics are primarily simple line drawings, which break up the copy and add to the newsletters' overall appeal. In addition to updates on schedule changes and modernization projects, some issues of the newsletter are expanded to a larger, 16½-by-11-inch format that folds to form six panels of the standard 5½-by-11 size, in order to carry detailed summaries of on-time performance and customer satisfaction reports.

"Customer surveys indicate that passenger satisfaction with the railroad's communications program consistently receives scores of 90 percent and higher," according to Donna Evans, director of corporate and media relations for Metro-North. "This is due in part to the regular appearance of the newsletter."

Print Versus E-Mail

With the advent of e-mail newsletters, many organizations have gotten away from traditional newsletters, thereby saving considerably on printing and mailing costs. Some people, however, particularly older segments of the population, either don't have or aren't comfortable with computers, so for them an online newsletter isn't an option. This means that the old-fashioned paper newsletter will continue to be a basic public relations tool for some time to come.

Frequency

A newsletter can appear monthly, bimonthly, quarterly, semiannually, or occasionally. How often it appears may be a function of how many people are spending time producing it.

Many organizations opt for quarterly newsletters, feeling that once every three months, more or less in tune with the changing seasons, is often enough to build a newsletter of real value to readers without demanding so much time that it precludes doing other things.

If you are launching a newsletter, you may want to begin with a quarterly schedule and then, after things are geared up and running smoothly, shift to a monthly

No More Glue Pots

There was a time when laying out a newsletter meant literally laying out type and photos on graph paper. Doing a newsletter required hours of working hunched over a light box with rulers and T-squares, dabbing rubber cement on the backs of screened photos.

It was messy and time-consuming and seemed always to be done in a rush to get the job off to the printer. When the newsletter came back neatly printed and folded, it was always something of a surprise that anything that looked so "fresh" could have come out of all the mess on the composing table.

My father taught me the trade of layout. He was a Linotype operator and had worked at some of New York City's biggest newspapers. Seated at the huge black machine, pounding away at a keyboard much like a typewriter's, he was one of the men who created the lead "slugs" of movable type that newspapers used in making up their pages before the advent of electronic typesetting.

One Sunday when my sister and I were very young, my father took us to the shop where he worked. While we watched, overwhelmed by the bang and clatter of the huge machines, he sat down at his Linotype, hit a few keys, and magically created lead slugs bearing our names, one for each of us. I remember being delighted by the way the finely molded letters spelled out my name along the edge of that slim piece of metal.

Technology eventually replaced lead slugs, Linotype machines, and aging Linotype operators like my father, who, too old to master a new trade, quietly retired from the workforce.

"It took me a lifetime to master my trade," my father would observe ruefully. "Today any kid with a computer can set type."

The steamroller of new technology replaced a generation of printers virtually overnight. Along the way, it also replaced the light boxes, T-squares, and glue pots used in composing newsletters.

Putting a newsletter together with rubber cement is a lost art—and, if I may speak for everyone who ever spent long, tedious hours hunched over graph paper, trying to get everything in place, it is an art that can *stay* lost. Using any one of a host of graphics programs, such as QuarkXPress, InDesign, or PageMaker, someone with even the lowest-end computer can create a very professional-looking job in a small fraction of the time it used to take.

But, although the production methods have changed dramatically, the basic elements that make up a newsletter have not. Likewise, the basic purpose of a newsletter remains the same: keeping members and supporters involved in and committed to the organization.

schedule. Once you decide on a publication schedule, keep to it. You want your members to be contacted on a regular basis so that they look forward to receiving your newsletter, as one aspect of your efforts to keep momentum strong for your organization's activities.

There may be enough going on at your organization to fill a monthly newsletter, but a monthly newsletter could be too much of a good thing. Even if you skip one or two months in the summer, as some organizations do, on the assumption that their readers are away on vacation, meeting a monthly schedule during the rest of the year can be a grueling chore.

A lot of work goes into producing a newsletter. It always takes longer than you think it will. If you are committed to turning out a new issue every four weeks, you may find that you're left with little time and energy, and not enough to devote more profitably to other things.

Publishing occasionally, whenever time and budgets allow, tends not to be as effective as appearing on a regular schedule. The haphazard nature of occasional publication misses one of the prime attractions of a newsletter: regular, ongoing contact with your readership. People like the familiarity of receiving a publication on a consistent basis. They come to expect it and look for it.

Date your newsletters, and keep track with a volume-numbering system. All the issues published in the first year of publication are part of volume 1, with each individual issue numbered sequentially. The first issue is volume 1, issue 1; the next issue is volume 1, issue 2; and so on. The next year, it starts all over again with volume 2, issue 1. In addition to enabling you to keep track of your newsletter's printing history, this system gives you some added flexibility. If you fall behind, as sometimes happens, the volume and issue markers do not so obviously flag the fact that you missed a month.

How Many Pages?

The simplest newsletter is a one-pager, a brief letter to supporters from the organization—sometimes from the president or chapter chair—full of up-to-date news about the latest projects. Print it on both sides of the paper, and you have a two-pager. Easy to produce, and in a format that works well in either a print or online version, a "letter to supporters" can be the easiest way to launch an organizational newsletter. You may choose later to expand it into a longer and more elaborate version.

One degree up in complexity is the 11-by-17-inch sheet of paper printed on both sides and folded in half to create four 8½-by-11 pages. Combine two such sheets, and you have an eight-pager, which is how most organizational newsletters are usually done. Add a third sheet, and your newsletter now has twelve pages. A fourth sheet makes sixteen pages, and five sheets give you twenty pages. Sometimes staples are inserted through the "spine" of the newsletter, from the outside in, to hold everything together. The final version can be mailed flat in a 9-by-13-inch envelope, or it can be folded in half to 5½ by 8½ inches and held closed with a wafer seal or tape, or it can be folded twice so that it fits into a #10 business envelope or can be mailed on its own.

If you have too much material for four pages and not enough for eight, you may want to opt for six. A simple, popular design begins with an 11-by-25½-inch sheet printed on both sides and folded twice to create a six-page 8½-by-11-inch newsletter. Newsletters like this are relatively inexpensive and require no stapling but can be a little awkward to hold, since they open up so wide.

Whatever the number of pages, the newsletter should be printed on light-colored stock. White, off-white, cream, or very light gray are common choices. Keep the paper light and the ink dark, and the newsletter will be easy to read.

How Many Colors?

How many colors do you want to use for printing? Easiest is one color, using black or a dark blue. You can keep costs down and get the effect of a second color by using the main color and a lighter tint of that color, which for black would be a shade of gray. Sometimes a dark blue is used for the single color. It is almost as easy to read as black, but it presents a problem when it comes to printing photos. A blue-tinted photo of a building or a tree may just look silly, but photos of people printed in blue are almost weird. A blue face peering out of the page somehow lacks credibility. Photos are best printed in black.

If your budget allows, for added punch you can make it a two-color job, using the second color as a design element to emphasize headlines and graphics. A second color does not significantly boost the price, and it makes the final product much easier on the eyes.

A four-color job means full color. Costs for full color have dropped, and many jobs that used to be done as one- or two-color jobs are now done in full color. Compare costs with your printer.

Keep in mind that a newsletter for a nonprofit is expected to be a simple, unpretentious vehicle for getting news out to interested supporters. It is not supposed to be a glossy sales piece. If the newsletter looks too slick, you run the risk of harvesting a bumper crop of complaints about contributors' money being wasted on fancy frills instead of going to the projects for which donations were intended. Given the storm of protest that a "too fancy" newsletter can generate, a two-color job may be the best choice.

Writing Style

Like all public relations writing, newsletters need to be written in clear, easy-to-follow prose. Make sure your grammar and punctuation are correct. Have someone who has not worked on the newsletter proofread it closely with fresh eyes. Avoid over-long sentences, and keep the style conversational and intelligent but not ponderous.

Remember, this is a *news*letter. It should read like a letter sent to friends who are interested in the doings of the organization. If there is no one in house who can write it, consider hiring a freelancer. Ask your printer to recommend someone. You can also find freelance writers and editors in the Yellow Pages under "Editing" or "Proof-reading Services" and online at elanceonline.com and www.wordsmitten.com. If money is tight (and for many nonprofits, money often is), you can also turn to the journalism or English departments of local colleges. Many aspiring journalists and authors just starting out are eager to add some real-world experience to their résumés and will be willing to work for a relatively small hourly rate or to donate their services entirely, especially to a worthy cause.

Design

Consider the image you want your organization to convey. Slick and glossy? Warm and earthy? Straight from the shoulder and no nonsense? The design of your newsletter should be consistent with the design of your other informational and promotional pieces.

People tend to associate an organization with a certain look, and being consistent can help to establish your identity in their consciousness. Make your design distinctive, recognizable, and consistent in order to build recognition and awareness. Your goal is that, in time, recipients will come to welcome your newsletter as a visit from an old friend, brimming over with the latest news.

We are all buried under mail, and the amount we receive every day seems to grow at an exponential rate. No one has time to read all the mail she gets every day, and yet some of that mail actually does get read. To increase the chances of your newsletter being read by your target audience, make it attractive and easy to read.

You can find a graphic designer in the Yellow Pages or online. You can also ask local printers to recommend designers they have worked with. Ask designers to show you samples of work they have produced for other clients. As in finding an editor, you may discover that a local college presents a viable low-cost solution. Contact the art department, and ask for a notice to be posted, indicating that you are looking for someone to do newsletter design and layout for a modest fee and a chance to build a portfolio. Students who respond may not have printed samples to show you, so ask to see samples of class projects instead.

Whether you do the work in house or bring in someone from outside, familiarity with the basics of design can be very helpful in creating a consistent, professional look for the organization. The basic rules of design outlined in Chapter Seven, on brochures, apply to newsletters as well. Properly applied, they can make all the difference.

- Use plenty of white space to prevent a cluttered, jammed-together look.
- Avoid big, unbroken blocks of type that can intimidate the reader and may send her looking for something else to read—maybe even the newsletter of a rival organization.
- Use headlines, graphic elements, and good photos creatively to make the newsletter readable and hold readers' attention.
- Limit the number of typefaces used in your newsletter.

Two Columns or Three?

Decide whether you want to use two columns per page or three. Three is the more common choice. The columns are narrower than in a two-column format and tend to be easier to read. The longer length of the lines in a two column page tends to tire the eye.

Nevertheless, the two-column format, just because it is less common, can be more distinctive. Whatever you choose, it is usually best to stick to it. Some newsletters use different formats for different pages, but the results often look haphazard. Being consistent is a virtue; readers are more comfortable with a single format to which they have become accustomed.

Mailing Panel

Newsletters are usually mailed without an envelope. If you will be sending the newsletter on its own, you'll need to allot a panel for your return address and the mailing address of the recipient. Once you've roughed out your design, take it to the post office to make sure it conforms to postal regulations. It can be very expensive to discover that the piece on which you have lavished so much time and energy cannot be mailed.

If you plan to send the newsletter out in an envelope, you won't need to take up space with a mailing panel, but you will incur the added expense of an envelope. One virtue of an envelope is that you can include other materials, such as a letter, a brochure, or a business card. Of course, even if you do design a mailing panel, you can still send the newsletter in an envelope when the occasion calls for it.

Masthead

The masthead is the section at the top of the first page that bears the name of the newsletter, usually in a distinctive typeface. The name of the newsletter should be something related to the name and goals of the organization. It should be simple, easy to read, and easy to remember. The name and logo of the organization should also be clearly displayed in the masthead.

The masthead should be pleasing to the eye, even when printed at reduced size on the editorial page, and it should be easily photocopied. If you design a masthead composed of red letters on a black background, for example, you may create problems later on when you are making black-and-white photocopies because the red type will show up as black and be impossible to distinguish from the black background.

Contents

There is no hard-and-fast rule regarding what must go into a newsletter, but most contain certain common elements:

- *A letter from the president,* often accompanied by a professionally shot photo. The letter addresses current issues of interest to the membership. The president's letter is typically about seven hundred fifty words long.
- *A calendar of upcoming events,* with promotional sidebars to encourage members to attend and participate.
- *Feature articles* about organizational events, such as conferences, expositions, exhibits, field trips, missions, VIP visits, and celebrations.
- *Photos of recent events,* including photos of organizational leaders and of honorees with their awards. A newsletter should make judicious use of photos depicting events, projects, and individuals. Photos with short, well-written captions can get the major points across quickly for readers who may not take the time to actually read every page. They also serve to brighten the layout of the page. Many photos and captions give the page "air" and make it more appealing. Faced with tough choices in selecting photos, editors sometimes run too many on a page. One good photo is better than three run so small that they are all but impossible to see.
- *Organizational history,* with highlights of past accomplishments, sometimes linked to important anniversaries of important programs or to other dates of significance to readers.
- *Success stories.* These are always popular. Typical stories focus on people who have been served by the organization and who, thanks to that help, have gone on to significant achievements. Another kind of success story might concentrate on wetlands preserved or historic buildings refurbished or a disease kept under control. People like to read about success. It makes them feel that they belong to a winning team.
- *Biographical profiles* of leaders, award recipients, and employees, often accompanied by photos of the featured subjects.

- *Highlights of new materials* produced by the organization, or that are of special interest to readers of the newsletter, such as books, articles, brochures, videos, or DVDs, or new areas on the organization's Web site.
- *Interviews* with people of interest to the members. The interviews can often be conducted at or before major conferences and can be used to extend the impact of those events.
- *Forums* featuring highlights of discussions among noteworthy individuals in the area of the organization's concentration.
- *Question-and-answer columns.* These are popular, especially if the people writing the columns have wit and good writing style.
- *Firsthand reports from the "front"*—that is, accounts of current programs by people who have visited and shared their impressions.
- *News items* related to the organization's area of concern. Even if you can assume that your readers already know about an event by the time the newsletter reaches them, if the news story appears in your newsletter, presented with an organizational slant, you can heighten the relevance of your activities to the larger scene.
- *How-to articles and columns* offering helpful hints. These are always popular and usually take the form of advice from experts on doing something of interest to your readers.
- *A look at projects and programs* that are planned for the future.
- *Contributor lists.* Make sure to spell all the names right and not to leave anyone out. Hell hath no fury like a contributor scorned.

Additional elements include quizzes, contests, and "Did you know . . . ?" sections of interesting facts. A newsletter can also be a great place to reuse other materials. Press releases or printed newspaper clips, excerpts from speeches and reports produced for other purposes, letters to the editor, op-ed columns, and feature articles are all potential recyclables for the newsletter.

Production Schedules

Print-based newsletters have always suffered from a certain lack of immediacy. A look at the production schedule for a typical nonprofit newsletter reveals why this is so.

The Human Resources Association of New York (www.hrny.org), a chapter of the national organization Society for Human Resource Management, meets regularly every month except July and August. An important role of the association's newsletter, *Inside HR/NY,* is to publicize upcoming meetings, so that is the starting point for creating the production schedule.

The November issue, for example, needed to arrive in members' hands in time to promote the meeting on November 15—ideally, no later than three weeks before that meeting, which means that the newsletter must arrive in the mail no later than October 25. Therefore, the newsletter, which travels at the not-for-profit rate and may take a week or more to reach members, must go into the mail on October 19. To allow enough time for editing, layout, printing, folding, and getting the newsletter to the post office, the deadline for submission of copy is set at September 25. Putting everything together, and allowing for times of the year when holidays make the production schedule even longer, means that articles in the newsletter may reach readers as long as eight weeks after they were written—not exactly the speed of light.

E-Mail Newsletters

Electronic or e-mail newsletters (sometimes called *e-zines*), sent via e-mail and posted on Web sites, are becoming increasingly popular, and for good reason. For starters, e-mail newsletters tend to be a lot less expensive than traditional print-based newsletters. They require no paper, no printing, and no mailing costs. If a recipient prefers to have the material, or portions of it, on paper, she can easily print it out. The e-newsletter also tends to be more current, unlike paper newsletters, which often seem obsolete and dated by the time they reach supporters' mailboxes.

An e-newsletter typically includes a "contact us" area that readers can use for responding to things of interest, asking questions, suggesting topics for future issues, and generally providing instant feedback. That easy interactivity makes it possible for the organization to stay in direct contact with its members, who in turn feel that they are personally connected to the organization. These are all strong factors in favor of electronic newsletters.

Print-based newsletters are still popular, but it may be only a matter of time before they start to look like just another step along the continuing evolution away from the world of graph paper and glue pots.

CHAPTER NINE

PRODUCING ANNUAL REPORTS

In the for-profit world, publicly traded corporations are legally required to publish annual reports. Small, privately held businesses are generally not required to issue annual reports, and they usually don't. Sometimes a small business will issue an annual report as a clever marketing strategy, just because it isn't required; the annual report is sent to its customers as a way of helping the company stand out from the crowd. For a nonprofit organization, however, the annual report is an important document.

Why an Annual Report?

According to Michael S. Kutzin, an adjunct faculty member at New York University's George H. Heyman, Jr. Center for Philanthropy and Fundraising and a partner in the New York law firm of Goldfarb Abrandt Salzman & Kutzin (www.seniorlaw.com), the majority of states require nonprofits that solicit charitable contributions within state borders to file an annual report with the state attorney general's office or with another, equivalent agency that has supervisory power over nonprofits. Depending on the state and the amount of revenue the nonprofit generates, the nonprofit may have to file its federal Form 990 in addition to other required financial disclosures, either in audited or unaudited format, and with varying requirements with respect to certification by officers and accountants. Of course, the legal requirements for annual reports do not take into account the aesthetic or marketing potential of a well-prepared annual report that not only provides the raw financial data required in federal Form 990 and under the laws of the various states but also tells the organization's story to the world. In addition to the legally required information, which usually appears at the "back of the book," the annual report commonly offers the reader a fairly comprehensive look at the organization and its activities. Incorporating articles, reports, statistical analyses, and photos, and augmented by attractive graphics, the annual report presents the organization to the public at large.

Because they tend to be fairly elaborate, annual reports that exceed the minimal legal requirements are often expensive to produce. Is all that effort worthwhile? The answer depends on who is going to be receiving it and on what it is intended to accomplish.

Fundraising

Properly designed and used, an annual report can be a very productive element in an organization's fundraising campaign. By drawing on its own resources, an organization may be able to create an annual report that works as a powerful fundraising tool and as an invaluable asset to the organization's campaign.

How one nonprofit set about doing just that, and how the bottom-line results affected the fundraising campaign, can be instructive for any nonprofit seeking to use its annual report as a natural fundraising tool. Like many other nonprofits, the Hebrew Immigrant Aid Society (HIAS) (www.hias.org) had a wealth of past and current accomplishments to draw on. But the organization's annual report was not capturing the excitement and human drama of more than a century of work that HIAS had done to help 4.5 million immigrants worldwide with rescue, settlement, and reunion. HIAS had no shortage of amazing stories to tell, but they were not appearing in the annual report.

But that had not always been the case, as Morris Ardoin, director of communications, discovered. Researching the organization's archives, Ardoin did see that the annual reports of recent years were not inspiring. "We found the typical, clichéd profiles on people, some dull charts, and not much else," he says. But, he adds, he "did some more digging and discovered that we were sitting on a rich but largely unused archive of old photos and annual reports dating back to 1917." He also found that in the peak immigration years of the 1930s and 1940s, the HIAS annual reports were fascinating documents, telling inspiring stories of heroic rescues and incredible courage. He was convinced that the HIAS story today, while different, was no less compelling, and that telling the story of the organization's history of accomplishment could be a powerful fundraising tool. Ardoin was determined to capture all that drama once again in the annual report.

Ardoin had the same budget—$35,000—for creating the annual report that had been allotted in previous years, and so his discovery of a treasure trove of free material was a considerable windfall. The previous annual report had been the usual twenty-four-page model, with few photos. Ardoin decided to use the newly discovered vintage photos and annual reports to create a retrospective report that would commemorate the organization's 120th anniversary. It would save money, and it would be more meaningful than a report using staged, costly new photos and clichéd "profile" copy.

Ardoin envisioned an annual report that, at thirty-two pages, would be fully one-third longer—an impossible objective, at first glance. "But," he says, "since most of the photos didn't cost us anything—we did have to buy the rights to use one picture, that of Tsar Alexander—and we were able to do all the copywriting in-house, our only costs would be for design and printing."

After Ardoin found a designer and a printer prepared to work within the budget, the project began to look truly doable, but it was going to require a significant amount of work on the part of the HIAS staff.

"We spent hours reviewing hundreds of photos in the archives," Ardoin recalls. "We pulled out dozens that we felt would be meaningful, telling, or simply beautiful. One staff person wrote the copy, one worked with the designer, and the third helped with proofreading and final fact checking. Since we are a three-person office, that represented a total allocation of staff."

The HIAS annual report was completed on time and within budget. Its thirty-two pages and front and back covers contained photos from the rich archives of the organization as well as cover art from annual reports dating back to 1917. The report also included an all-important fundraising component, something that had not appeared in earlier annual reports. The new section was used to thank major donors and to list the names of people who had made contributions. An initial mailing to 1,200 key contributors and potential donors generated more than $100,000, an unprecedented amount for the organization.

Nearly five thousand copies of the annual report were mailed to friends of the organization, donors, key legislators, resettlement agencies, libraries, museums, and other institutions. In addition to its obvious fundraising applications, the annual report now serves as a valuable resource for historians, researchers, authors, and producers of documentary films. Since the publication of the annual report, HIAS has worked with eleven documentary filmmakers, each of whom has used the report for research and idea-generating purposes. The completed films, which will heighten the organization's visibility, can be seen as another by-product of the annual report.

To make this success even sweeter, the 2000–2001 HIAS annual report was the winning entry in the "Big Apple" awards competition of the Public Relations Society of America. It is particularly gratifying when a public relations piece earns both money for the organization and recognition for its creators.

Who Gets the Report?

Typically, the annual report is sent to board members, major contributors, and a range of organizational leaders, lay and professional. These are the people who have a stake in the organization and its operations. The annual report is intended as a kind of "state of the organization" presentation, a look at everything that is going on and the plans that are in place at the moment.

The annual report is a declaration and a statement. It is the organization saying, "Look at us, look at what we've accomplished. Look at what we are *going* to accomplish."

Both an educational and a motivational tool, the annual report is intended to heighten support among the major decision makers for the organization's activities. That is an important mission, which is why so much goes into it.

The annual report is also often sent, as a courtesy, to sister organizations working in the same and related fields. It is also sent to government agencies—state, federal, and local—as a way of underscoring that the organization is a serious "player" in the nonprofit world.

Copies of the annual report are usually displayed at the organization's office and at major meetings, conferences, and special events. They are often included in delegates' kits at conventions. Any occasion that calls for making the best possible impression presents an opportunity to use the annual report.

Unlike some other public relations pieces, an annual report has a very definite shelf life. It comes with a date stamp that makes it look obsolete—literally, last year's news—at the changing of the year. Last year's annual report may be included in press kits and given away at conferences for a while beyond that date, but it is not nearly as interesting as the current issue.

Media as an Audience

Although it is not intended to be sent along with every press release, the annual report can be a valuable source of information about the organization for use by the media. When a journalist is doing a story about the organization or interviewing one of its leaders, an annual report can be a very useful tool. It provides a factual snapshot of the organization at the moment, full of key facts and figures. When the annual report is included in a press kit, it literally adds weight and substance.

Many media people now prefer getting their information online. Therefore, in addition to printing the standard paper version, many organizations are putting their annual reports on their Web sites. Journalists are invited to visit the site, where they can view the annual report and download all or part of it in PDF format. Many nonjournalists also prefer the digital format to paper. As more people become comfortable retrieving information online, the printed annual report may become an endangered species.

At a kind of midway point between online and "on paper" is the CD-ROM. Some organizations have opted to copy their annual reports onto read-only CDs, which can be cheaper to produce and distribute in bulk than traditional paper versions of the annual report. Security can be a concern, however, since the threat of contamination by a virus makes some people think twice before inserting CDs into their computers.

Elements of the Annual Report

The well-produced report manages to convey a sense of simplicity that appeals to its readers. A good graphic designer can put the elements of an annual report together in a way that will effectively communicate the heart and soul of the organization's mission. The following sections describe some of the more common elements.

Financial Data

Financials, often with graphics to make them more accessible to the reader, are the one essential element of the annual report. Because most people find numbers boring, these tallies of revenue coming into the organization and expenses going out tend to appear toward the end, at what is referred to as the "back of the book." The name of the accounting firm responsible for the audit is always included along with the numbers.

Name, Logo, and Tag Line

The name of the organization, together with the logo and a powerful tag line, should be prominently featured early in the annual report, usually on the front cover. Many reports repeat all three elements throughout the book.

Letter from the Chair or President

The letter from the chairperson or president should be accompanied by a photo. The volunteer or lay leader is the living embodiment of the organization and as such should be prominently featured, usually toward the beginning of the book. These leaders traditionally get top billing over the professional head of the organization.

Letter from the Professional Head of the Organization

This letter, whether from the executive director or the CEO, is also accompanied by a photo. The office of president is often an honorary one, with people rotating into and out of the position each year, but the professional head is frequently recognized as the real force behind the organization's accomplishments. As such, his or her comments carry weight.

Many annual reports feature both heads, volunteer and professional, on one page, presenting a single message jointly signed. For example, the first page of the annual report issued by Girl Scouts of the USA (www.girlscouts.org) features a joint letter from the national president and the national executive director, with a photo of each of them heading the page.

Mission Statement

Sometimes overlooked, the mission statement is very important. It is the declaration of the organization's reason for existing and the driving force behind all the wheels that have turned and all the activities that have taken place. The mission statement says why it all matters. It should be prominently featured early in the annual report.

Contact Information

The organization's mailing address, phone and fax numbers, and Web site and e-mail addresses should all be easy to find. This information does not usually belong on the front cover, which should be devoted to a high-impact image, but it should be easily accessible. Many annual reports put such information on the inside of the front cover or on the outside or inside of the back cover. Make it easy for people to contact you for more information about the organization or the specific programs they may want to support.

Lists

Some annual reports devote page after page to listing the names of contributors, usually by category of contributions. Such lists may seem unbearably boring at first glance, but to the people whose names appear, few things make for more fascinating reading.

The listings also reveal levels of support. Headings like "Golden Circle" and "Silver Circle" can serve as a not-so-gentle prod to donors to increase their support next year. Because the levels of giving are stated so plainly, as a matter of public record, the annual reports of other organizations are also favorite reading matter for fundraising professionals.

Other types of lists can and do fill the pages of annual reports. Including lists of board members, chapter presidents, division heads, officers, or senior staff members, often with photos, is a way for an organization to promote a sense of connectedness among its various constituencies.

Articles

Articles about ongoing projects, often accompanied by photos, bring the reader into the world of the organization's activities. Articles usually include highlights of the past year and statistics to convey the scope of operations.

There can be many creative approaches to telling an organization's story. United Cerebral Palsy of New York City (www.ucpnyc.org) used a "one day" approach to illustrate the scope of its services. The first client profile carries a time stamp of 6:00 A.M. and features a story and article about an early-morning program. The next page is headed 8:42 A.M. and focuses on a different program taking place later that day. Each page carries the time line forward until the final profile, which is headed "Lights Out at 9:20 P.M."

American ORT (www.aort.org), which operates vocational schools in countries around the world, used a similar idea in its annual report. Noting that the sun never sets on its global operations, it highlighted programs taking place at a single moment in time. At the same time that ORT students in New York were beginning their school day, ORT students in France were finishing up their afternoon classes, and ORT students in Israel were already doing their homework. Using photos and a graphic time line, the annual report conveyed the global scope of operations in simple human terms.

Interviews

The annual report can feature interviews with people the organization has helped, workers in the field, leaders who have visited operational sites, and important heads of state or of other organizations. Interviews, often accompanied by photos, provide individual perspectives on projects and activities.

Profiles

Profiles of people involved in some way with the organization are an interesting way to present the human side of operations.

Maps

Maps are a big favorite in annual reports. There are as many people who really like maps as there are who really dislike them. Maps are a great way to visually convey the scope of operations, but they should not be overdone.

Photo Essays

Photo essays work well because the annual report has space for them. With minimal captions, or perhaps just a brief heading on the page, a series of good photos can be worth far more than the proverbial thousand words. It is important not to print the photos too small—better fewer photos that can actually be seen than a larger selection, each of which is an indistinguishable blur.

Graphics

In the age of photography, line drawings can add a nice touch. Girls Incorporated (www.girlsinc.org) opted to give prominent placement to the architect's rendering of its new National Resource Center, in Indianapolis. In addition to being a dramatic addition to the page, the drawing provided a forward look at a major upcoming project of the organization. It also afforded an opportunity to highlight the generosity of a leadership grant by the organization's longtime supporter, the Lilly Endowment.

Horizons National Student Enrichment Program, Inc. (www.horizonskids national.org), of New Canaan, Connecticut, achieved a different kind of dramatic effect when it used photos of colorful crayon drawings by students in the program to brighten up its annual report.

Exceptions prove the rule. Photos and graphics can give life to the pages of an annual report, but not using them can also have a drama of its own. The New York–based National Minority Supplier Development Council (www.nmsdcus.org) chose not to use any photos or graphics in its annual report. Instead, an attractive typeface and a creative design combined to create a stark, but appealing look.

Reprints of Articles

Articles about the organization that originally appeared in other publications, along with those publications' mastheads, convey a good "in the news" feel about your work. In addition, favorable comments from an outside observer provide added credibility and serve as a third-party endorsement. Mastheads and published articles, of course, are the property of the respective publications, and permission must be obtained to use them in your annual report.

Highlights of the Volunteer Year

A "look back" page, featuring photos taken at special events during the year, can be very appealing. Typical photos show supporters at such organizational functions as award ceremonies, conferences, and conventions.

The annual report of the United Nations Association of the United States of America (www.unausa.org), for example, includes a two-page spread of photos showing a wide range of supporters from the worlds of business, finance, and the arts. Featured with supporters in the photos are UN secretary general Kofi Annan, former South African president Nelson Mandela, and Princess Firyal of Jordan. The obvious reason for featuring such photos is to underscore the significance and wide appeal of the organization.

Membership Tallies

In its annual report, Girl Scouts of the USA lists its membership in a table, by state. The table serves to emphasize the nationwide scope of the organization and to enhance pride in its widespread presence.

Historical Perspectives

A brief history of the organization, or of one of its aspects, can help put current operations into perspective. The inclusion of vintage photos can add an interesting touch to a layout.

Campaign Promotion

The entire annual report can be considered advertising for the organization, but its pages also provide an excellent platform to "pitch" specific programs. This ability should not be overdone, or you risk turning the reader off, but brief promotions can work well.

For example, the annual report published by St. Francis College in Brooklyn (www.stfranciscollege.edu) uses a half-page panel to briefly explain the benefits of its planned giving program. It features a photo of a statue of Saint Francis of Assisi, for whom the school is named, and urges readers to call for more information.

Allotting half a page or so to a promotional column can generate considerable response. Because the annual report goes to selected supporters, including those who are affluent and committed to the organization, it can be an excellent vehicle for connecting with prequalified potential supporters of a particular program.

Response Envelope

One theory of fundraising maintains that no one should ever be denied an opportunity to contribute. In line with that philosophy, many annual reports arrive with a response envelope tucked neatly into the binding. The reader cannot miss this none-too-subtle request for funds—but, then again, subtle may not be the name of the game.

After leafing through the annual report and getting all the latest news about the organization's accomplishments, the reader may well be moved to write a check and send it back in the conveniently provided response envelope. Organizations like United Cerebral Palsy (www.ucp.org) and Human Rights Watch (www.hrw.org) use this device in their annual reports.

Because there is no postage on the envelope, there is no cost to the organization for postage. But these envelopes do rely on the person who is sending the check to find a stamp—maybe a small chore, but sometimes that can be just enough to slow the giving impulse as the letter goes into the "I'll take care of it later" pile.

Some nonprofit organizations, like the Christian Children's Fund (www. ChristianChildren'sFund.org) and the Jewish Braille Institute (www.jbilibrary.org), opt to include a prepaid business reply envelope in their annual reports. The organization pays the postage only for those envelopes that are actually returned to them.

Some annual reports opt for a response coupon instead of an envelope. Although it is cheaper to do it this way, the reader has to find a pair of scissors, cut out the coupon (leaving the annual report with a missing chunk), locate an envelope, and find a stamp. That is more effort than most people are willing to make.

Mailing Panel

The annual report is usually mailed in a 9-by-13-inch envelope and is, or should be, accompanied by a personalized letter from the organization's leaders. Some organizations mail the reports on their own. To facilitate this practice, they reserve a white panel on the back cover for the mailing address.

Paper

Most annual reports are made of 17-by-11-inch sheets printed on both sides, folded in half, and saddle-stitched together with several other sheets to make an 8½-by-11-inch book. The typical page count tends to range from 8 to 36 pages, with 24 pages being the average.

Some annual reports are printed on uncoated or dull-coat text-weight stock, which gives a warm, earthy feel. Most, however, are printed on coated text stock that is designed to show off photos to advantage. The cover is often heavier—a cover-weight stock that gives the book more body. There are no hard-and-fast rules, and annual reports vary.

The Christian Children's Fund annual report, for example, uses a lightweight text stock inside and also for the cover, giving its report more the feeling of a tabloid magazine, or something you might pick up from a magazine rack in a store. As a result, the report's stories and pictures about kids around the world seem more like news stories, and this quality adds to the sense of immediacy and urgency. The lower half of the back cover is reserved for the mailing panel, and this feature makes the report a very effective self-mailer. A prepaid business reply envelope tucked into the center of the report encourages readers to make a contribution while the faces of the children they've seen smiling out at them from the pages of the report are still fresh in their minds.

CHAPTER TEN

MAKING DIRECT MAIL WORK

D irect mail is so named because it goes directly to the person to whom it is addressed. According to Senny Boone, executive director of the Nonprofit Federation of the Direct Marketing Association (DMA) (www.nonprofitfederation.org), Washington, D.C., "The beauty of direct marketing is that you are speaking directly, one on one, with the person you want to reach." Direct mail, she notes, "is both a methodology and an art form."

In a 2004 study of trends and benchmarks in nonprofit direct marketing, the DMA offered some telling statistics on the effectiveness of direct mail for nonprofits. When it comes to fundraising, DMA studies show that 59 percent of adults respond to solicitations for contributions made by direct mail. By comparison, only 45 percent of people respond to special-event fundraisers, and only 41 percent respond to word-of-mouth solicitations.

The Basics

The basics of direct mail are simple. You mail something—perhaps an informational piece accompanied by an appeal for a contribution—to a list of qualified prospects. You hope the recipient will take the time to open the envelope, read the material, and send back the response card or envelope—all very straightforward. Put together a list of prospects, send out some mail, and just wait for the money to come back to you. So what's the problem?

For starters, too many people are doing the same thing. The average U.S. household receives more than a hundred pieces of direct mail every week. Many nonprofit groups use direct mail to raise up to 90 percent of their funds. Prospects are buried under a growing avalanche of direct mail.

The first challenge is finding ways to make your mailing stand out from the ton of things the recipient gets in the mail every day—all those flyers, postcards, catalogues, newsletters, magazines, and other mail.

On average, less than 1 percent of a direct mailing elicits the intended response. With direct mail, a response rate of 2 percent is generally considered a success. This means that out of one hundred envelopes sent out in the mail, ninety-eight end up in the garbage. And that's in a *successful* campaign.

With numbers like that, why would anyone—or any organization—ever choose to mount a direct-mail campaign? The answer is: look at that 2 percent. Those relatively few people who respond positively more than make up for the vast majority who toss your material, unread, into the trash. The strength of direct mail is that you can target *exactly* the people who are most likely to be interested in your product, or, in the case of a nonprofit, your organization.

A Successful Technique?

According to the DMA, direct mail is successfully used as a fundraising technique by 64 percent of fundraisers, far surpassing telephone solicitations at 39 percent and the Internet and e-mail at 18 percent and 19 percent, respectively. Direct mail compares favorably with special events, which are used successfully by 69 percent of fundraisers.

From the other side of the equation, 70 percent of people responding to fundraising appeals have rated direct mail a successful technique, which compares favorably with the 64 percent who consider special events a successful technique. Only 38 percent thought telephone solicitations were a successful technique, 30 percent thought use of the Internet was a successful fundraising technique, and 29 percent held that opinion about the use of e-mail. Outstripping these, however, were opinions about major gifts campaigns, at 86 percent, and planned giving, at 82 percent, as successful fundraising techniques.

Nonprofits with the Best Direct-Mail Results

When it comes to donating money, says the DMA, more than half (52 percent) of the people responding to appeals donate their money to organizations involved with issues of health. Next in popularity are organizations involved with issues of food and hunger (41 percent of donors) and community services (40 percent). Organizations that focus their efforts on children receive contributions from 39 percent of people making donations to nonprofits. Other nonprofits cited in the DMA study are those involved with religious causes outside of church (a 39 percent donor rate), disaster relief (37 percent), homeless shelters (36 percent), education (27 percent), animals and environmental groups (22 percent), and social services (15 percent). Political groups bring up the rear with a response rate among donors of 14 percent.

Elements of Direct Mail

The three elements of a direct-mail campaign are the product or offer, the creative package, and the list. For a nonprofit, the product or offer is the organization's call to action—the message and campaign pitch intended to motivate support for the organization. The creative package is the writing and design—how your mailing looks and reads affects the results, so don't stint on the time and effort needed to make it as good as you can. The list is the mailing list—the key to the success of any direct-mail campaign.

The Offer

To be effective in a direct-mail piece, the call to action has to have the impact and "sales appeal" of an irresistible product offer. If you were selling widgets, an appealing offer might highlight the terrific product benefits, cite testimonials from celebrities, and create a sense of urgency with a message to "call now" to get a bargain price. You aren't selling widgets, but you *are* making an offer of sorts. You are offering the reader an opportunity to join with your organization and become a part of something that matters very much.

In constructing an offer, direct marketers stress the importance of answering the question, "Why should I?" You need to provide both rational and emotional answers to that question.

Your mailing should convey a sense of urgency. The reader must understand that if she does not act immediately, tomorrow may be too late. "If not now, when?" asked the first-century Jewish sage Hillel. Your mailing must pose the same question.

The mailing should create a personal connection between the organization and the reader. Speak in the reader's language, and make it clear that you are writing directly to her, that you know who she is and have her in mind. Know what is important to her, and refer to it in your mailings. Know her "hot buttons," and be smart about how you push them.

Let your mailing teach the reader things she will care about. Don't bury her in statistics, but do not hesitate to use some important numbers to illustrate the scope of the problem and the urgency of the need: so many children at risk, so many acres being laid waste, so many cures desperately needed. Use facts as tools to present the scope of the problem, and show the ways in which the organization aims to provide the solution. Talk to the reader as if she is a potential partner in the cause, and she is more likely to become a partner.

The Creative Package

Outside Envelope. Most direct mail ends up getting thrown away unopened and unread. If the recipient just reflexively throws away the envelope and its contents, it won't matter how brilliantly designed the material inside is, or how incredibly incisive the copy. Therefore, your first job is to consider how to give the outside envelope the best possible chance of surviving the initial selection process. Do anything you have to do to get the envelope opened.

The outside envelope must really do two jobs. First, it must stand out from among the piles of letters, bills, and magazines and be noticed. Second, it has to sell—it has to offer the recipient a reason to open it.

The New York City Rescue Mission (www.nycrescue.org) has developed a direct-mail piece that does both. Every fall, as Thanksgiving approaches, it launches its annual, and very distinctive, direct-mail campaign. The mission's mailing piece measures 5½ by 8¼ inches—the same size as the oversize postcards and letters used in so many direct-mail campaigns. Those oversize pieces make up about 10 percent of direct mail received in people's homes, according to the Direct Mail Association, so it would be easy for the mailing to get lost in the crowd. But this mailing is different.

The envelope is a miniature brown grocery bag. On one side, above the address label, are the organization's name and its logo, which features a dove flying over a city. On the other side is a compelling message that begins with the intriguing headline "There's a complete Thanksgiving dinner in this little bag!" (see Exhibit 10.1).

The body copy on this envelope disguised as a grocery bag goes on to make the appeal. The subhead reads, "You can help feed one hungry person a complete Thanksgiving dinner for just $1.94." Inside the envelope is a response form and a postage-paid business reply envelope. The package is designed so the recipient can remove the response material without tearing open the outside envelope—very clever, very distinctive, and, according to Joe Little, the mission's donor relations manager, very effective. "People tend to notice our mailings," says Little. "Response to our little brown grocery bag has been very favorable."

The New York City Rescue Mission draws on the nature of its operations to create a direct-mail piece that captures the essence and the spirit of its work.

**EXHIBIT 10.1. NEW YORK CITY RESCUE MISSION'S
DIRECT-MAIL APPEAL.**

There's a complete Thanksgiving dinner in this little bag!

We're counting on this bag to help us feed thousands of hot, nutritious dinners to hungry, homeless and hurting people this Thanksgiving. Tender turkey with all the trimmings. Cranberry sauce. Even pumpkin pie. We want to do our part to make sure that everyone in need in York City has a happy Thanksgiving. But frankly, we can't do it without your help.

You can help feed one hungry person a complete Thanksgiving dinner for just $1.94.

$11.64 will feed 6 people! $23.28 will provide 12 delicious holiday dinners. Or, your gift can provide the safe shelter, Christian guidance and other vital care right here at **New York City Rescue Mission**.

So here's what we'd like you to do. Write out a generous check and mail it with the reply form in the enclosed envelope.

Once you've mailed your gift, we hope you'll reuse this bag as a reminder of the help you're giving others!

Thanks to you, needy men, women and children right here in our community will have a very satisfying Thanksgiving—complete with a turkey dinner. And that ought to give you a satisfying holiday of your own.

Thank you, and may God bless you!

Source: New York City Rescue Mission "Thanksgiving dinner in this little bag!" direct mail appeal, courtesy of the Russ Reid Company.

Kittens and Puppies

The American Society for the Prevention of Cruelty to Animals (ASPCA) (www. aspca.org) also makes use of its own "natural resources" to create a direct-mail piece that captures the essence of what it does. The outside envelope for its mailings features the words "ASPCA Membership Card Enclosed!" The membership card itself is visible through a little window in the corner of the envelope. The recipient's name appears on the card, just beneath the letters "ASPCA" and an appealing color photo of an irresistible kitten and an adorable puppy. The mailing also includes a response card and a business reply envelope as well as a letter about the organization and a decal, again featuring a cute puppy and a kitten.

Once a contributor's level of support has made her eligible for membership in the ASPCA Founder's Society, the mailing becomes more elaborate. It arrives in an oversized envelope and includes a CD accompanied by an invitation to "share our vision." On the CD is a picture not of a kitten and a puppy but of three very happy-looking dogs. Just looking at the picture makes you smile.

One benefit your recipient enjoys by opening your envelope is the opportunity to consider becoming actively allied with a cause that touches her personally. If she is already a supporter, then the name of your organization may be enough to evoke an impulse to offer further support. If she is a potential supporter, perhaps someone whose name you acquired from a mailing list, then your organization's name may need to be supplemented with a clear message indicating just what you do and why she may care about it.

Give some thought to using artwork on the envelope—maybe a line drawing of something significant to the recipient, or perhaps a building or a mountain, or even an arresting logo. Also consider using a photo of something that will elicit a reaction—say, a photo on the face of the envelope of an appealing child or an endangered whale or a cute puppy. Be creative in considering what will resonate with your target market, and don't hesitate to use it on your outside envelope.

The outside envelope is the first thing the recipient sees when she gets her mail, and so it is your first point of attack. The envelope must interest her enough so that she will open it and read the contents. You have three seconds. That is how long the average person takes to decide whether to open an envelope or throw it away. And in an era when many people are fiercely determined to eliminate clutter from their lives, you may actually have less than that, so the envelope has to be good.

Often the organization's name on the outside envelope is the most potent selling tool. If that's true of your organization, then make sure its name appears prominently, printed big and clear and easy to read.

In the heated competition to get the envelope opened and read, your organization's name, and the name recognition it has among your supporters, has the power to tip the scales in your favor. According to a U.S. Postal Service survey, current members will open 72 percent of the mail you send them, and one-third of the people who are familiar with your organization but not currently members or supporters will open and read mail you send them. And you can even do more than prominently feature the name of your organization. Because you are already printing your address on the face of the envelope, there is little or no additional cost for also printing a provocative "teaser line" or a compelling line drawing or photo under the return address or along the bottom of the envelope. An envelope with a teaser line on its face is likely to get a better response than an envelope without one.

When you consider what to print on the envelope, remember that the first purpose of the envelope is to overcome the recipient's impulse to throw it into the trash, and the second purpose is to get her to open the envelope and read what is inside. Whet the recipient's curiosity; remind her of a significant accomplishment, an important anniversary, or an upcoming event.

The recipient's name—and it should be the person's name, never "Dear Friend of Our Organization"—is either printed directly on the envelope or on a label that is pasted on or that appears through a clear plastic window. Whenever possible, the name should be imprinted directly on the envelope and not on a paste-on label. Mailing labels should generally be avoided; few things are more impersonal.

Because the outside envelope is so critical to the overall package, outside envelopes have been carefully studied for years as direct mailers have sought ways to boost their response rate. Those studies have led to the interesting discovery that postage stamps work better than metered postage when it comes to getting people to open the envelope. And the stamps work even better if they are put on a little crooked. No one knows exactly why this is so—some speculate that it gives the impression that a flawed human affixed the stamp rather than a precise but impersonal machine.

Letter. Once the recipient opens the outside envelope and begins to read the letter inside, the clock is ticking. How long do you have to make your "sale"? Not long. Unless you catch the reader's attention in the first few seconds, all you will have done is delay the ultimate moment when she tosses your whole package into the trash. You need to exercise a lot of thought and creativity in crafting your letter.

The opening sentence needs to irresistibly pull the reader in. Direct marketers offer a helpful hint: the two most effective words for connecting with a reader are *I* and *you*.

The letter should be the first thing the recipient sees when she opens the envelope, and her name should be visible immediately. Begin by taking advantage of the ability of direct mail to personalize. Personalization increases responses. Make your salutation as personal as is appropriate, but avoid offending with overly personal names.

First Class or Third?

As a registered nonprofit organization, you probably qualify for a third-class nonprofit indicia. This is a special imprint that the U.S. Postal Service allows you to use in place of stamps. It entitles you to mail at a special low nonprofit rate. Check with your post office to see if you qualify. There is no appreciable difference in response to mailings sent out by third class as opposed to first class, and you can save money by taking advantage of the special nonprofit postal rate.

Third class is cheaper, which is a plus, but misaddressed third-class envelopes won't be returned to you, which is a drawback when it comes to keeping your mailing list current. From time to time, send a mailing to your in-house list by first-class mail so that incorrectly addressed pieces will be returned to you. You can then correct any mistakes in your database and update your list.

Structure. The letter is composed of three parts: the opening, the argument, and the call to action.

The opening, or hook, is designed to catch the reader's eye and get her to read on. It serves the same purpose as a headline does in an ad. You know the people in your target market. You know what will get their attention, what will excite them. Use that knowledge when creating the opening to the letter that will hook the reader's attention and pull her into the letter.

The argument is the part of the letter that answers the question "Why should I care about the problem?" Once you have made the reader care about the problem, you need to answer three related questions: "Why should I care about what your organization does about the problem? Why should I get involved? Why should I take the action you are urging me to take?"

Make your case as clearly and powerfully as possible. Testimonials from people the organization has helped, or people whose good opinion will carry weight with the reader, are a good way to add impact to the letter.

Tell a story—short, to the point, but dramatic and, if possible, heartwarming. People like stories; it helps them relate to others. Be sure the stories are believable, however, and make sure you get your facts right. Your credibility is one of your most precious assets. The letter should make the reader feel deeply about both the importance and the urgency of taking action.

The call to action as embodied in the letter is the raison d'être of the whole package. This is where you get the reader to do what you want her to do.

The Johnson Box

The Johnson Box was invented by Frank Johnson in the hugely successful letters he created for the direct-mail campaign of *American Heritage* magazine. It is a common opening device for sales letters that can also be used by nonprofits. It is a summary of the offer, sometimes enclosed in a box, printed at the top of the letter, ahead of the salutation. Often presented in a larger, bolder typeface than the bulk of the letter, it announces to the reader that something of personal interest is going to follow in the letter she is about to read. Many nonprofits use the Johnson Box to good effect, employing the boxed area not to tout their products but to highlight the urgent need that has prompted the letter.

The letter needs to clearly state the problem and indicate how action on the part of the reader can help solve that problem. The letter should make very clear exactly what the reader is being asked to do. Often it is to write a check. Sometimes it is to reserve a place at a function. Whatever the action requested, nothing should be taken for granted; the necessary steps should be clearly indicated.

The letter should include contact information indicating how the reader can reach the organization with questions or feedback. The address of the organization's Web site, its e-mail address, and its fax number and main phone number, ideally toll-free, should be clearly indicated. Make it clear that your organization is accessible to its supporters, and that it welcomes and encourages ongoing communication. The reader's action is not the end of the campaign; it is one step in a continuous action plan to join the organization in its mission.

Length. How long should the letter be? There is a long-standing dispute in direct-mail circles about what works better: short letters or long ones.

In the 1920s, Claude Hopkins, one of the giants of twentieth-century advertising, wrote what was to become a direct-marketing rule of thumb: "The more you tell, the more you sell." He believed that the best way to get a message across, whether about a product or about an organization, was to do it thoroughly.

A more contemporary school of thought argues that the Hopkins approach is outdated. Today, this argument runs, most people have short attention spans, and as a rule they don't like to read. People are accustomed to a sound-bite culture that dictates a "get right to the point" approach.

Some studies show that a four-page appeal letter has a better effect than a two-pager. The longer length allows for a more in-depth "chat" feel, with space and time for background and case histories, which give the reader a feeling that important information is being shared. Other studies seem to indicate that the key to success is brevity. The jury is still out on the most effective length for a direct-mail letter, so this is a good area to begin testing. Try doing it both ways. Tell your story with a short letter and a long one, and see which generates the stronger response.

Appearance, Style, and Tone. However long the letter is, it should be easy to read. It should have plenty of white space and subheads and short rather than long blocks of type. Make it easy on the eyes, and it is more likely to be read. Photos, with or without captions, illustrations, headlines, bullets, and callouts can be used to break up the page and make it easier for the reader to get through the letter.

The letter is a communication from one person to another. That is important to remember because it is easy to fall into the mind-set that the "organization" is "doing" a mailing to a "current or potential supporter." While that may be true, the letter should not be written in that tone. Someone signed the letter, and someone else is receiving it. It should be written that way.

The letter is and should read like a personal communication that really speaks to the person who is holding the letter in her hands and reading it. Keep that direct personal aspect, the sincere me-to-you tone, in mind as you prepare the copy. You are establishing and continuing a relationship. Communicate with an audience of one.

Write in the language of the people who are receiving the letter. That may seem obvious, but it means more than just formal language. Whereas broad market-based advertising avoids jargon, slang, and buzz words, direct mail can be an ideal medium for them.

If you use words or expressions, technical terms, or phrases from other languages that you *know* are familiar to supporters of your organization, you can effectively underscore the bond between the letter writer and the letter reader. You establish an "in crowd" feeling that can be very useful in bonding with current and future supporters of the cause.

Because humor doesn't always travel well, it is usually a good idea to avoid trying to be funny. Convey warmth, convey urgency, but stay away from jokes. If the reader doesn't "get" them, you risk turning her off and losing a potential supporter.

The letter should be signed by someone of significance, and her organizational title, even if it is only honorary, should always accompany her name. The letter is presented as coming from the person whose name appears at the end. This may be a convenient fiction, but that tone should be maintained in the letter.

Postscript. The postscript, or P.S., is one part of a letter that almost always gets read, and a letter with a postscript gets a better response than a letter without one. In fact, the P.S. is the part of the letter that the reader is most likely to look at, after her own name and the name of the person who signed the letter. In a single-page letter, the reader's eye often drops to the P.S. first. Because the P.S. tends to get read more often than the main text of the letter, it offers an opportunity to make a very short, compelling statement that will whet the reader's appetite for more. Therefore, it is usually a good idea to use a P.S.

Although the P.S. comes at the end of the letter, think of it as a provocative introduction. If you were selling a product, this would be the ideal place to stress its most compelling benefit. Because you are, in effect, "selling" your organization, the P.S. is an ideal place to stress the urgency of the need to take action.

Response Vehicle. The outside envelope gets the package to the reader. The letter inside makes the case. The response vehicle facilitates the desired action.

By enclosing a response card or envelope, you make it easy for the recipient to take action. Her name and address may already be preprinted on the card, but be sure to allow enough space for her to fill in any other requested information, including her level of contribution. A hard-to-follow or off-putting response card can mean that a frustrated recipient throws it in the trash instead of sending it to back you.

Restate your main appeal on your response form, and, again, make it easy for the reader to take the action you want her to take. If there are several choices to be made, be sure the boxes to be checked are clearly indicated. Indicate what credit cards you accept, and leave enough space for her to fill in her credit card number and its expiration date.

Your response card should also list the address of your organization's Web site, the organization's e-mail address, and a toll-free phone number so that the person filling out the response card can easily contact your organization with any questions that come to mind. Add a thank-you line or a quick statement of appreciation for the recipient to read as she completes the form so she will be reminded of how much her support matters.

In some cases, a simple preaddressed response card can be enough for your purposes. If you want the recipient to send back a check, or if you are requesting personal information, such as a phone number or a credit card number, you should always provide a response envelope. The response form should fit comfortably into the response envelope, and both, obviously, should be smaller than the outside envelope so that they fit inside comfortably. Check with your printer or stationery supplier in advance, to be sure that everything actually does fit where it is supposed to.

Double-check that the organization's return address is correct, and indicate any special department or individual to whom the card should go. This is especially important for tracking the response rates from different mailing lists or to packages with varying components.

You may want to include postage as well—again, to make it easier and more convenient for the recipient to respond. It adds to your cost, but it saves the respondent time, and that can make all the difference.

There are several ways to include postage on a return card or envelope. One way is a postage stamp or metered postage. Another is with a prepaid business reply envelope or business reply card. The response envelope or card travels by first-class mail, and you pay only for envelopes or cards that are actually returned to you. You can arrange for business reply mail at the post office.

Additional Enclosures. In addition to the letter and the response card or envelope, it is often a good idea to include an article reprint. A favorable article about your organization that appeared in a newspaper or magazine adds credibility to who you are and what you do.

You may want to highlight a sentence or two in the article for the reader to glance at, since she may not read the entire article. Attaching a "thought this would interest you" note to the article, especially if it bears the name of the president of the organization or chapter, serves to personalize the enclosure and adds a nice touch.

In the direct-mail field, such an added piece is known as a "lift note," so called because it is an extra piece in the mailing designed to lift response levels. It is usually a folded piece of paper of a different color from anything else in the mailing, and it constitutes an added voice in the selling pitch, an added push from someone else. An article that is clearly in someone else's voice can serve the same function in your mailing, working as a "lift note" to boost response.

If you are enclosing an article or other additional pieces in your mailing, such as raffle tickets, passes to an event, and the like, be sure to take a mock-up to the post office to check that your mailing hasn't become so heavy that it is pushed into a higher postage bracket.

Also avoid anything breakable or with sharp edges, including improperly applied staples, that could tear through the envelope or hurt the recipient—not a good way to encourage a favorable response.

The List

One direct-mail study attributes the success or failure of a campaign as follows: 60 percent of its success depends on the list, 30 percent on the "offer," and 10 percent on the creative package. Most direct-mail professionals regard list choice as the single most critical element in determining the success of a mailing.

You already own one of the best possible mailing lists: your own membership list, what professionals call a "house" list, is an excellent starting point. Direct mailers say that a list of current customers is "golden."

An organization's members are like current customers. They have already demonstrated their interest in the organization and what it does. They represent the very best prospects for any mailing. If you diligently maintain your member database and keep it current, you can effectively mine it for your mailing.

To expand your mailing, you need to get additional names. That means defining your target audience, or several target audiences, and acquiring a list of people who fall within those parameters. You have several options.

You can rent a list from another organization, one that deals with a similar target market. (People commonly talk about buying mailing lists, but you don't actually buy a list; you rent it, and when you contract for a list, you pay for the right to use it a specific number of times.) You can rent lists from publications—magazines, newspapers, and newsletters—that serve the market you want to reach. You can also get additional names from a list broker, who will offer a wide selection of possible lists along with some advice and guidance. The cost of renting a list tends to be the same whether you rent from a private source or a broker, because the owner of the list pays the broker's fee. You can find list brokers online or in the Yellow Pages under the heading "Mailing Lists." You can also consult the *Directory of Mailing List Houses* in your library's reference section. Another good source is the U.S. Postal Service's Web site (www.usps.com/directmail).

Deciding which list to use requires a very clear and precise sense of whom you want to reach. The more you know about the people in your target market, the more accurately you can match their profiles with the right list. Carefully consider such demographic factors as age, education, income, and geographical location.

Consider, too, what marketers call the *psychographics*. These are factors that define segments of the population according to other criteria, such as lifestyle activities, hobbies, and interest affiliations. For nonprofits, these factors are particularly useful in zeroing in on the most promising target market. A good rule is to begin by renting lists of people who match the characteristics of your current supporters. Then branch out from there.

In the world of sales, the secret of success is to concentrate on prospects, not suspects. It is important to know the difference. Prospects are consumers who are ready, willing, and able to buy; suspects are merely eligible to buy. Communicating with prospects is a much more fruitful expenditure of resources than communicating with suspects, a pursuit that spreads your resources too thin. In creating your mailing list, narrow your focus to concentrate on target markets that represent likely prospects before you widen your approach to include people who are only eligible suspects.

There are some eighteen thousand published lists in the United States, and they are constantly being updated. Consumer lists go out of date at the rate of 2 percent per month, or 24 percent per year. Business lists go out of date even faster, at the rate of 1 percent per week, or about 50 percent per year. With all that moving around, how can you keep your list current? That is a problem for every direct-mail practitioner. The solution, as it is for so many other things in the realm of direct mail, is to contact your post office. Ask about keeping your database of names current through the National Change of Address Program (NCOA), which works with the U.S. Postal Service to keep addresses current.

When you rent a mailing list and get responses, the names of your respondents are yours to keep. You are free to mail to them as often as you like and even to rent their names to others. Embedded within any list you rent, however, are a number of disguised names that bring your mailing back to the list broker. That is how the broker knows when you are using his list. If you use it for more than the agreed number of times, you are breaking the contract.

The cost of renting a mailing list varies. Prices are generally given in terms of cost per one thousand names. The cost of a consumer list that reaches people at their homes tends to range between $50 and $200 per thousand names. Business lists, which reach people at work, tend to be more expensive.

Mailing Houses. If you are doing a small mailing (several thousand pieces or fewer), you may find it easiest to handle the whole thing in house. Staff members and volunteers can be given stacks of letters, response vehicles, and outside envelopes and can stuff them during meetings or while on the phone. After all, multitasking is all the rage. You can check with your local post office or office supply store for postal scales, feeders, sealers, and instructions for handling metered mail or mailing permits.

If that is impractical, or if the mailing is larger than you can comfortably handle, you may want to turn to a professional. Many printers provide complete mailing services for an added fee. Check with several printers, to get an idea of the range of prices. You can also check the Yellow Pages, under the headings "Mailing" and "Marketing."

Test, Test, Test. "In developing mailing pieces, you need to test and test again," says Senny Boone. "The DMA regularly holds educational conferences on the subject. Little things can make a big difference to the success of a direct-mail piece—things like is your envelope white or off-white, is there a foil liner inside the envelope—all of that can dramatically affect response to a mailing."

Indeed, direct marketers say that the three most important things to do in developing a direct-mail campaign are to test, test, and test. When you rent a list from a list broker, ask to rent a few thousand names from each of several different lists. Send the same mailing to each list, and see which has the best response rate. Be sure to code your response card so you know which response came from which list.

Here is a standard formula: if a list has one hundred thousand names, test five thousand of them. Ask your list broker for an "nth name selection," which means that you will get every twentieth name from that list of one hundred thousand. Mail to the five thousand names. If the mailing is successful, go back to the list broker for another twenty-five thousand names. If the success continues, mail to the entire list. And, of course, keep track of the results, to compare them with similar tests of other lists.

Don't just settle for a mailing that works nicely. Constantly tweak it. Try changing the envelope, the wording and look of the letter, the enclosures, and the response card. Keep testing. Track and measure your results so you can make it the best direct-mail piece possible.

Your organization provides different services to different populations. Try emphasizing one kind of service in one mailing and another kind in another mailing, to see which generates the better response. You may well find that different activities appeal to different segments of your supporters. You may want to craft different appeals that will resonate with each specific group.

Follow-Up. A single mailing may not achieve the desired results. Direct mail, like advertising, often requires repeated exposures to its target market to be effective. How many mailings? Two or three follow-up mailings is not a lot. As many as five follow-up letters is not unusual, and you may want to consider including a phone call or two in the mix.

Some nonprofits send out mailings on a monthly or semimonthly basis. If all those repeated mailings seem excessive, consider that in advertising it is generally accepted that a print ad must appear a minimum of six times before its target is actually moved to take action.

For additional guidelines in using direct mail, you can consult Direct Mail World (www.dmworld.com) and Direct Mail News (www.dmnews.com). Consider the Direct Marketing Association, too, the oldest and largest trade association devoted to the direct marketing field, with a membership of more than three thousand advertisers and marketers. And, again, the U.S. Postal Service is always a good resource (www.usps.com/directmail).

CHAPTER ELEVEN

UNDERSTANDING ADVERTISING

What's the difference between advertising and public relations? Advertising is publicity you pay for; public relations is publicity you pray for. One of the advantages of paying for something is that you get to decide where and when it will appear.

"Advertising is essential when you want to control the placement and the timing of your message," says Ken Brown, public relations director for New York University's School of Continuing and Professional Studies. New York University is a sizable nonprofit organization with a considerable budget for advertising. Advertising, says Brown, is "ideal for keeping the nonprofit in the public's mind and announcing programs. But since people are so bombarded with advertising, they tend to be skeptical of any claims made in a paid ad. It is always preferable to have other people say nice things about you than to say them yourself."

Done properly, advertising can overcome that initial skepticism. A good ad, well conceived and effectively presented in the right media, can be a key element of a successful public relations campaign.

This chapter presents basic principles and tools of advertising in various media, beginning with a discussion of the advertising message and moving on to explanations of how to calculate a favorable advertising rate and how to test an ad with a target market, before presenting basic facts about advertising in print and on radio and television.

AIDA and the USP

Advertising professionals cite the "rule of AIDA," the four things a good ad must do: draw *attention,* excite *interest,* stimulate *desire,* and get the target to take *action.*

Every ad must begin by grabbing the attention of the target audience. One way to do that is to highlight the organization's unique selling proposition, or USP. The USP is a concept pioneered by Rosser Reeves in his book *Reality in Advertising.* Reeves, chairman of the Ted Bates & Co. ad agency, was one of the founders of modern advertising. He created the "hammer in the head" ads for Anacin in the early days of television and, later, the famous tag line for M&M's: "Melts in your mouth, not in your hand." According to Reeves, a product's USP is something that the competition either cannot or does not offer. The USP may be important, trivial, or totally concocted as long as it catches the attention of consumers and distinguishes the product from its competition.

To stand out from the crowd, a nonprofit organization also needs a USP. The nonprofit may provide essentially the same services and may serve the same populations as other nonprofits, but it can select one aspect of its operations to highlight in its public relations and advertising campaigns. Putting the focus on the USP can position the organization in the mind of the public as *the* organization in its field.

Staying on Message with the "Big Idea"

Nonprofits are not in the business of selling soap. They are engaged in important human issues, dealing with things that matter. In every ad, presented in all types of media, the organization's message should reflect the importance of its mission. The following principles describe effective advertising for nonprofits:

- An ad should concentrate on one big, central idea and link the organization's name inseparably with that big idea.
- Standing out from the competition is essential. The ad should focus on a characteristic that sets the organization apart from its competitors. The message should be expressed in a way that is unique to the organization.
- The ad must involve the target market. It must have an immediate dramatic impact in order to arouse interest and hold it. The target market must perceive the message as relevant to the things it cares about.
- It is important to establish a relationship with the target market. A kinship, a community of shared concern, should be stated and underscored. The situations shown,

the styles of presentation, the people depicted, the language, and the tone of voice should all reveal that the organization has an understanding of and sympathy with the target market's lifestyle and values. "We are in this together" should be communicated in every aspect of the advertising. Subsequent ads should continue to develop that relationship further.

- Whatever else it is, an ad must be credible. Statements made and statistics cited, as well as photos, maps, and any supporting material used in the ad, must be believable. Even when the presentation involves humor or a tongue-in-cheek approach, the organization itself must always be perceived as trustworthy and reliable.

- The message and the wording must be simple and clear. Chances are that anything that can be misunderstood *will* be misunderstood. Too many messages or impressions will confuse the issue and lose the attention of the target market.

- The idea must be "campaignable." The ad should not be seen as something that stands alone, but rather as part of an ongoing campaign.

- The ad and the way it links the name of the organization to the "big idea" must help to build the organization's "personality." Each advertisement affects the target market's perception of the organization. Each ad helps to build and reinforce the established personality of the organization. Each ad in the campaign must be in character. Its style, manner, and tone of voice must be consistent with the organization's tone of voice. If any one advertisement conflicts with that perception, it will weaken the established personality. Several such ads can effectively erase it altogether. It is therefore important to ensure consistency in the organization's advertising.

- Each ad must take full advantage of the capabilities of the medium in which it appears. The big idea is fundamental and remains consistent in all media, but it will be expressed differently in a print ad, in direct mail, and on radio and TV. Each medium has its own characteristics that should be used to best advantage.

Cost per Thousand

When you are deciding how to spend your advertising budget, it can be helpful to determine which media, and which vehicles within those media, are the most cost-effective. What are their relative costs per actual exposure? In the advertising industry, a common measure of comparable efficiency or productivity is *cost per thousand*, or CPM.

CPM refers to the dollar cost of reaching one thousand prospects. Its chief advantage is its simplicity. By measuring comparative CPM, you can easily compare the potential effectiveness of an ad placed in one publication with that of an ad placed in another publication. Because CPM provides a common basis for comparison, it is also useful for comparing the potential of different media—say, the potential of a print ad with that of a radio ad, or "spot."

Getting the CPM right is essential to making smart decisions about your advertising. To calculate the CPM, you take the ad rate and divide it by the publication's circulation (or the radio or TV station's viewers).

Suppose, for example, that you are targeting women thirty-five and older. Assume that one publication has an audited circulation of 1 million readers. Its readership profile information reveals that 28 percent of the readership falls into your target market's demographic of women aged thirty-five and older. That means the publication reaches 280,000 readers whom you want to target.

Say, further, that the cost of a half-page ad in the publication is $1,000. By dividing the $1,000 cost of the ad by the 280,000 readers who may see it, you get $0.00357, or just over one-third of a cent, which is what it costs for your ad to reach each of those female readers over the age of thirty-five. To avoid working with such awkward decimal points, that number is multiplied by 1,000 to get the cost per thousand female readers aged thirty-five and over. The result—the CPM, or cost to reach one thousand readers—is $3.57.

Now suppose you are also considering advertising in another magazine. Say the second magazine has an audited readership of 2 million, of whom 40 percent fall into your target demographic of women thirty-five and over. As a larger publication, it will charge $1,500 to run the same half-page ad. Which of the two publications is offering the better deal? You begin making that decision by comparing relative CPM.

Because 40 percent of the second magazine's 2 million readers fall into the targeted demographic of women over thirty-five, there is a total of 800,000 readers in your target market. Divide the cost of the ad, which is $1,500, by the number of readers, which is 800,000, and you get a per-reader cost of $0.001875. Multiply that number by 1,000, and your cost per thousand for the second publication is just under $1.88.

If you compare that to the CPM of the first publication, $3.57 to reach one thousand readers, the bigger publication looks much better. If you were to base your decision on the CPM alone, the better buy would clearly be the larger publication. There are, of course, many other factors to consider, but CPM can help put your options in perspective.

If you were comparing one of those publications with a radio or TV station, you would base the CPM on the number of the station's listeners or viewers and divide the cost of the spot by that number. For example, a thirty-second spot on a popular radio station during the expensive morning drive time slot (6:00–9:00 A.M.) might cost $5,000 and promise an audience of 3 million listeners. Of those 3 million, however, you may have determined that only 15 percent fall into your target market. That means you are reaching 450,000 people you want to reach. By dividing $5,000 by 450,000, you determine that the cost to reach a single target listener is $0.0111. Multiply by 1,000, and you get $11.11 to reach one thousand people you want to reach. That is a relatively high CPM by comparison with what either of the two publications offers. You haven't finished making your decision—there are other factors to consider—but knowing the relative CPMs of the media you are considering is a good starting point.

Committees and Focus Groups: Test with Your Target Market

Once you have created an ad, it is always a good idea to test it before going to the expense of actually running it. Seek out members of your target audience. Convene focus groups.

Advertising agencies regularly conduct focus groups for their clients. Seated around a big conference table, eight or ten people will respond to questions posed by a facilitator probing their reactions to various ads.

One wall of the room is usually made of opaque glass, and behind that wall are several people from the advertising agency that created the ad, along with a video camera recording the proceedings for later review. Reactions of the people in the focus group are thus monitored and later evaluated in conjunction with reactions of other focus groups. It is quite an elaborate process and not all that foolproof, because some major advertising mistakes have been made despite all the research and testing. But the procedure remains a generally accepted step in the launching of any major advertising campaign. Such focus groups typically cost about $5,000.

Nonprofits with limited resources, which means most nonprofits, can find focus-group testing more affordable if it is done in a more informal way. Gathering groups of people in a comfortable setting and asking them to evaluate several ads according to a definite set of criteria can be very helpful in fine-tuning the ads. Go on testing with focus groups as you develop new ads in the future. The input can help identify the "hot buttons" that will get you the responses you are looking for.

Advertising in Print

Job One: Grab the Reader's Attention

A print ad works only if the reader keeps looking at the page. The problem is that people turn the page—every two seconds, on average, as they flip through a magazine or newspaper. That is how long your ad has to grab the reader's attention. If you succeed, he will at least notice your ad and may begin reading. If not, he is on to the next page, and your copy will go unread. Therefore, the first task of any ad is to be noticed.

A good start is having one single, clear focal point for your ad, something the eye is powerfully drawn to and that it automatically goes to first. That focal point can be a great photo, a riveting headline, or a stunning design, but it has to be compelling enough to literally grab the reader by the chin and say, "Hey, look over here!"

Guide the Reader Through the Ad

Once you've got his attention, don't waste it. Make sure that your ad provides a clear path for the eye to follow. A well-constructed ad, like a well-constructed house, has a natural flow to it. The eye is led along easily, skipping from one element to another.

Research shows that American readers read a page from left to right, and from up to down. This means that once the reader's eye has been to the upper right of an ad, it won't naturally return to the upper left. Similarly, once it looks down, it will not usually look back up again but instead will continue right off the page. You can use that information to keep the reader's eye looking at your ad and guiding it through from point to point.

For example, if you know that most people, after looking at a photo or graphic, will look down, you can consider using a great photo or graphic as the most important element at the top of the page and placing the ad's next most important element— usually the headline—under it.

Avoid blocking off portions of the ad with borders. People prefer things that are a unit to things that are segmented. Eyes prefer unity of impression; give it to them in your ad.

After people look at a photo their eyes tend to look down. Therefore, putting copy next to the photo means putting it where it will likely not be read—not a smart idea.

Studies show that when readers arrive at the bottom of a page, they have a strong tendency to turn the page. Don't expect them to look back up at an important message point in your ad.

Printing words over a picture makes them harder to read, so they are less likely to be read. Avoid printing words over pictures.

Make an Emotional Connection

Advertising is not about the head; it is about the heart. Nonprofits have an edge in the "heart department" because they tend to deal with dramatic, human situations. Create a headline that complements the illustration and combines with it to grab the reader's heart.

People love stories, and nonprofits typically have wonderful stories to tell. Readers may well forget the facts and the figures you muster to make your organization's case, but a good story, fraught with drama and suspense, will stay with them. With a strong graphic or photo and a few powerful words, your ad can tell a moving human story that touches your audience. Make people care and connect with your organization on an emotional level, and you boost the chances that they will read on with interest and even experience a desire to take action.

Use Photos to Advantage

Use photos to help you tell your stories. A good photo can "sell" the organization and its message better than words. Consider not only the subject of the photo but also how it will appear.

Color photos attract the eye. The human eye is particularly drawn to blue and green hues. Generally, if you can afford color, you should use it.

Black-and-white photography lacks the eye appeal of color but it has a documentary flavor. Color pulls; black-and-white explains. Black-and-white forces the reader to consider the abstract idea behind the photo itself and can be good at convincing, providing an authoritative, seeing-is-believing documentary approach.

Craft Complementary Headlines, Subheads, and Body Copy

A headline should excite the reader's interest. Keep the headline simple. Use a single typeface and font and a single type size for the headline, and don't break the line. If you split a headline, with half of it above a photo and half below, you will break the natural flow, and readers will generally not follow in sequence to put the parts of the headline together again.

A headline should give the reader a reason to read more. In his book *Confessions of an Advertising Man,* David Ogilvy notes that in a well-designed ad, either the illustration or the headline is the most important element, the element that does the lion's share of getting the message across. If the headline is the lead player, he says, make it the most prominent element, and let a simple photo support it. If the photo is the major element, keep the headline simple, and have it complement the photo. The ad is telling a story. Let the pictures and the words work together in their best combination to tell that story effectively.

Subheads focus on different aspects of the main message. They should be subordinate to the headline in size and importance. Their function is to carry readers through the ad, not stop them dead in their tracks.

The body copy of an ad has to be, above all, readable: simple, straightforward, pleasant to read, with shorter rather than longer sentences and action words wherever possible. Grammar and wording need to be clear and easy to follow, and the story the copy tells must be compelling.

Determine Copy Length

There is a long-standing disagreement about short ads versus long ads. Most advertising pros recommend short copy, on the theory that less is more and people's attention spans are limited. In *Ogilvy on Advertising,* however, David Ogilvy opts for longer because, in his experience, long copy does a more effective job of selling. For many nonprofits, with stories to tell as opposed to products to sell, long copy may be the right option. Ogilvy cautions, however, that in a passage of long copy, the first paragraph has to be arresting.

Track Responses to Your Ad

If your ad asks the reader to contact you, take advantage of the opportunity for tracking the ad. Indicate a separate telephone extension for readers to call in ads that run in different publications so you can track and compare rates of response. Indicate a Web site dedicated specifically to tracking responses to that ad. Indicate a name or department or a box number to which responses should be sent. This also enables you to see which responses were stimulated by which ads.

Evaluate Options for Placing the Ad

Once you know your target market and have identified several publications that reach that audience, how do you choose where to run your ad? You begin by contacting the publications and requesting an advertiser's package, or kit. There is no cost, and the kit can be very helpful in your decision-making process. Order kits from all the publications you are considering, and compare readerships, rates, and publication schedules to get a sense of where your ad can appear to best effect. While the data is also generally available on the publication's Web site, it can be helpful in evaluating a range of publications to lay out their print materials on a table and compare the information.

Elements of an Advertiser's Kit. An advertiser's kit contains two types of information: on readership and on advertising rates.

Circulation and Readership Information. The advertiser's kit typically arrives in a two-pocket folder that contains a sample issue of the publication and sheets of demographic information about the publication's readers. It also includes a piece of information that is of significant interest to prospective advertisers—a publisher's statement, with data on the publication's circulation or readership. The name of the audit bureau that certifies those numbers to be accurate usually appears on the first page of the statement—for example, "Audit Bureau of Circulation, Schaumburg, Illinois, (847) 605-0909." Some smaller publications may not use an audit bureau, in which case you should take their circulation numbers with the proverbial grain of salt.

A common device used by smaller publications, especially small neighborhood weeklies, is to cite pass-along "readership." This involves taking the total number of copies distributed and then multiplying that figure by four, basing that final number on the premise that every person in the family—with an average size of four—will read some part of the paper every week. Somewhat arbitrary and unreliable, these numbers should not be taken too seriously.

The purpose of the kit is to convince prospective advertisers to advertise in the publication. Because most advertisers are interested in a target market that is affluent, the statistics usually present the publication's readers as possessed of impressive buying power.

Readership demographics cited include gender, age, household income, marital status, level of education, number of children, number and make of cars, and number of vacations taken each year. Other favorites include the percentage of readers who own their own homes, have an IRA, own a computer, and are planning to remodel their kitchens.

If the publication serves a niche market (for example, the residents of a particular geographical area) or a special-interest group, there will be often be further statistics showing that the publication's readers loyally patronize businesses whose ads appear in its pages. Also usually included is an advertising schedule, indicating the closing date for placing ads in the publication's various editions, and a calendar of special-interest and holiday supplements that provide an opportunity to target specific audiences. With a detailed picture of each publication's readership you can compare and evaluate and choose those that seem the best fit with the demographics of your target market.

Rate Card. The rate card that comes with the an advertiser's kit indicates the cost of various sizes of ads, including ads printed in black and white, with one color added and, when applicable, in full color. If the publication appears in different editions in different locations, the kit will include details on each edition's readership and offer combination rates for placing your ad in several of those editions.

Most publications will offer a frequency discount. If you decide to run your ad several times, consider buying a multiple insertion. With a commitment to a series of ads, the cost of each insertion goes down. The longer the run, the better the discount.

Publications usually offer a 5 percent discount for placing an ad three times, 8 percent for six times, and 12 percent for placement in twelve or more issues. Some also have an eighteen-time rate. If the publication offers special rates for nonprofit organizations, these are also included. You may be able to get an added discount if, rather than requesting a specific placement, you tell the publication to put the ad wherever there is room. This arrangement is called *ROP,* which stands for "run of press."

Consider setting up an in-house ad agency, which will entitle you to a 15 percent agency discount on your ads. Believe it or not, all it takes is creating letterhead on your computer and calling yourself an agency. Place your ads through your agency, and you qualify for the discount. Check with the publication to be sure that this won't cancel out any special nonprofit rates.

Reach and Frequency

As used in advertising, the term *reach* generally refers to the number of different targeted audience members who will be exposed at least once to an advertiser's message within a predetermined time frame. Reaching just anybody may not help sell the product. Reaching the right people, the targeted people, is what counts in spending your advertising dollars. *Frequency* refers to the number of times each person will be exposed. Both reach and frequency are important, but frequency usually weighs more heavily. Repetition leads to familiarity, and nonprofits want to be known to their target markets.

A final note about rate cards: they need not be taken too literally. They are frequently just a starting point for negotiations. You can usually arrange a better rate, and it is always a good idea to ask.

Advertising on Radio

Every medium offers its own particular benefits. Radio offers intimacy. For relatively little cost, your organization's message can be delivered to your target audience in a warm, intense, often one-to-one environment. You can reach people when they are alone, in their cars, or at home. That personal intimacy gives radio the potential to be a highly effective medium for nonprofits.

Radio is also pervasive. It is literally everywhere. According to the New York–based Radio Advertising Bureau, radio reaches 77 percent of consumers daily and 95 percent weekly, and 82 percent of adults eighteen and over listen to the radio while they drive.

There is no shortage of opportunities to place a spokesperson from your organization on a radio show. In North America, there are 459 national talk radio shows, 251 syndicated talk radio shows, and 5,102 local talk radio shows. Approximately one-third of those shows feature a range of general-interest topics; the others specialize in everything from business to sports.

Nonprofits can use radio advertising for ads that call for direct action as well as for ads geared to gaining organizational name recognition. Because many people consider radio to be retailer-oriented, many nonprofits overlook what can be a very effective medium for accomplishing organizational goals.

Most radio advertising is composed of direct-action ads placed by local retailers. The instructions are simple and repeated often throughout the ad. Call for a free something or other, come in to our store and get a discount when you mention this ad, and so on. Just as radio ads can promote a free widget with every order placed, ads for nonprofits can direct listeners to a toll-free number or a Web site for more information and to get involved in a cause.

The fact that radio stations and programs are aimed at very specific markets makes it possible to reach the demographic segment of the population that represents your target audience. You can also fine-tune your radio selection to very specific geographical areas, controlling the reach and the frequency of your ads. Demographic information for all radio stations is available nationwide from SRDS (www.srds.com), Des Plaines, Illinois, at (800) 851-7737 or (847) 375-5000. SRDS also publishes a quarterly publication, *Radio Advertising Source,* that is augmented by daily electronic updates.

Radio has the additional benefit of being relatively inexpensive when compared to other media, with a CPM that is considerably less than that for ads on TV or in newspapers and magazines. One corollary, however, is that radio spots have the least impact of any of the major media. One of the reasons for the lower cost, and the lower impact, is that people tend to consider radio as background noise and do not always give it the attention they give to other media. This is especially the case for music stations. But it also holds true, though to a lesser extent, for talk radio, news shows, sports shows, and religious programming. Although these programs provide a better climate for nonprofit ads—their listeners are already in the mode of listening to the spoken word— there is still the need to overcome the radio-as-background effect. To be effective, an ad must grab the listener's attention right from the beginning.

Many stations offer special low rates to nonprofit organizations. You may also be able to take advantage of buying ads on an ROS basis (the term *ROS,* analogous to *ROP,* stands for "run of station"). It means the station will run the ad when it chooses to, usually sometime within a one- or two-week period. The station likes the arrangement because it enables it to make use of unsold airtime. By running an ad ROS, you can save as much as half the usual cost of the ad. If your message is not time-specific, ROS can be worth considering.

As in print advertising, when it comes to advertising on radio, don't take rate cards seriously. All advertising is negotiable, and radio advertising is more negotiable than most other kinds. If a radio station doesn't sell an ad for a time slot, that slot represents a loss of money. Following the logic that it is better to sell that time slot for something than to leave it empty and gain nothing at all, stations are open to negotiating prices. Stations also hope to establish ongoing relationships with new clients, so they are often receptive to opening the door with an attractive initial offer.

Target Market

When you are considering radio advertising, make it a point to study all the radio stations and programs in your area, to find those that reach out to your target market. Because radio stations appeal to different segments of the market, they offer the ability to reach a very precise demographic. It is possible that advertising on just one program, broadcast on just one station, will enable you to reach exactly the audience you want to reach. If so, that may be enough for your purposes. If you decide to advertise on more than one station, or even on more than one program on the same station, provide slightly different contact information for each one.

If, for example, you are inviting listeners to call for information, give a different contact name or extension on each program on which your ad appears. By tracking comparative responses, you will be able to identify those programs and stations that work best. Measuring response is important if you are to fine-tune your campaign and maximize results.

Also consider the best time to reach your target market. Many advertisers prefer drive-time radio, either in the morning, when people are on their way to work, or at the end of the day, when people are heading home. Of the two, afternoon drive time is usually preferred because people's thoughts are less likely to be concentrated on work matters. But if, for example, your audience consists of stay-at-home parents, or of retirees who are likely to be at home in the mornings, then to reach that audience, you may choose to advertise on a morning radio show that airs at 10:00 A.M.

Structure of a Radio Ad

Lead your commercial off with a powerful, attention-getting sound. The first three seconds of the ad are crucial and serve the same function that a headline does in a print ad. Either you get your targets' attention in those first three seconds or you lose them for the whole ad. Choose carefully what they will hear in those three seconds.

A good choice could be the sound of a distinctive voice or the familiar name of someone who figures large in the world of your target audience. It might be the sound of birds migrating or surf crashing or children playing: any attention-getting sound that can be linked to your organization's mission. Because sounds on their own may not always be clearly recognizable, have the voiceover identify the sound for the listener: "The neighborhood is echoing with the sound of children at play . . ."; "When the blue-crested loon calls to its mate, you know that . . ."

A typical thirty-second radio spot has 70 words. Most sixty-second spots run about 140 words. The cost of a thirty-second ad is usually more than 50 percent of the cost of a sixty-second ad, so it may be cost-effective to spend extra money to get the longer ad.

Chances are that you can probably say what you need to say in the shorter time frame, and you may have a better chance of holding the attention of your audience with a shorter ad. If your message is complex and requires a longer time frame, however, the longer ad might be the better choice.

A common structure for a thirty-second ad is what is called a "doughnut." This consists of a taped opening of approximately ten seconds, followed by fifteen seconds of taped music but no words—because this is where the announcer is going to read your copy—and then a final taped five seconds to close the spot. Retail stores use this format a lot because it allows for easy changes of the middle portion so that new sales and specials can be announced. When adapted for nonprofits, the middle section is used for announcing new upcoming events.

The doughnut format is easy to update and has the added benefit of establishing a recognizable on-air presence for the organization. People come to associate the opening and closing portions with your organization, and that helps to reinforce its identity in the public mind.

A variation of the doughnut format for radio ads is the "tag," which has a taped fifteen-second message followed by fifteen seconds of script delivered by the announcer.

An alternative to having the announcer read a script is to prerecord a tape, either at the radio station or at an outside studio, and provide the entire prerecorded commercial to the station. Even trained announcers can stumble over difficult pronunciations, and if the ad includes complex words, such as medical or technical terms, or if it features hard-to-pronounce names, it may make sense to opt for the prerecorded ad. That way, you can avoid the risk of an on-air announcer making mistakes that will distract listeners from the important message you want to deliver.

Producing the Ad

Sometimes, out of a sense of public-spiritedness or community pride, the station will offer to write the script for you. Think carefully about the offer. It is usually better for you to write the copy. You know your organization a lot better than an outsider. You know the message points you want to convey and what resonates with your target market. Unless your message is so standard as to be indistinguishable from that of any other nonprofit—which it should not be—it is generally a better idea to write the ad yourself.

If, however, the station offers to produce the ad, that can be a good idea. The station may charge you a nominal fee, but almost certainly less than what you would pay at an outside studio. Check that you can get involved with the production process, to be sure the results meet your expectations.

Music can make a big difference. Played in the background, under the voice of the announcer, it can serve as the underpinning of the message. It can also carry the emotional note you need to convey your message effectively. You can take the music from the music library owned by the station or an independent studio, in which case you may be charged a "needle drop" fee for each cut you use in your ad, or you may negotiate an all-in-one arrangement.

Alternatively, you can have a "hungry" musician create and play an original music track in exchange for the right to include the ad on his demo reel. The professionals producing the ad for you will set the audio levels of the background music. You don't want the music to drown out the speaker, but you also don't want it so faint that it contributes nothing to the final piece. Properly used, music can be the wind beneath the wings of your ad copy.

Stations and studios also have libraries of standard sound effects. You can rent the sounds of a thunderstorm or an earthquake for a nominal fee. Consider carefully before you get carried away with sound effects. You want to keep your message simple. Too many distractions can muddle what you are trying to say.

Radio as Storyteller

Radio is a great medium for storytelling. Consider the great radio serials of the pre-TV days, like *The Green Hornet* and *The Shadow,* not to mention soap operas that began on radio, like *As the World Turns.* Radio listeners become vicarious participants, naturally using their imaginations to "see" what they hear.

You can harness the listener's imagination to your cause by using radio to tell your stories. By creating powerful word pictures, you can share with your listener a slice of the human drama that is your organization's mission.

Take the listener into the world in which you work; get a statement from someone you have helped, or from an official who has been impressed by what you do. It can all be done in seconds, and to great effect, with a simple, powerful radio commercial that mobilizes the attention and the imagination of the listener.

Another technique that works well for nonprofits is to tape an interview with a leader of the organization. Do the interview in a professional sound booth, to ensure professional quality, and let the interview run for several minutes. Guide the interview in a way that leads the interview subject to articulate key points in short, punchy sound bites. Obviously you can just give the subject a list of preselected sound bites to read, but they tend to sound more natural if they are taken from an actual interview. Use those sound bites in a series of commercials, changing them over time to keep the commercials fresh while still conforming to your established format.

Besides conveying the "real people" aspects of your organization, this technique has the added benefit of turning the organization's leaders into media stars of sorts, often earning them semicelebrity status in the community and thus enhancing their effectiveness as spokespeople for the organization.

Once you have the listener's attention, you can call on him to take direct action. Urge him to call for further information, visit your Web site, come to a rally, run for the cure. Repeat the name of the organization frequently along with the contact information. Run the ad repeatedly. Repetition is key to successful radio advertising.

Advertising on TV

There are many advantages to advertising on TV. Your ad will reach a large audience. You can segment and select the market in which you are interested. TV's combination of visual image, music, narration, and special effects provides a dynamic and absorbing medium with which to tell your organization's story. You can actually show what your organization does, whom it serves, and even the results of your good efforts. Television is an indisputably powerful and effective medium for conveying a story. Advertising on TV can be expensive, but it is an option that nonprofits should explore and consider.

Ad Rates on TV

Competition for advertising dollars is fierce. Prime-time television is still beyond the reach of most nonprofit advertising budgets, but fringe time on major networks and good time slots on cable and satellite TV can be surprisingly affordable. Once you have identified your target market, you can usually find a station and a program that targets it.

Local TV stations, like their radio counterparts, typically offer special low rates for nonprofit organizations. They also typically offer the option to purchase your ad on an ROS basis. As in radio advertising, ROS means the station will run the ad when it chooses to, usually sometime within a one- or two-week period, and running an ad ROS can save half the usual cost. Again, as in print and radio advertising, don't make the mistake of taking published rates seriously. The rate cards are a starting point for negotiations and should be viewed as such.

Producing the TV Ad

Television audiences are accustomed to watching professionally produced programs with high production values. If your ad looks second-rate, your organization will be perceived as second-rate and will not be taken seriously. If you are considering advertising on television, consult with an experienced production company. You should not do a shoddy job. If you can't do TV advertising right, it's better not to do it at all.

Like radio stations, however, many television stations will offer to produce your ad for little or no money. It is always best to write your own script or have it written by someone who can convey the important elements of your story with impact. But if the station wants to make its equipment and personnel available to produce your ad, that can be a cost-effective way to get your ad done professionally. Some formats readily lend themselves to in-studio production.

One popular format for nonprofit television advertising is the celebrity endorsement, in which a well-known figure briefly presents an urgent problem and suggests the organization as a solution. Often combining the celebrity's "talking head" with cuts to scenes of the organization at work on the problem, such an ad can be effective, especially if the celebrity is well known and his or her connection with the nonprofit is compelling.

Another popular commercial style is the ministory, in which the problem is dramatized for viewers and the organization is shown to be the solution to the problem. Such an ad generally requires more than in-studio shoots. The Christian Children's Fund, for example, shows footage in its ads of a three-year-old girl scavenging in a garbage dump. For only a few cents a day, the on-camera narrator informs us, Maria can receive clean water, nutritious food, medical attention, shoes, and an education that will lift her out of the slums. The effectiveness of the ad lies in its portrayal of the real-life Maria in a way calculated to stir the compassion of the audience.

Because people typically watch television with a remote-control device close at hand, ready for use at the first sign of a commercial, the opening seconds or even milliseconds of your ad must be compelling enough to grab viewers' attention before the ad is zapped. Compelling visuals and music can work toward that end. People often talk over commercials or turn the sound off, so it is a good idea to design the commercial with the organization's name and logo superimposed over the image at the bottom right-hand corner of the screen. Anything you can do to help win the battle for the hearts and minds of your target market should be considered.

Like all other advertising, a TV ad must grab viewers' attention at the outset. A good ad on TV, like a good ad in any other medium, should excite the viewers' interest, stimulate their desire, and motivate them to take action. The purpose of most commercials is to get prospects to take action. Whatever action you want your targets to take—call for information, write a check, visit the Web site—make the directions clear and easy to follow.

Track the response to a TV ad as you would track the response to any other type of ad, with coded response keys. Properly used, television advertising can be very effective.

Producing video footage for use in commercials and other fundraising vehicles can be quite complex. The process is covered in detail in Chapter Thirteen.

Choosing the "Right TV"

If you do decide to advertise on TV, the next question to ask is "*Where* on TV?" Which stations? Which programs? Prime time, evening, or late night?

The first thing to consider, of course, is who your target market is. Like the print media, the electronic media aim at different demographics. You should request advertiser's kits from television stations for the programs on which you are considering placing ads. You can also access demographic studies through Simmons Market Research Bureau at (212) 373-8900, Mediamark Research, or the SRDS *TV & Cable Source,* copies of which are available at good business libraries.

The industry standard for TV advertising is the data provided by the A. C. Nielsen research firm Nielsen Media Research (www.nielsenmedia.com), which tracks the number of viewers who are actually watching individual programs. The statistics available include numbers on how many people are viewing specific programs in different geographical areas. The Nielsen Television Index measures audiences in major media markets for specific programs during four "sweeps week" surveys, when networks typically air their best offerings. Television advertisers talk about audience "share," which is another way of saying "percentage."

Ratings are calculated in gross rating points, or GRP. For example, 1 percent of the TV sets in a given area equals one GRP. If there are 500,000 households with televisions in a city, and if 50,000, or 10 percent, of those households are tuned to a particular program, then that program gets an audience share of 10, or 10 GRP. The cost of advertising on TV is determined by the GRP of the particular program. Prices per GRP vary in different markets—cheaper in small towns, more expensive in big cities. The cost per GRP goes up everywhere during the Christmas advertising season, October through late December.

Knowing a program's GRP, or share number, is a start, but it is not enough to determine whether or not to advertise on that program. You need to calculate the CPM for the program you are considering and compare it with the CPM of advertising on other programs and with the cost of advertising in other media.

If, for example, the cost of advertising on program A, with 1 million viewers, is $2,000, then each set of a thousand viewers costs you $2 to reach, so program A has a CPM of $2. You arrive at that number by dividing the $2,000 cost by 1,000 (the number of thousands in 1 million) to get the figure of $2 per thousand.

Suppose program B has twice the audience, or 2 million viewers, and also charges $2,000 to run your commercial. In that case, each thousand of that program's viewers costs you only $1 to reach, so program B has a CPM of $1. (You divide the $2,000 cost by 2,000, the number of thousands in 2 million.) Advertising on program B will cost you only half as much as advertising on program A—seems like a bargain.

But you may be comparing apples with oranges. In order to compare apples with apples, you have to compare the cost of reaching not just a broad audience but also the portion of the audience that is composed of people in your target market. Demographic surveys will help you see what proportion of the audience is composed of the targets you want to reach. You are not really interested in the cost per thousand but rather in the cost per prospect.

If, for example, of the 1 million people watching program A, only 30 percent fall into the demographic profile you want to reach, then your commercial will effectively reach only 300,000 people in the target market that you care about—only 300,000 prospects. (The rest of the audience, for purposes of your advertising dollar, does not matter.) This means that you are effectively spending your $2,000 to reach not 1 million people but only 300,000. Considering only the prospects in your audience, the CPM for program A is effectively $6.67 (which is what you get when you divide $2,000 by 300, the number of thousands in 300,000).

Meanwhile, of the 2 million viewers of program B, which seemed like such a good bargain in terms of absolute number of viewers, suppose that only 12 percent fall into the demographic categories you are targeting. This means that your commercial will effectively reach only 240,000 of the people in your target market—only 240,000 prospects—which means that for those prospects, your CPM ($2,000 divided by 240) will be $8.33. Compared to the CPM of $6.67 for program A, program B no longer looks like a bargain. Program A is a much better choice for your ad.

When you consider your options, TV can make a lot of sense—but only if you do your homework.

Public Service Announcements: When Ad Space Is Donated

To enhance support for its programs, Teach For America (www.teachforamerica.org), a nonprofit based in New York City, had decided to launch a PSA campaign aimed at major national magazines. That kind of paid advertising campaign doesn't come cheap. It can easily run into the hundreds of thousands of dollars. But Teach For America was determined to do it for free.

Melissa Golden, the organization's vice president of marketing and communication, tapped into a contact who had done work for Teach For America in the past, and her contact in turn connected her with a small new Boston ad agency. The agency agreed to take the project on a pro bono basis, to create the actual ads, and to handle all the production, including the photos. The agency created a series of three ads, each one featuring a photo of one person along with a headline and a paragraph of body copy.

The first ad shows a man in a suit waving to an unseen crowd as he emerges from a car. The headline reads, "This politician has ulterior motives" (see Exhibit 11.1). The other two ads in the series follow the same general pattern, but in place of "politician" one has "lawyer" and the other has "doctor." The body copy conveys the idea that if a person spends two years as a teacher in a rural or urban school in a low-income

EXHIBIT 11.1. AD FROM TEACH FOR AMERICA.

Source: "Lead a Life with Purpose" print ad courtesy of Teach For America.

community immediately after graduating from college, the experience will enable him to have a direct impact on the lives of children and will also make him more effective at whatever profession he chooses to pursue later in life. In addition, he will come to see firsthand the challenges facing children growing up in low-income communities and these children's great potential.

Getting the ads made was only the first step of the campaign. Teach For America's goal was to get them placed in major national magazines. For that, Golden says, the organization turned to one of the most basic PR tools: personal relationships.

"The president of Teach For America spoke at a national conference of executive women," says Golden. "During the conference, she established relationships with a number of people who ultimately proved to be very helpful to the organization, including a high-ranking executive at Time Warner who was committed to our mission. She gave our president the names of people to contact at a number of Time Warner publications. Then it became a matter of calling and reaching out to them."

Golden says the campaign has required time, energy, and perseverance, but the results have been gratifying.

"Our full-page ads have appeared in major national publications, including *Time*, *People*, *Fortune*, and *Business 2.0*, all at no cost to the organization. Response to the ads has been very positive. We've enhanced the organization's visibility and boosted our recruitment numbers."

Golden notes that when publications find themselves with empty pages, they will often donate space to nonprofits for PSAs. "They may not have been able to sell the page, or the advertiser who had committed to it may have pulled their ad at the last minute. The publication has to run *something* on that page. Some publications keep a selection of ads from nonprofits in reserve, ready to use in that eventuality. The trick is to become one of the favored nonprofits. That all comes down to establishing relationships with people at the magazine."

In connecting with the media, Golden advises nonprofits to tap into every possible resource. Board members and supporters should be asked for the names of any contacts they may have. The nonprofit should use those contacts to gain entrée to the people who can donate ad space and help get out the organization's message.

But you cannot count on angels appearing to help you with your ad campaign. More typically, it is a matter of carefully reviewing and comparing options and making the best choice.

CHAPTER TWELVE

PITCHING AND PLACING: RADIO

R adio stations target very specific market segments. Once you have defined your target market and identified the radio stations and programs that reach your market, radio can be a powerful tool to connect your organization with a receptive audience.

Choosing Stations and Programs

Study the format of every radio station that reaches your target market's area. You can eliminate the majority of FM stations. A few do interviews, but most have all-music formats. Most all-news and all-talk stations are on AM. Avoid the "schlock" radio stations. Even if you get the airtime, having your organization affiliated with offensive programs can do unnecessary damage to its image.

See which programs air stories about the kinds of issues that are your organization's focus. Look for ways you can connect with events in the news, and look for things of immediate interest to the audience. Note which stations run public service announcements.

The popularity and the range of programs on talk radio provide many opportunities for an organization's spokespeople to reach their target market. Talk show producers have one to three hours of airtime to fill. They need interesting programming to keep their listeners tuned in. Many welcome spokespeople from nonprofits, especially if they are bright, knowledgeable, and articulate and can provide entertaining programming. Because radio interviews are often conducted over the phone, with the interview subject comfortably at home or in her office, it is possible to conduct a virtual radio "tour" of the country without ever leaving home base.

Whom to Pitch

When you have identified a program that is a good fit with your organization and have listened to get a feel for it, you are ready to pitch the show's producer. You can do it with a phone call and some basic follow-up material.

Who should you call? You can consult a directory such as those listed at the end of Chapter Four or a Web site like www.radiopublicity.com to find the name of the person you should talk to. But people in radio tend to move around a lot, so names and titles keep changing. The simplest way to get the name of the person you need to pitch is to call the station. The best time to call is the hour immediately after the end of the program you are interested in. That is when the people you want to talk to are generally unwinding after the show and getting ready to put together future programs.

If you are pitching an interview for a talk show, call four weeks in advance. Ask if the show has a producer or a guest booker or whether the host of the program does her own planning and scheduling. Ask to speak to her, and always begin the conversation with the question "Is this a good time for a one-minute pitch?" If it is not a good time, ask when to call back. Introduce yourself, make a brief pitch, and then stop talking. Your brevity will be appreciated. One approach is to propose that your spokesperson be interviewed upon his return from participating in an important conference or symposium. He will thus be able to report on the latest developments and future prospects. When you pitch an interview for a news show, as opposed to a talk show, you should contact the news director one week before the projected date. Be sure not to call during or just before a news broadcast. No one is going to speak with you then. If you want to place a PSA (see "Public Service Announcements," later in this chapter), contact the station's public service director. Ask for the station's policy statement and any guidelines the station can provide. And no matter what you are pitching, connecting with the station manager is always a good idea.

Pitching Tips

Stephan Schiffman, president of D.E.I. Management Group in New York, is the author of a dozen books on cold calling and sales skills and is himself a frequent guest on radio and television programs around the country.

"There are a million guests a year on radio," Schiffman says, "so there is a real, continuing need for guests. It is essentially an unlimited opportunity."

Guest Spots on the Radio

The Kathryn Zox Show airs daily on AM station WSDE (1190) and on WSDE.com from Albany, New York. It is typical of many talk radio shows. Zox's one-hour interview program reaches audiences across the state of New York, in Massachusetts, and on the World Wide Web. Her interviews are live and unedited. Guests from all over the globe call in from the comfort of their own homes or offices.

Zox advises nonprofits that want to get their messages out on the airwaves to identify the stations and programs that serve their target audiences and to contact them via e-mail, fax, or regular mail, stating why the show's listeners would be interested.

"Stations are always looking for guests," she points out. "I interview two experts a day on *The Kathryn Zox Show* and at least two more on my *Morning Magazine Show*. Radio talk show hosts welcome guests. We *need* them to survive. There are thousands of radio stations out there, and we all need guests."

Once a guest has been booked for her show, Zox invites him or her to submit a list of questions for possible interview material. She engages her audiences with a warm and friendly conversational approach. Zox values guests who are articulate and entertaining and have something unique to share.

Zox's program, typical of the hourlong radio format, is divided into segments. Her show follows the news and weather updates that run from noon to 12:06. The first interview runs from 12:06 to 12:15, pauses for a short commercial break, and then continues until the bottom of the hour. Zox then picks up a second interview. After a third-quarter break, Zox returns until she says good-bye to her second guest, at 12:57, making way for news and weather at the top of the hour.

Like all radio talk show hosts, Zox needs stimulating interviews to keep her listeners current and informed. A nonprofit with a good story to tell and, as she puts it, a "willing and enthusiastic spokesperson" to tell it, is a welcome and valued guest.

Schiffman sees cold calling to pitch the media as a three-step process: focus, write a script, and follow up.

Focus. Schiffman advises setting a scheduled time to spend on the phone making pitches and then working that time slot. "Different programs need different kinds of guests," he says. "In pitching a program, you need to understand what the program is looking for. Once you understand that, your goal is to pitch the interview as something that is of real interest to the program's audience."

Write a Script. Schiffman recommends preparing a script for your pitches.

"Write down what you are going to say, and prepare for the responses you are likely to hear," he advises. "Plan what you will say to turn around objections—by, for example, pointing out the practical value to the audience of what the guest has to say."

Suggest hot topics the spokesperson can talk about. The best way is to prepare a list of suggested questions that the show's host will be able to ask the guest. Pose the first few questions in your pitch, and show how fascinating the answers will be.

Make your pitch clear, concise, and interesting. You are selling something that will be of interest to the station's audience. Make it sound that way.

Follow Up. Follow up with a phone call. When you call, be prepared to offer additional ideas or information.

Many people are concerned about seeming to be pests, but there is a difference between being persistent and being annoying. You need to develop a sense of when to press and when to back off.

"Remember," Schiffman says, "there is a real need for good guests. A three-hour talk radio program, with guests coming on for twenty-minute segments, needs as many as nine guests." The goal is to make one of those guests someone from your organization.

"Send Me Something"

Nine out of ten pitches may result in a reply of "Not interested." You need to have a thick skin, advises Ken Sunshine of the New York–based PR firm Ken Sunshine Consultants. But, he says, "PR people are in the business of getting rejected."

If you keep at it, however, your perseverance will pay off, and a producer will say, "Sounds interesting. Send me something."

What do you send? First you need to prepare a pitch letter or a pitch press release. Keep it short—no more than a single page. Tailor it to the specific program, and refer to its listeners' interests. Make it punchy. Use lots of white space and bullets in a *who, what, where,* and *when* format. Stress the interview's entertainment value, and emphasize the idea that listeners will be fascinated by what they will learn from the interview.

Don't bother writing long paragraphs of copy. The pace at radio stations can be hectic, and radio producers probably won't read the whole thing anyway.

To bolster your pitch, include a press kit. Keep it "lean." Many producers receive two to three hundred press kits in the mail every day, and they do not look favorably on folders bulging with information. Even a limited selection of materials may receive only a cursory glance, so choose carefully.

Include a biography of the spokesperson, a backgrounder about the organization, a brochure, an article about the organization from an outside publication, a list of the spokesperson's previous media appearances, if any, and perhaps an audiotape of a previous appearance, to demonstrate that the spokesperson is a good interview subject. Most important, include a page with suggested interview questions. Also called a *tip sheet*, it helps the producer prepare the program. At a smaller station, your tip sheet of suggested questions will often be used as is, particularly for a shorter interview, according to Stephan Schiffman. "There is no spontaneity," he says. "Typically, the producer just hands the list of questions to the host, who then poses those questions to the guest."

Staying in Touch

After you've made your initial pitch and sent in your materials, follow up with a phone call three or four days later, and then with another phone call or e-mail a week after that. Be persistent. Producers are busy people, occupied with keeping many different balls in the air at the same time. You and your organization are easily forgotten in the rush. Persistence pays off.

It can be helpful to regularly reach out to the producer with e-mails offering additional information and relating your organization to breaking developments in the news. Forward articles about your organization that have appeared in newspapers and magazines. Attach a personal note, with a reminder that some aspect of your organization's activities would make a wonderful segment on the program.

After you've made the connection, be sure to keep yourself available to the station. If someone calls you with a question, get back to her promptly. It is both the courteous and the professional thing to do and will be appreciated. You want to cultivate a reputation as someone who is reliable and efficient, the consummate professional who is a pleasure to work with. That reputation can go a long way toward smoothing the way for future pitches.

The Numbers Game

The procedure for pitching is fairly straightforward. Contact the station, ask for the name of the program producer, call her with your pitch, send a press kit, send an e-mail, call to follow up, and then follow up again. Like any other kind of sales program, it is a numbers game. Make enough pitches, and you'll get on the air.

Public Service Announcements

Radio provides talk, music, commercials, and public service announcements. PSAs— announcements about activities and events going on in the community—were created for nonprofits and are an easy, if somewhat haphazard, way to get free publicity for your organization.

The Federal Communications Commission requires that radio and television stations provide a certain amount of airtime at no charge to serve the public interest. Local broadcast media typically meet that requirement by reporting on local events sponsored by nonprofit organizations by means of PSAs. A station that is on the air every day, around the clock, will usually air about sixty PSAs each week.

Radio announcers read PSAs at random. If a station has unsold advertising time, it can find itself with extra airtime and will fill some of it with PSAs. There is no charge to the organization, but there is also no guarantee that yours will be one of the PSAs that gets read, or that it won't be read at three in the morning. But PSAs are free and relatively easy to prepare, and they are worth doing.

Call the radio station and ask for the name of the person who is responsible for receiving public service announcements. Sometimes there is a public service or community service director. Often this is the responsibility of the news department or a clerical person. Get the person's name, and send the PSA directly to her. Ask how she prefers to receive material—by e-mail, fax, or regular mail—and ask for the station's PSA guidelines. Read the station's guidelines carefully, and be sure that your pitch conforms to its format.

As a rule, PSAs are ten-second, thirty-second, or sometimes sixty-second spots. Often a station will ask you to submit your spot in all three versions (see Exhibit 12.1). Be sure you know the time frame, and then write a script to be read within that time. Speakers usually talk at the rate of 125 words per minute, so a sixty-second PSA should be about 125 words, a thirty-second PSA should be about 60 words, and a fifteen-second PSA should be about 30 words.

Sometimes the station will specify the number of words it will accept. If, for example, a station limits PSAs to 100 words, then observe the limit. Keep in mind the station's needs and the interests of its audience. Shape your materials accordingly.

In some cases, the station staff will rewrite your PSA and make it suitable for on-air reading. Generally, however, station personnel are under far too much time pressure to edit and rewrite, and they rely on the organization to send in acceptable copy, ready to go.

Prepare a PSA on a single sheet of paper—the organization's letterhead is good—that includes your organization's name and contact information. Like a press release, the PSA should include the name and phone number of a person who can be reached to answer any questions.

Make the PSA warm, lively, and conversational in tone and content. Include the basic news information: who, what, where, when, why, and how. Stay on message, and include a call to action. Be sure the contact information is stated clearly and that it is repeated so listeners can write it down. Include a number for listeners to call, double-check that it is accurate (stories are legion of wrong numbers that have been broadcast), and make sure that there is someone or at least an answering machine to answer

EXHIBIT 12.1. THREE VERSIONS OF A RADIO PSA FOR THE ADOPTIVE PARENTS COMMITTEE.

10-second spot
Considering adoption as a way of building a family? The Adoptive Parents Committee's 24th annual conference will be held on November 21st at Long Island University's Brooklyn Campus. Call 917-432-0234 for details.

30-second Spot
Considering adoption as a way of building a family? Come to the Adoptive Parents Committee's 24th annual Adoption Conference, "Adoption—*ALL YOU NEED IS LOVE."* This day-long conference will be held on Sunday, November 21st, at Long Island University's Brooklyn Campus. There will be over 100 workshops and more than 50 exhibitors. For information, call 917-432-0234, or get registration forms at www.adoptiveparents.org. That's 917-432-0234.

60-second spot
Considering adoption as a way of building a family? Come to the Adoptive Parents Committee's 24th annual Adoption Conference, "Adoption—*ALL YOU NEED IS LOVE."* This day-long conference will be held on Sunday, November 21st, at Long Island University's Brooklyn Campus. The conference is for those considering adoption, for those who have already adopted, and for professionals and advocates who are involved in the adoption and foster care fields.

There will be over 100 workshops covering a wide range of adoption and parenting topics and led by professionals in the adoption field. Adoptive parents and adoptees will also lead workshops. Topics include international, agency, and independent adoptions and information to support foster care.
There will also be more than 50 exhibitors representing adoption agencies, social workers and support organizations.
For more information, call 917-432-0234, or to get registration forms for the conference go to www.adoptiveparents.org. That's 917-432-0234.

Source: Courtesy of Adoptive Parents Committee.

calls. List your Web site as well, and be sure that information about the event appears on the site.

Keep sentences short and easy to read. Try reading the PSA aloud several times to test for "speakability." If you find yourself gasping for breath, your sentences are too long.

When you can, avoid words that are hard to pronounce or easily misunderstood. If you must include words or names that can be tricky to pronounce, spell them out phonetically, and indicate which syllables should be emphasized.

Grab the audience's attention right from the outset. Sometimes the voice of a celebrity saying, "Hi, this is So-and-So, and I'd like to tell you about . . ." is an effective if not terribly original way to get the audience's attention.

A straightforward statement of a need can also work well: "Every night, six thousand children in this city go to bed hungry. . . ." So can a hope: "Wouldn't it be wonderful if everyone had a chance to follow their dream . . . ?"

If the station does run your PSA, be sure to write a thank-you note to the station manager. Everyone likes to be appreciated. In addition to being the right thing to do, it paves the way for the next PSA you submit to the station, or even for a pitch for a feature story about your organization.

A First-Time PSA

Sandra Calandruccio is manager of volunteer services at Guiding Eyes for the Blind (www.guidingeyes.org), a nonprofit forty miles north of New York City, in Westchester County. With a full-time staff of 115, the organization trains Seeing Eye dogs for the blind and the visually impaired.

Guiding Eyes had no public relations person on staff. As the date approached for the organization's thirtieth annual "New Leash on Life" walkathon and its first annual 5K run, Calandruccio volunteered to try to get some media coverage for the event. She called the community affairs director at the FM station Q104.3 ("New York's *only* classic rock station") and was promptly invited to submit a script for a PSA.

"I had never written a PSA before," says Calandruccio. "Actually, I didn't even know what a PSA was, exactly. I had to ask."

She obviously learned quickly, because the PSA she wrote was aired by the station more than thirty times. The community affairs director was so impressed with the work of the organization, and so pleased that the Guiding Eyes walkathon was being held in the town where he had grown up, that he agreed the station would become a sponsor of the event and cover the whole thing live.

On the day of the walkathon, a studio van rolled into FDR Park in Yorktown Heights, complete with broadcasting equipment and two on-air personalities who spent the next four hours reporting the event live. The station usually charges a fee for event appearances of its people, as is common practice, but in this case the fee was waived. The station also posted a notice of the event on its Web site.

In exchange for all the free publicity, Guiding Eyes agreed to feature the station's logo on the event brochures as well as on its Web site, accompanied by a notice indicating that the station was a proud sponsor.

Calandruccio's PSA got additional airtime on other stations as well, including the popular New York rock station Z-100. The considerable air time given to the radio spots brought a record turnout to the Guiding Eyes for the Blind event, thanks to the first-time PSA that appears in Exhibit 12.2.

EXHIBIT 12.2. RADIO PSA FOR GUIDING EYES FOR THE BLIND.

On Sunday, October 10, 2004, Guiding Eyes for the Blind will host its 30th annual "New Leash on Life" walkathon and 1st annual 5K run at FDR State Park, in Yorktown Heights, New York.

Since 1974, Guiding Eyes graduates have made this event a celebration of the mobility and independence their guide dogs have helped them achieve. They travel from all over the United States and are joined by volunteers, friends, and supporters as they walk 10 kilometers through the park. An exciting new addition to the event is the 5K run, which will kick off the day's festivities at 9:00 AM. The 10K walk will begin at 11:00 AM.

It costs Guiding Eyes approximately $40,000 to prepare each graduating guide dog team. Yet the dogs, training, travel costs, room and board for 26 days, and lifetime follow-up support are all provided free of charge. Guiding Eyes receives no government funding and instead relies solely on the generosity of people like you.

So bring your family . . . bring your dog and join Guiding Eyes for a day of fun-filled activities:

- A fun run for the kids
- A talent contest for your dogs
- Pooch and people photos
- Face painting and crafts for the kids
- Working-dog demonstrations
- Free T-shirts and barbeque lunch for registered participants
- Free goody bags for the first 300 participants at the park
- And . . . meet Clifford, the Big Red Dog!

Registration for the 5K run begins at 8:30.
Registration for the 10K walk begins at 10:00.
For more details and registration information, call 1-800-942-0149, or visit www.guidingeyes.org/bin/upeventsl.

Source: Courtesy of Guiding Eyes for the Blind.

Radio Actualities: Audio News Releases

Radio news actualities are welcomed by small and midsized stations that lack the resources of the larger stations. Whereas larger stations have staffs to cover news stories themselves, smaller stations often rely on taped material provided by outside sources.

The radio actuality gives smaller stations the ability to cover news events, such as conferences, rallies, and marches, by way of the audiotaped material you provide, typically in the form of a sixty-second segment they can air as part of their news coverage. It conforms to the "doughnut" format of a typical radio ad as discussed in Chapter Eleven.

It opens with an introduction by a narrator that sets the stage by giving the standard *who, what, where, when, why,* and *how* of the event. That is followed by a thirty-second sound bite by an organization spokesperson or perhaps an honored guest at the scene, commenting on the significance of the event. That in turn is followed by brief concluding remarks by the narrator.

A radio news actuality is an audio version of a news release and so, not surprisingly, it includes the same basic elements found in a written press release. In a written news release, the name and contact information of the organization's media relations person appears at the top of the page for reporter follow-up. In a radio actuality, the contact information is given at the end of the tape. That contact information, along with information about the subject of the tape and the date, should also be clearly printed on the face label of the tape.

A station will often substitute its own on-air announcer for the taped intro and "outro," using only the taped sound bite. That doesn't matter to a nonprofit, of course, whose goal is to get airtime for the event and the spokesperson.

Relatively easy to make, at a cost of a few hundred dollars, a radio actuality can be sent to every radio station in the target area. It should be accompanied by a simple information sheet or brochure about the organization and a brief note addressed by name to the producer, to personalize the mailing.

Radio Features

If your organization has a project or ongoing operation that lends itself to a radio feature, prepare a pitch about it for the station's features editor. If there is no one specifically responsible for features, pitch the station manager.

Include in your follow-up materials news clips, if you have them, as well as a brochure and a brief summary of the proposed story. Highlight why the station's listeners will find the story fascinating. Find a local angle, or tie the story in with something in the news. In your cover note, offer to assist in arranging logistics and interview subjects in the preparation of the story.

After you have sent the materials, make a follow-up call "just to check that the package arrived" and to offer another juicy fact or two. This gives you a second chance to pitch the story, and the updated information may make the idea even more appealing.

Radio Interviews

Become familiar with the program's format and host. If possible, listen to several shows to become familiar with the style so you will be comfortable during the interview, if you are the subject. Find out, too, about the audience. A good way to do that is to ask the producer to have the station's advertising department send you an advertiser's package. As outlined in Chapter Eleven, this is a package of information designed for potential advertisers that presents the demographics of the audience. By reviewing that information, you can learn something about the people who will be listening to the interview and perhaps calling in with questions..

If the program does include a call-in segment, it may be a good idea to arrange for several people to call with prepared questions. This will provide another opportunity to get key message points across. It will also avoid the possible awkwardness of a silent phone line, just in case no one in the listening audience calls in.

In most cases, radio interviews are not confrontational but informational and focused on human interest stories. Short interviews tend to stick to the questions you have prepared in advance.

A longer interview provides room for spontaneity and more freewheeling discussion. Of course, that carries with it its own risk because the opportunity to speak freely may sometimes open the door to the guest saying something she will later regret or going off on tangents instead of staying on message.

Carefully prepare three to five message points that are to be conveyed. Also prepare several brief, heartwarming anecdotes that illustrate what the organization does and why it is important. Remember, radio is a great medium for telling stories.

Coach the spokesperson to review her notes before the interview. Prepare her to cite a few significant numbers and statistics, to reinforce her credibility as an expert. It is all right for her to jot things down on index cards, to have them readily at hand, but she should be comfortably knowledgeable and have a body of facts at her fingertips.

It is important to have a short, one- or two-sentence answer to the question "Just what does your organization do?" The answer must be clear and easily graspable by an audience that, while listening, may also be negotiating traffic on the freeway or moving laundry into the dryer. Keep it short, simple, and positive.

Rehearsal

If media interviews are going to be a serious part of a PR campaign, it is always wise for spokespeople to get professional media training (see Chapter Thirteen).

It may be a good idea to rehearse an upcoming interview. Tape a mock radio interview and then listen critically as it is played back. Did she speak clearly? Did she sound relaxed and confident? Was her conversation punctuated too often by "uh" and "mmm"? Those sounds are a sign that a person is not sure of herself. Did she use a lot of technical terms and jargon or speak in long, convoluted sentences? Did she ramble and take forever to get to the point, or did she communicate in clear, punchy sound bites? Did she make good use of facts and figures to back up her arguments? To ensure a polished presentation, it is helpful to identify any weak points and correct them before the interview.

At the Studio

When the interview will be conducted in a studio, plan on arriving at the studio early. Leave extra time in case of traffic problems or bad weather. Few things are as frustrating as being stuck in traffic a mile away from the studio at 8:15 with an interview scheduled for 8:30. It happens, but it should not happen to you.

Get to the studio at least an hour early, and look for a coffee shop within walking distance of the studio, where you can review your notes. When you walk in the door of the station, you will be relaxed and confident, and that will come across in the interview.

Your interview begins the moment you walk into the station. Be polite and friendly to everyone there. Word gets around a station quickly if a guest is difficult to work with. You don't want to send the wrong impression.

Be sure to arrange for a tape of the interview. Most stations will provide one if you make the request in advance. Remember to bring a blank audiotape with you. As a backup measure, ask someone at home or at the office to make a professional-quality tape, using a radio that is combined with a tape recorder. The tape will not sound professional if a tape recorder is simply placed next to the radio.

Keep recordings of your radio appearances. They can be posted on your Web site as transcripts or as audio files, and copies can be sent to other stations you are pitching, to demonstrate your proficiency as an interview subject. Copies can also be sent to organizational leaders as a kind of audio newsletter. A taped interview also underscores the fact that the organization is being featured in the media.

During the Interview

You can hear a smile. It is always a good idea to smile during an interview, even though you are on the radio. It will soften up your tone and your entire presentation. It will come across in your voice.

During the interview, you want to be bright and interesting and, above all, brief. You should usually limit your answers to less than thirty seconds. Be sure the key points you want to make are conveyed within that time frame. Practice getting your answers out in a polished, pleasant, concise manner. You want to keep up the momentum of the conversation, not deliver a one-sided lecture. If you do try to monopolize the conversation, the interviewer will cut you off even if you have not made the point you set out to make.

Come to the interview prepared with a few brief anecdotes that dramatically illustrate what your organization does and why it matters so much. Don't be afraid to use a little humor to convey your message, although it is usually a good idea to avoid telling jokes. A warm, touching story that brings a smile to the lips is the right tone for humor.

Repeat part of the interviewer's questions back in your answers. Use the questions as springboards to the answers you have prepared and the information you want to convey. Sometimes an interviewer will lead the conversation into unexpected paths. She may start asking questions that are far off the topic, and for which you are not prepared. If that happens, take the initiative. Speak to her point briefly and then politely guide the conversation back to what you want to speak about. Be friendly and cooperative, but also be firm. You are there to serve *your* agenda, not hers.

Keep things cordial. Call the interviewer by name once or twice (more seems forced), and treat the interview as a conversation. It makes for a good interview and a better chance of being invited back.

The interview format can be an excellent platform for a call to action. If you want people to come out for a rally, volunteer to wrap Christmas presents, or refurbish a school, you can frame the announcement as a personal invitation. Be sure that the contact information you give is accurate.

Radio Interviews via Telephone

Radio interviews are frequently done over the phone, with the interview subject comfortably seated at home or in the office. If you are doing an interview on the phone, here are some helpful basics. Make sure to have a glass of water close at hand. Before you begin, remove anything disruptive, like jewelry that might bang against a tabletop and make a distracting noise. Get the air conditioning or heating the way you like it because you won't be able to adjust it in the middle of the interview.

Have any facts or figures you may need for the interview within easy reach and "easy read" so that you don't have to rustle through papers when you are on the air. Have a blank sheet of paper and a pen handy, too, so you can jot down thoughts you may want to include in the interview. Have the objectives of the interview written out big and bold on a piece of paper in front of you so that you can keep them in mind and stay on message throughout the interview.

Turn off your answering machine and any other phones that can be heard. Take the call in a room where you can close the door and close out the world, and make sure anyone else in the area knows to be quiet and not to interrupt you—no matter what.

Just before you go on, take a deep breath and then another. Relax, and focus on the conversation you are about to have. It can help to think of it as just that—a conversation. The interviewer is simply someone who is interested in hearing what you have to say but doesn't have much time, so you'll need to stay on track. And remember to smile during the interview, to keep your tone warm and relaxed. You really can hear a smile.

After the Interview

It takes a little time, but it is always a good idea to send a brief note of thanks to the people you worked with at the station. The classiest way is in the form of a handwritten note, but an e-mail sent out right after the interview is also very much appreciated. Besides making you stand out as a courteous, appreciative professional, a timely "thank you" lays the groundwork for your next call and your next pitch.

Think of the connection as a relationship, and be on the lookout for ways to be helpful and to stay on the producer's radar. If you know she is planning to produce a segment on something, and you happen to run across an article on that topic in a magazine she probably doesn't read, send her the article along with a very brief cover note.

Ask the program host or producer for a letter, or at least an e-mail, stating that you were a good interview subject. Photocopies of such testimonials in your press kit can be invaluable for future pitches to the media and demonstrate that you know how to handle yourself in an interview and will be an entertaining, informative asset to the show. When you make future pitches, include a list of recent media appearances along with several testimonials to further convince the producer that you can be relied on to deliver a consistently good performance as a guest.

Radio Tours

Authors do radio tours to promote their new books, and tours work well for nonprofits as well. A radio tour is simply a series of radio interviews, done from a studio or from the subject's home or office, with as many stations and programs as can be scheduled into a specific time period. It requires some planning and logistics, but a radio tour can provide a lot of valuable exposure in a short time.

When a publisher sets up a radio tour for an author, the first interview is typically scheduled for 5:00 A.M. on the East Coast, and the rest are worked in through the morning, to take advantage of differences in time zones so the last interview in the series ends at 9:00 A.M. on the West Coast. That adds up to hours of saying the same thing and answering the same questions to a blur of different interviewers. It is exhausting, but it can be effective.

When a radio tour is arranged professionally, the interviewer is usually set up in a soundproof studio with sophisticated switching equipment and a technician to handle connections. A less sophisticated but still effective way to conduct the series of interviews that make up a radio tour is to operate from a quiet office or home. Arrange each interview on the "tour" in advance, the way you would arrange a single interview, and then follow the established schedule.

To reach as many stations as possible, it is also a good idea to connect with statewide networks of stations that can feed the program to all their affiliates throughout the state. Typically located in the state capital, a large network can reach as many as a hundred local stations, giving your organization considerable exposure.

Become a Resource

Talk radio shows are always looking for experts prepared to speak on subjects that become hot topics in the news. Establish your organization as an expert by making yourself known to local radio station managers. Make sure station managers have your direct number, and be prepared to have a spokesperson ready to be interviewed at a moment's notice. You can also let stations know that you are prepared to supply a spokesperson to be interviewed if a previously scheduled guest cancels at the last minute.

You can broaden your scope by listing your organization and its spokespeople with directories that radio producers turn to in search of instant expertise, such as *Newsmaker Interviews,* which lists potential guests and their topics, and *The Yearbook of Experts, Authorities, and Spokespersons* (www.yearbooknews.com). You can also consider placing an ad in *Radio-TV Interview Report: The Magazine Producers Read to Find Guests.* Known simply as the *RTIR,* it is published three times a year and is mailed to more than four thousand radio and TV producers in North America.

CHAPTER THIRTEEN

PITCHING AND PLACING: TELEVISION

It is an understatement to say that television reaches a mass audience. There are more than 220 million television sets in the United States. A total of 98 percent of homes in the country have at least one TV set. And in homes with children, television is on an average of nearly sixty hours a week.

Broadcast television reaches a huge general market. Specific target markets can be reached by way of specific programs and time slots, by the use of local television stations, and by the judicious use of cable and satellite TV that is tailored to very specific audiences.

Getting an organization on TV is a process. You begin by reviewing all the stations that reach your target market, identifying the programs that are aimed at your market segment, and selecting a good match with your organization. Local programs are generally easier to get on than national and are a good place to start.

Making a Connection

Options for publicity for nonprofits exist at most TV stations. It's all a matter of finding out whom to contact and then making that contact for your organization.

Who to Contact

Once you have identified the programs on which you want your organization to appear, contact the appropriate person at the TV station. To find the name and contact information of the right person, you can consult one of the directories listed at the end of Chapter Four. You can also find the names and contact information of assignment editors and program producers by going to the station's Web site.

Television producers change jobs frequently, so be sure your information is current. Call the station, explain the nature of your story or interview subject, and ask whom you should contact. Be sure to get the correct spelling of his name and the correct contact information. Also find out how he prefers to receive material, whether by e-mail, fax, or regular mail.

At local TV stations, there are typically a daytime assignment editor, a nighttime assignment editor, and a weekend assignment editor. Contact the editor responsible for the time slot of the program you are interested in. For talk shows, contact the show's producer.

When to Call—and When Not To

For an interview on a local TV news show, contact the station one week before the projected date. For an interview on a local TV talk show, send materials one month in advance of the date you would like the interview to take place. National television is different. Call the show you are interested in to find out its preferred lead time. Some book a week ahead, and others need two months. For holiday specials, six weeks is a fairly typical lead time.

When you call a TV station, there are times to avoid. Never contact a TV station when a news program is on the air. Everyone will be watching his own program and the competition on adjoining monitors.

A station typically holds its morning meeting at 9:00. This meeting includes the assignment editor, the producer, the executive producer, and the news director. At 3:00, the same cast of characters meets for the afternoon meeting. Calling at either 9:00 A.M. or 3:00 P.M. is pointless. All the decision makers you would want to talk to are in one of these meetings. Call before or after.

What to Say

When you call, always ask if it is a good time to talk. If the answer is no, set a convenient time to call back. When you do connect, limit your pitch to no more than two minutes.

Always remember that television is a visual medium. When you pitch, think and speak in terms of visuals. Be prepared to briefly describe a number of powerful visual images the story will generate. Think human interest.

If you have professionally shot video footage of your organization in action, be sure to let the station know. Smaller stations will often welcome this footage because it saves them time and expense.

If you are pitching an interview with an organizational spokesperson, mention a few of the most impressive programs on which he has appeared. If this is his first time out, stress his warmth and personality. Make it clear to the producer that what you are "selling" is a great program segment with a guest who will provide a great interview.

What to Send

Prepare a one-page pitch letter, press release, or media alert. TV news people tend to like faxes. Grab the producer's attention with a headline that smacks of urgency. Stress the visual elements. Concentrate on what the viewer will see on screen.

To bolster your pitch, either include additional background material or indicate the Web site address where the information can be easily found. If you are contacting the station by e-mail, you can include a direct link to the information.

Never just send material to the station blindly. Always address it to a specific individual by name.

It is sometimes a good idea to send a press kit along with your one-page pitch letter, press release, or media alert. At other times, you may want to have a press kit prepared and ready to go if the producer requests it. A press kit should include a backgrounder, a brochure, and articles about your organization.

Producers are impressed by article reprints from first-rank newspapers and magazines. Even publications of less than the first rank can have an impact, and reprints from them suggest that there is enough "meat" in your story to make for a good program segment. Don't overwhelm the producer with a bulging folder; two or three articles are usually enough.

If you are pitching an interview, include a brief biography of the spokesperson and a good photo. It should be at least 5 by 7 inches and can be either black-and-white or color but should always be professionally done. If the subject has been interviewed by significant publications, include copies of published interviews, and mention the most impressive titles among the others.

It is important to include a page of suggested interview questions, also called a "tip sheet," because it provides tips to the producer about the kinds of questions the interview subject can be asked. Print journalists typically resist such spoon-feeding, but radio and television interviewers work at a more frantic pace, and such aids are usually welcomed. Often the producer will use your list of suggested questions pretty much as is or will alter the questions only slightly before giving them to the interviewer. The interviewer in turn will simply ask those questions.

Include a list of previous media appearances and, if possible, a video with highlights of TV interviews the subject has done in the past. Producers like to be assured that the spokesperson is comfortable in front of the camera and won't freeze up when the interview begins.

Following Up

After you've sent your materials to the producer, follow up with a phone call. It is best to call in the morning, when things are relatively relaxed. In the afternoon, a station tends to get pretty frantic as people scramble to prepare for the evening news program. Again, don't call at 9:00 A.M. or 3:00 P.M., when show meetings are generally held and no one is free to answer your call.

Ask if there are any questions you can answer. Offer an added bit of information. If the producer isn't interested in the story, try to find out why not. Sometimes you can come up with a new angle for the story while you are on the phone with the producer that will make the story a "go."

If you don't sell the producer on the story, don't despair—90 percent and more of pitches come up empty. Consider the conversation a preliminary building block in a long-standing relationship. Don't antagonize the producer; you will be pitching him another story on another day, and you want to leave him with positive feelings about you and your organization.

The same applies to pitching an interview. You want to convince the producer that the interview will be a terrific program segment. But if there is no interest, withdraw gracefully. There will be future opportunities.

Media Advisory

A good way to get TV coverage is by way of special events. If the organization is doing something with a strong visual appeal that lends itself to television coverage, you can issue a media advisory to local TV stations.

A media advisory, also called a media alert, is a one-page notice resembling an invitation. It looks like something intended to be posted on a bulletin board. It features a big, bold headline to capture the attention of the reader and tell what the event is. It covers the same basic information as a press release, but it often includes bulleted items and uses lots of white space.

After the key words *who, what, where,* and *when,* and sometimes *why* and *how,* the information is listed clearly and succinctly. Also listed are the times set aside for photo opportunities, in addition to a contact name and the contact's direct phone number.

Good Timing

You can sometimes make a successful pitch by simply sending a well-timed fax. As information about upcoming events and story ideas comes into a TV newsroom, it is put into a calendar file by the date of the event. Usually at the end of the day, the assignment editor reviews what has been collected for the following day. The following morning, the editor makes recommendations to the producers.

Because television stations make their final decisions about what stories to cover around 9:00 A.M., if you time your fax right, it may arrive just at the moment of decision. That can sometimes be enough, especially if you have a track record with the producer, or if you can link your organization to a breaking news story. You can get lucky and find a camera crew on your doorstep that day.

It may be a good idea to make a follow-up call the night before or that morning, just to give the story that extra little push.

Because Sundays, holidays, and the days after holidays tend to be slow news days, assignment editors may welcome your contact and the chance to fill airtime with an interesting story. You have a better chance of having your story covered on these days.

The media advisory is usually faxed directly to the appropriate producer at the station and then followed up with a phone call, to make sure it arrived and to answer any questions the producer may have. (See Exhibit 13.1.)

It is also a good idea to send the media advisory to the local Associated Press (AP) Daybook, which forwards news about stories and events to producers at TV stations throughout the country. AP has a number of bureaus, each with its own Associated Press Daybook for its region. You can find the contact information for your local AP bureau in the standard media directories listed at the end of Chapter Four.

After the Pitch

After you've made the connection, you may get a call from the station with a question or a detail that needs to be finalized. Be sure to take the call or return it promptly. People in the television environment work at a fast pace and appreciate the courtesy and efficiency of a quick callback. It will stand you in good stead to establish a reputation as someone who is courteous, efficient, and reliable. The next time you make a pitch, your good name will precede you.

EXHIBIT 13.1. SAMPLE MEDIA ADVISORY (CONGRESSWOMAN VELÁZQUEZ).

NEWS FROM CONGRESSWOMAN NYDIA M. VELÁZQUEZ

Representing New York's 12th Congressional District
Brooklyn, Manhattan & Queens
Ranking Democratic Member, House Small Business Committee

For Immediate Release   CONTACT: Wendy Belzer, Kate Davis
October 23, 2003   202-225-2361

MEDIA ADVISORY

Velázquez to Speak at
Women Entrepreneurs Business Conference

Conference will advise women entrepreneurs on how to finance their businesses

NEW YORK—Congresswoman Nydia M. Velázquez (D-N.Y.), Ranking Democratic Member of the House Small Business Committee, will be the keynote speaker at the *We Can! Women Entrepreneurs Capital Access Networking Business Conference* at St. Francis College hosted by the Brooklyn Women's Business Center (BWBC) at the Local Development Corporations of East New York.

Small businesses are the backbone of the New York City economy, and those firms owned by women and minorities are a growing force. In fact, as of 2002, there were an estimated 230,000 women-owned firms, which employed more than 250,000 workers and generated over $34.2 billion in sales.

Reflected in the high number of entrepreneurs who finance their businesses with credit cards, access to affordable capital remains a significant barrier to start-up and growth. The *We Can!* business conference seeks to provide both aspiring entrepreneurs and established business owners with practical information on getting the capital they need to launch and expand their businesses. Sessions will be offered on preparing to borrow as well as "borrowing for your business" from banks and microlenders.

When and Where:

When: Tuesday, October 28, 2003, from 8:30 A.M. to 2:30 P.M.
            Congresswoman Velázquez will speak at 9:00 A.M.*

Where: St. Francis College, Callahan Center/Founders Hall
            180 Remsen Street, downtown Brooklyn

Who: Congresswoman Nydia M. Velázquez
            Representatives from the Small Business Administration
            (SBA) and the Brooklyn Women's Business Center
            Lending Experts
            Local entrepreneurs and business owners

###

Source: Courtesy of the Office of Congresswoman Nydia M. Velázquez.

Arranging Logistics "On Location"

If you do manage to interest a TV station in doing a story about you and they are planning to send a camera crew, be sure that you handle all the logistics involved. Check with the location in advance, to be sure you have permission for the camera crew to come on site. Many TV camera crews have stories of getting to the door, only to be stopped in their tracks by a store manager or warehouse foreman who had not been told to let them inside. Be sure to get permission, in writing if possible, from someone in authority, and be there on the day of the shoot to handle details and deal with any problems.

Start Local, Go Global

Small local stations are easier to get on than the larger network shows. Local publicity has a powerful impact all its own, so local TV should not be scorned. Besides providing an excellent arena for honing interview skills, a videotape of the interview is an essential marketing tool for going on to the next step. Larger programs and stations will typically ask to see a sample of how a spokesperson has done on TV. A tape of an actual TV interview on a local station will demonstrate that he is "good television."

You have the best chance of getting airtime if you pitch the less popular time slots. Sundays are slow for broadcast stations. The months of July and August, when program directors are scrambling for guests, can be an excellent time to pitch a novice spokesperson.

Local TV in West Palm Beach and New York. Getting an organization on local TV is often a combination of personal relationships and a great story idea. The Richard David Kann Melanoma Foundation in West Palm Beach, Florida, teamed up with a local Brownie troop for a feature story on WPTV, the local NBC affiliate.

The Brownies had been looking for a project. By a happy coincidence, the grandmother of one of the little girls was a friend of a Melanoma Foundation board member. The connection between the two organizations was quickly made, and the foundation helped the Brownies with their project: collecting sun block to send to American troops stationed in Iraq. Appearing on the station's 5:30 news program, the Brownies were interviewed by local anchor Chandra Bill, who is on the advisory board of the Melanoma Foundation.

Looking cute and very telegenic, the girls spoke on camera about their project. With charming enthusiasm, they conveyed the Melanoma Foundation's message about the dangers of overexposure to the sun and the need to use sun block. It was a warm, appealing story segment on the local news that garnered considerable local visibility for both the Brownies and the Melanoma Foundation. And, like so many stories that make it into the news, it was based on personal relationships.

Melvin Taylor, media specialist for the New York Urban League, knows that the community relations department of a local television station can be an excellent resource for spokespersons. Taylor approached the community relations department of WPIX-TV (Channel 11) to request that Vanessa Tyler, a popular African American newscaster, serve as a spokesperson for the organization's outreach to New York's African American community. For a back-to-school initiative targeted at Latino high school students, Taylor approached PBS station WNET (Channel 13) to request Rafael Pi Roman as an on-air spokesperson. In these and other cases, the stations and the on-air personalities were happy to lend their names, without charge, to positive efforts on behalf of the local community—excellent publicity for the Urban League and its work, and great exposure for the spokespeople and the stations. As in most instances of smart PR, everybody won.

Publicity on Local TV. Nonprofits can and should take advantage of the free advertising available to them on local TV. All local stations have community bulletin boards and calendars. The community affairs department of your local television station routinely announces events of interest to the public via on-air announcers and community bulletin boards.

A case in point, says Anna Carbonell, vice president of press and public affairs for WNBC (Channel 4) and the Spanish language WNJU (Telemundo 47), in New York, is WNBC's "Best Bets" segment, which the station features during its weekend editions of *Today in New York*. For a Spanish-speaking audience, another good vehicle for promoting events, says Carbonell, is Telemundo, which has a community calendar that carries announcements of upcoming nonprofit events.

To get a story on a local TV station, Carbonell advises nonprofits to send an e-mail to the station's community affairs director and follow up with a phone call.

Ojeda Hall-Phillips makes regular use of local TV outlets as director of the Women's Business Center of the Local Development Corporation of East New York. Based in the East New York section of Brooklyn, the organization works primarily with minority women entrepreneurs. She also regularly sends announcements to public access TV.

Connecting with Public Access TV. Typical of community access television stations, Brooklyn Community Access Television (BCAT) (www.bcat.tv) makes its free community calendar service available to not-for-profit organizations such as cultural organizations, PTAs, government agencies, and school boards, as well as for-profit organizations that are offering free services or events to the Brooklyn community. Nonprofits are required to file their 501(c)(3) certificates with the station in order to establish their not-for-profit status before BCAT will accept their announcements. Once that form has been received, the station enters the organization into its database and provides a community calendar announcement form by e-mail, fax, or regular mail.

The form can also be downloaded from the station's Web site. Most announcements are submitted through the online database on the BCAT Web site. The information is shared by the online calendar and the cablecast calendar.

The BCAT deadline for announcements, also fairly typical for community access television, is three weeks prior to the scheduled event. The simple form requests basic information: the name, date, exact time, and location of the event or service, the name of the sponsoring organization, and a phone number to contact for additional information.

"We've found the community calendar an invaluable way to communicate with the public," Hall-Phillips says. "People do check it to find out what's going on, and it helps deliver a big turnout for our events."

"Public access television is often underused by nonprofits," says JoAnne Meyers, director of marketing for Brooklyn Information and Culture (BRIC), which oversees BCAT's operations. BCAT's major users include the Brooklyn Museum, the Brooklyn Public Library, and local high schools, which make use of the station's resources to tape and air cultural events. But, says Meyers, as is often true of public access stations across the country, a lot of local nonprofits overlook BCAT as a tool. Many public access television stations conduct outreach programs to make the availability of their services better known in their local nonprofit communities.

Like many such stations, BCAT functions on a first-come, first-served basis, and its mandate is to serve the local community. In addition to encouraging organizations to post events on its community calendar, BCAT produces public service announcements for nonprofits at no charge. BCAT also offers free training for nonprofits on how to use the BCAT equipment to make their own PSAs. Once a PSA is made, the station puts it on the air at no charge.

It is the mandate of all public access stations to offer locally based nonprofits the channel space to host their own show, free of charge. With the cost of video cameras and at-home editing systems going down, public access television is an increasingly popular way to reach audiences. For those who don't own their own equipment, BCAT, like most public access stations across the country, also offers low-cost training on how to use professional video equipment. At BCAT, that extends to making the television studio and media center available to nonprofits to create their own programs, which can be cablecast, at no additional charge, weekly, monthly, or as a onetime special.

Some public access stations help nonprofits make full-blown promotional videos that run as long as twenty-eight minutes or even an hour. The nonprofit can use the master to make copies for promotional and fundraising purposes. Rules, regulations, and procedures for community access TV vary from one municipality to another. Every public access station has to deal with a variety of city, state, and federal regulations, some of which occasionally contradict each other. Although local resources vary, public access TV is a valuable and underused resource for nonprofits.

The TV Interview

Preparation: Practice, Practice, and More Practice

The key to a successful interview is preparation. Carefully prepare your spokesperson for the interview. Have him watch several shows in advance, to become familiar with the format and the interviewer's style. Use the tip sheet of suggested questions to conduct mock interviews in rehearsals. One advantage of having prepared the questions is that you can also prepare the answers. The interviewer may not always follow the list of suggested questions, so it is a good idea to become familiar with the kinds of questions the interviewer likes to ask. Find out if there will be other guests on the program with your spokesperson, and try to find out something about them by way of preparation. A guest appearance on television is a performance, and like any performance, it should be rehearsed to ensure the best results.

Videotape a mock interview with your spokesperson. Watch the playback together, and offer constructive criticism and encouragement as he watches the tape. The goal is to help him appear confident and at ease when he is on camera so that he will look and sound sincere and credible.

Point out how much more effective short answers are than long ones. Assure the spokesperson that nodding and smiling and using gestures adds to the overall impression. Look for flaws in his presentation. When he speaks, does he fail to make eye contact with the interviewer? Does he fumble or use too many "uh" and "mmm" sounds? Be on the lookout for overuse of technical terms and jargon as well as confusing, convoluted sentences. Does he deflect questions that lead away from the topic, and does he guide the interview back to what he wants to talk about? Does he stay on message? How effective is his use of facts and figures to complement his arguments? Does he use sound bites effectively?

Staying on Message

Be sure the spokesperson has three or four key message points prepared, things that are important to convey to the audience. The interview represents a wonderful opportunity to convey those key message points, and it would be a shame to waste that opportunity. Coach your spokesperson on getting those points across in the interview. Skilled interviewees are good at answering the questions they want to answer, no matter what questions they are actually asked. The key to this is learning how to bridge.

A good bridging technique is to respond by saying, "That's an interesting question" and then follow that observation with a brief, polite comment and a smooth return to the topic you actually want to talk about.

There is also the "Oops, I forgot" bridge. When the interviewer asks a question, reply with a bridge, such as "I'm really excited about that aspect of our program, but I forgot to mention the ABC earlier. In the ABC, we do XYZ, which has a lot in common with the program you just asked me about . . . ," and then continue to answer the interviewer's question. Another useful device is the "And we also" bridge, which puts the material at the end of your answer: "And in addition to that, we also recently expanded our ABC, which does XYZ."

It is important for the person being interviewed to take control, to remember that it is his interview. Rather than waiting for the interviewer to ask the right questions, he should guide the conversation to the main points.

If the interviewer asks a question to which the spokesperson does not know the answer, it is all right for the spokesperson to say, "That's not my area of expertise. I'll get back to you on that." The trick is to get past the question as gracefully as possible and then move on to the next question. It is never a good idea to make things up or lie.

Find out in advance if the station will agree to broadcast the organization's contact information. If it will, make sure the station has the correct information before the interview. Have the spokesperson bring an extra copy of the information with him to the studio, just in case what you sent has been misplaced.

The Soul of Wit

Shakespeare called brevity the soul of wit. It is also the essence of good interviewing. Coach your spokesperson to keep things short and to the point. As an exercise, get him to try speaking in "headlines," making short, declarative statements of thirty seconds or less—preferably less. The electronic medium is a fast-paced world where the sound bite is king. Learning to handle it is, in some ways, like learning a new language.

Radio and TV like stories. Brief anecdotes, full of warmth and humor, can be very effective. Prepare several good anecdotes that convey the importance of what the organization does in simple, human interest terms. The organization should obviously figure in the telling of the story, but the idea is not to deliver a commercial. Interviewers and audiences are savvy and object to promotion that is too blatant.

Media Training

If media interviews are going to become a regular part of a PR campaign, it may be a good idea to get professional media training. Many public relations firms will not work with a client unless he agrees to media training. Most PR firms either offer it themselves or work closely with outside media trainers.

Rick Frishman, president of Planned Television Arts, an independent division of Ruder-Finn, Inc., insists that any client his firm represents must have media training. The cost can vary from $2,000 or $2,500 in an office to $5,000 at a studio. "Whatever the cost," Frishman says, "its worth it."

Media training can help a novice appear relaxed and spontaneous on air, according to Virgil Scudder, who prepares CEOs to handle radio and TV interviews at the Manhattan-based Virgil Scudder & Associates. Scudder's clients range from Fortune 500 corporations like Gillette and UPS to nonprofits like the National Restaurant Association and the New York Public Library. He has prepared a dozen basic guidelines that he says are key to a successful media interview (see Exhibit 13.2). Not surprisingly, first on the list is preparation.

EXHIBIT 13.2. MEDIA GUIDELINES.

1. Preparation is the key to success in any interview situation. Prepare your agenda thoroughly before the interview begins.

2. Be responsive, but steer the interview to your key topics. You have a right to state your points—and restate them.

3. Take control of the interview at your earliest opportunity. You never do an interview to answer questions; interviews are done to make points.

4. Tailor the message to the media and the audience. The "must air" points for one interview will not necessarily be the right ones for the next interview.

5. Keep it tight. Long answers invite misinterpretation of your positions and diminish your effectiveness and credibility. Give a headline response, and then elaborate only to the degree that is appropriate.

6. Eye contact is critical to credibility. Look the interviewer right in the eye, especially when the questioning is hostile or negative.

7. Use examples, illustrations, and comparisons to help your interviewer or audience understand your positions.

8. Don't be defensive. Put your points across firmly and confidently. The interview is a chance for you to tell your story.

9. "Bottom line first" is the key to a successful response. If you wind gradually into your conclusion, you invite misunderstanding and suspicion.

10. Always be friendly and courteous with interviewers even if they don't return the favor. But don't be timid and passive.

11. Clear language and concise responses are essential to success.

12. Debrief after every exposure to the media. What did you do right, and what could you have done better? This is how great newsmakers get to be great.

Source: Courtesy of Virgil Scudder & Associates.

Details and Logistics

If you haven't already done so as part of your pitch, when you book the interview you should send some basic information to the producer of the show, including a one-page fact sheet on the organization, a one-page biography of the spokesperson, and some sample questions. On the day before the interview, call to make sure the station has all the materials you sent earlier. Stations can be hectic places. Be prepared to hand-deliver anything that has gone missing.

Always call to confirm the details of the interview. Be sure that you are clear about exactly where the spokesperson has to be, and when. Make sure you have the name of a contact and his direct phone number, and a backup name too, if possible, so the spokesperson can ask for someone by name when she arrives.

Also find out in advance if there will be a hair and makeup person to do a touch-up before the guest goes on. You and the spokesperson should be friendly and polite to him and ask his name. A little courtesy will be appreciated, as he literally has the spokesperson's appearance in his hands. If there is no hair and makeup person, or if he has run out of time and can't work with the spokesperson, make sure the spokesperson takes the time to do the touch-up job herself in the restroom mirror. Little things, like a piece of spinach caught in her teeth, can have a disproportionate effect on the image she projects on the air.

The spokesperson should plan to arrive at the studio with time to spare. Half an hour is a good amount of lead time. If traffic may be a problem, she should get to the neighborhood of the studio earlier than that and use the extra time to review her notes over a cup of coffee. That way, if it does take longer than expected to get to the studio, she has a cushion and can still arrive in plenty of time, unhurried and relaxed.

Although your spokesperson may be a little distracted, especially if being interviewed is a new experience, it is nonetheless important to be polite and friendly to everyone, beginning with the receptionist. People tend to respond in kind, and it sets up a pleasant atmosphere that can help relieve any last-minute nervousness. Urge the spokesperson to take some time to get acclimated to the surroundings. If possible, encourage her to chat with the interviewer, to get comfortable with his style and try to establish a rapport.

It is always a good idea to bring along something to read during the wait in the green room, the holding area for guests. It will make the time go more quickly, and she will be less likely to build up a case of preshow jitters.

Tell your studio contact that you would like a copy of the program, and bring a blank 120-minute VHS tape with you to the interview. Sometimes, when more than one guest is being interviewed and the control room has only one free tape deck available, it is the guest with the foresight to bring a blank tape who walks away with a copy at the end. Most programs will promise to make a copy and send it on to you later.

They usually remember to do it. Others will do it, but only after a half-dozen phone calls renewing the request. It is much easier all around just to bring a blank tape to the interview.

Dressing for Success

Appearance is critical on TV interviews. Prior to the interview, watch the show and observe how the host and their guests dress. Have your spokesperson take her dress cue from the host and the bigger-name guests. She should dress comfortably. There is enough going on in the studio setting to make her ill at ease. She should counter that by wearing something that makes her feel confident and relaxed. If she normally wears a uniform in her "day job" and you are talking about something work-related, it may make sense for her to do the interview wearing the regular uniform.

For a television appearance, it is wise to dress neatly and conservatively and choose solid colors. Dark colors, blues and dark grays, are best. Checks and narrow striped patterns are distracting and may cause a rippling rainbow effect, called a moiré pattern, when seen on screen. You want your audience watching and listening to the message, not being distracted by a play of electric colors.

It is also smart to avoid big reflective jewelry. A white shirt or blouse under a jacket or sweater is all right, although blue is generally better, but she should stay away from an all-white look; it reflects the light and blinds the camera in the same way a snow-field blinds the eye. Men should be sure that their socks reach high enough on the leg so no naked calf will show if they cross their legs.

With all the last-minute adjustment of microphones, lights, and cables, it is easy for an interviewee's clothes to get a little mussed. Just before going on camera, it is a good idea to look at the monitor to make sure that everything is straight, that the right buttons are all buttoned, that the jacket is pulled down and the tie is pulled all the way up to the throat (it is surprising how often ties are askew in interviews). Clothing that is even a little out of place can be a distraction.

After she has checked and adjusted, the trick is to forget about her appearance during the interview. She should not continue checking herself in the monitor. If the camera catches her primping, she will look narcissistic and disorganized. Once the cameras roll, it is best just to concentrate on the conversation and on getting the message out as clearly as possible.

Speech and Body Language

The key is to look and sound relaxed. TV likes movement; the viewer's eye is attracted to motion and bored by lack of it. A stiff, unmoving body, a frozen stare, and barely moving lips all convey hostility. Worse, they convey the impression that the person speaking is not to be trusted. The viewer starts to wonder, "What is she so uptight about? What is she hiding?"

Remind her to gesture and nod her head, to lean forward as she listens to the interviewer, to smile and express her feelings just as she would in a "real" conversation. It can help a lot to actually listen to the interviewer and react to questions as if she were not on camera. An audience can tell when someone is not really listening, and it looks phony.

She should feel free to move and gesture, but it can help to have a basic "at rest" posture to return to. This is not intended to be a rigid pose but a starting point.

Some tips for looking alert, relaxed, and at ease include keeping both elbows on the chair armrests and keeping one hand folded over the other on the lap, with the hands not clasped but free for natural gesturing. It is fine for her to gesture with her hands if that is her natural style, but not wildly, and she should not point her finger at anything; it looks harsh on camera. Advise her to smile often and make eye contact with the host and other guests when she speaks. She should keep her jacket unbuttoned for ease of movement, and, if seated around a table in the setting so popular on some talk shows, she should cross her legs at the knee.

She should not lean back in the chair as though she is relaxing at home; the impression will be one of sloth and disinterest. She should lean forward, position herself on the edge of the chair, sit straight, and stay focused on the conversation.

She should not look at the monitor or at the camera but at the person doing the talking. If she needs to look at someone out of her direct line of sight, she should move her head, not her eyes. Eyes going to the side make a person look shifty. The exception is when the show takes telephone calls from viewers. In that case, because she is responding to someone "out there," it does make sense to look directly into the camera when responding to questions.

A relaxed, confident tone of voice conveys sincerity. Studio microphones work just fine; there is no need to talk loudly or quickly. A regular pace and a calm, well-modulated voice go a long way toward making a good impression. She should not be afraid to vary her tone and to speak with measured enthusiasm if the topic warrants it. Keeping the conversation interesting keeps the audience's attention focused on the spokesperson and on the message she is there to convey for the organization.

The lights in the studio are hot, and there is a lot going on behind the cameras and all around the set. It is easy to get disoriented and distracted. It is important to stay focused on the prepared message points and on appearing relaxed and confident. How she appears on camera will create an image in the minds of audience members that will be linked to how they think of the organization. It is important to get it right.

After the Interview

After any TV interview, always send a thank-you note to the people you worked with at the station or stations that aired it. A handwritten note is nice, but even an e-mailed thank-you is very much appreciated and makes you stand out. Remember to ask for a letter from the producer, stating that the spokesperson was a good interview subject. That letter will be part of the material you send when pitching appearances on other shows in the future.

Be sure to find out when the program is scheduled to air. Then make a point of letting the world know about it. Send an e-mail to the board, officers, supporters, other organizations, city and state agencies, foundations, and anyone else who will be impressed by the organization getting on the air. Even though most won't catch the program, you will still score points for letting them know about it, and the stock of both the spokesperson and the organization will rise as a result of the appearance.

When the program does air, if you don't already have a copy, be sure to videotape it. Send copies to selected leaders and supporters. Again, even if they don't actually watch it, you will make an impression just by sending it out. Always include a cordial cover note from the spokesperson or an organizational leader. Sending the video provides a nice way of touching base and heightening the organization's visibility.

The interview can also be posted on the organization's Web site, and an e-mail can be sent out to announce that it is available for viewing.

The footage can also be used as an element in the informational and promotional videos and DVDs that the organization produces itself (see Chapter Fourteen).

The Virtual Media Tour

Rather than sending an organizational spokesperson on a speaking tour from city to city, with all the attendant wear and tear and expense, it is possible to construct what is in effect a virtual speaking tour via satellite uplink. Modeled on the media tours that best-selling authors use to promote their latest books, virtual tours can be conducted from the comfort of a video studio.

As many as twenty interviews can be scheduled in a single day, if the spokesperson can manage that many. Arrangements are made in advance with TV stations to have their interviewers ready at a specific time. When a station's turn comes up, its interviewer phones his questions in to the spokesperson, who hears the questions over the studio's audio hookup and answers the interviewer directly. The local station can later edit in footage of its reporter asking the question on camera. The effect for the viewer is of a live interview, with all the same human give-and-take and immediacy, but with much less stress on the spokesperson.

The cost of such a media tour is about $5,000. But for a nonprofit with a message to communicate nationwide, it can be money well spent.

Demo Reels

When you have several interviews on tape, have a video studio use them to make a demo reel that is four to five minutes long. A professionally produced reel is key to getting interviews on national television. It should be a composite of highlights of several interviews, each brief segment opening with the setup piece—the host introducing the spokesperson and the topic—followed by the best part of the interview. With titles and bridge music added and a professional-looking label, the demo video is an excellent marketing tool for taking the next step and approaching the larger programs.

Public Service Announcements

Many TV stations air public service announcements. Like PSAs on the radio, PSAs on TV are free, and their placement is random.

At YAI/National Institute for People with Disabilities, senior media relations manager Lynn Uhlfelder Berman produced a PSA to rally support for YAI's annual Central Park Challenge in New York City. The experience can serve as a good example of how to make and use an effective PSA.

The thirty-second PSA opens with Keith Hernandez, formerly of the New York Mets, standing in Shea Stadium, with players practicing on the bright green field behind him. In the upper right-hand corner of the screen, in small letters, are superimposed the words "Time Warner Cable," which partnered with YAI to sponsor the event. Hernandez, a former gold glover at first base and now a popular sportscaster, looks handsome in a blue blazer. He smiles into the camera and says, "Everyone wants to be on a winning team."

As Hernandez's voice-over continues, the scene shifts to video footage of adults and children running, walking, and enjoying themselves at the previous year's event. "That's why I support YAI/National Institute for People with Disabilities," Hernandez's off-camera voice continues. "And you can, too, by attending YAI's Central Park Challenge at 8:30 A.M. on Saturday, June 5th. There's a 5K run, a 3K walk, and fun for the whole family. So be a winner—support people with disabilities on Saturday, June 5th, in Central Park. Call 212-273-6526."

For the final few words, the scene shifts back to Hernandez standing in Shea Stadium. As he gives the phone number, the number appears at the bottom of the screen. The last sound on the PSA is the sound of a bat hitting a ball in the background, which nicely complements Hernandez's smile. All in all, this PSA is a very satisfying thirty seconds of television (see Exhibit 13.3).

EXHIBIT 13.3. TV SCRIPT FOR A PSA: THIRTY-SECOND
AND FIFTEEN-SECOND VERSIONS.

:30 YAI CENTRAL PARK CHALLENGE PSA

HI. I'M KEITH HERNANDEZ. EVERYONE WANTS TO BE ON A WINNING TEAM.
THAT'S WHY I SUPPORT YAI/NATIONAL INSTITUTE FOR PEOPLE WITH DISABILITIES.
AND YOU CAN, TOO, BY ATTENDING YAI'S CENTRAL PARK CHALLENGE AT 8:30
A.M. ON SATURDAY, JUNE 5TH.

THERE'S A 5K RUN, A 3K WALK, AND FUN FOR THE WHOLE FAMILY.

SO BE A WINNER—SUPPORT PEOPLE WITH DISABILITIES ON SATURDAY, JUNE 5TH,
IN CENTRAL PARK. CALL 212-273-6526.

:15 YAI CENTRAL PARK CHALLENGE PSA

HI. I'M KEITH HERNANDEZ.

IF YOU WANT TO BE A WINNER, JOIN YAI/NATIONAL INSTITUTE FOR PEOPLE WITH
DISABILITIES' CENTRAL PARK CHALLENGE ON SATURDAY, JUNE 5TH.

SUPPORT PEOPLE WITH DISABILITIES.

CALL 212-273-6526.

Source: Courtesy of YAI/National Institute for People with Disabilities.

This PSA, as well as the fifteen-second version Berman made, which included
fewer scenes of past events, aired repeatedly on many stations throughout the New
York area in the weeks before the Central Park Challenge, and it helped bring more
than five thousand people out to the event. Berman says that establishing relationships
with the media, and especially with PSA directors, helps the organization spread the
word about its Central Park Challenge.

"We developed a relationship with Time Warner Cable," Berman says. "They are
a media sponsor in-kind for our event, so their logo is on the PSA, our Central Park
Challenge Web site, T-shirts, brochures, and posters. It also helps to know the people
at the stations who deal with PSAs. And to have them know about us. That comes from
working in the field and making every effort and using every opportunity to meet them
and get to know them personally, whenever possible. Time Warner ran the PSA hundreds of times. Buying that much airtime would have cost a fortune, but as a nonprofit,
we got it all for free."

Berman notes that shooting the footage at Shea Stadium presented its own set
of challenges. Every time Hernandez started to speak, a plane would fly over from

nearby La Guardia Airport, totally drowning him out. "It took take after take until we finally got it. It was very frustrating, but he was the soul of patience." Including post-production, Berman estimates that making the PSA took about twelve hours.

YAI also made a second version of the PSA, this one featuring actor Dominic Chianese, who plays Uncle Junior on the HBO series *The Sopranos*. Some stations preferred to run one version, and some chose the other. At one station, the PSA director didn't like the Mets and said she "preferred a spokesman from the Mafia." Her station aired the "Uncle Junior" spot.

To arrange for a PSA to be shown on TV, begin by contacting the station where you want it to air and find out who handles PSAs. It is often the public service director or, at a smaller station, the assignment editor. Request the station's PSA guidelines, and review them carefully. Some stations will produce a PSA for the organization and even write the copy. In that case, you need to provide the "raw material" of information along with suggestions for visuals.

If the station accepts written scripts, observe the guidelines for format, length, and style. Keep your sentences short and your prose punchy and attention-grabbing. Convey the basic facts, as with a news release: *who, what, where, when, why,* and *how.* Television PSAs typically run fifteen, twenty, thirty, or sixty seconds in length, and you need to be accurate. The average announcer can get out twenty words in every ten-second segment.

If the PSA is tied to a specific event, such as an anniversary or a holiday, clearly indicate that fact at the top of the page. Submit the script at least a month, and ideally two months, before the date of the event. Follow up with the station as you get closer to the date you want it to begin being aired. Most station guidelines will specify triple-spaced copy on plain 8½-by-11-inch white paper. Clearly indicate the visuals that will accompany the text.

Rather than producing the PSA yourself (see Chapter Fourteen) or having the station produce it, you may be able to get the production work donated by an ad agency, a PR agency, or an independent producer. If the agency believes in your cause, or if it is just starting out and needs to make a demo to showcase its abilities, or if you can establish a personal relationship, you may be able to avoid incurring the expense.

"Nonprofits can also often get corporate funding for PSAs in partnership arrangements or marketing deals," says Ed Lamoureaux, senior vice president of marketing at West Glen Communications (www.westglen.com), a broadcast communications company that produces and distributes many PSAs every year. "Many of those nonprofit PSAs are paid for out of corporate budgets. For nonprofits, this is definitely an option worth exploring."

Plan to produce three versions of the PSA, in fifteen, twenty, and thirty-second lengths. Stations like to have a selection to choose from.

B-Roll Footage and Video News Releases

According to George DeTorres, account manager at PR Newswire (www.prnewswire. com), a public relations research and distribution company, creating and distributing background ("B-roll") footage and video news releases can maximize the TV coverage of an organization. Both have become standard PR tools, and PR Newswire prepares both. Typical distribution includes two satellite uplinks, one for the morning and one for later in the day (some stations will have missed the earlier one). As production costs come down, more nonprofits are considering the use of these two tools.

B-Roll Footage

B-roll footage, also called simply *B-roll*, is video and natural sound that a station can use to tell an organization's story. TV stations have limited budgets, personnel, and time, so they are unable to send camera crews to every project or event they might like to cover. You can enhance your chances of getting coverage by providing video footage to the station yourself.

If you let a TV station know that you have professionally produced B-roll, it will increase your chances of having the station do the story. This is not a job for amateurs with a camcorder. TV stations generally won't broadcast homemade video unless it is of an approaching tornado. You need to hire a professional video crew with experience in this area.

Production companies that offer these services can be found online or in the Yellow Pages. You dispatch the crew to shoot a few minutes of interesting visuals that make for a good TV story. Then you supply the footage along with a press release and a voiceover script to local TV stations the same day. The cost can run to $10,000 or more, with, of course, no guarantee that any station will run any of it.

Alternatively, you can beam the images up to a satellite, contact the stations to let them know the images are available, and then let the stations download the images directly. Distributing visual images of your event via satellite uplink can cost up to $15,000.

There is a less expensive way to get professionally shot video, and that is to use moonlighting professionals. You can usually locate competent people by calling local stations and asking for a list of freelancers. Many stations have no objection to their videographers freelancing on their own time. These are pros who know how to shoot the kind of footage stations use and do it quickly. A typical rate is $1,200 a day.

Videographers usually provide their own professional equipment, which saves on expensive rental fees. For a few hundred dollars more, they can also usually round up any additional crew members needed to handle separate audio or light a difficult location. Many have their own editing facilities or can easily recommend one.

B-Roll for MTV and CNN

When MTV wanted scenes of college students for its Get Out the Vote campaign, it turned to Brooklyn College. The Brooklyn College Television Center was happy to provide B-roll of its students walking around campus and attending classes. George Casturani, producer and operations manager at the center, notes that in this "everybody wins" situation MTV got the free footage and Brooklyn College got free publicity. B-roll produced by the center was also used in a story that appeared on CNN and was later used again as part of an informational video shown at a gala dinner honoring Brooklyn College alumni.

The advent of affordable, high-quality digital equipment has made quality digital video (DV) production a viable option for nonprofits. Several major manufacturers, including Canon, Panasonic, and Sony, make mini-DV cameras for the "prosumer" market. Priced in the mid-$3,000 range, they provide better sound and image quality than the typical consumer cameras made for recording the family vacation. Although these cameras are not up to the level of truly professional equipment, their quality is generally accepted by network and cable stations. Moderately priced digital editing systems and software programs have also expanded the do-it-yourself possibilities for nonprofits.

Shots should be ten to fifteen seconds long, to give the stations that use the B-roll enough footage to work with. Make about ten copies in Beta SP (broadcast-quality analog videotape), the standard broadcast news format, for distribution to stations. Have copies made in digital format as well, for use on your Web site as streaming video. You may also be able to use some of the footage for PSAs as well as for promotional videos and DVDs (see Chapter Fourteen).

Video News Releases

Designed for stations that do not have complete news staffs to send out on stories, or to provide video content that news organizations would not typically have access to, the video news release (VNR) is more than just a series of visual images. A VNR is a complete feature story, with the look, sound, and "feel" of a network news story, prepackaged and ready to be aired. A VNR is often referred to as just that—a package.

The edited video runs ninety to one hundred twenty seconds and includes an excerpt from a prerecorded interview, broken into one or two sound bites. It is usually provided to a TV station in two versions, one with professional voiceover and one with all the background sounds and interview sound bites but without the voiceover. This allows the station the option of using its own people for the voiceover.

VNRs are used by both large and small stations. Small stations with limited resources are more likely to use the version as is, with the prerecorded voiceover. Larger stations usually edit them and generally prefer to add their own in-studio voiceovers. Just as a press release provides story ideas and information to newspaper reporters, a video news release does the same for television news reporters.

Production costs, including distribution, can run in the $20,000 range, according to Ed Lamoureaux at West Glen, which also produces and distributes VNRs. That price typically includes a fully produced and edited VNR distributed to stations via two satellite feeds, accompanied with several days of phone pitching to newsrooms. Lamoureaux points out that uplinking the VNR via satellite to make it available to TV producers is less expensive than sending out Beta SP tapes. If the VNR were to be distributed via tape, the total cost could double to $40,000 or more. A VNR is prohibitively expensive for most nonprofits, but even at that expense, a good placement can be very cost-effective when compared to the cost of some TV commercials.

"A VNR must have a strong, compelling story that is visually appealing so that stations will want to pick it up," says Bill Brobst, a PR consultant in suburban Maryland, outside Washington, D.C. Brobst produced a VNR for the Virginia Center for Innovative Technology (CIT) that was picked up and widely aired on evening news shows throughout the state, including on major stations in Richmond, Roanoke, and Newport News and on stations in suburban Washington, D.C. "It got the message out about the CIT's role in bringing technology to the state and was considered very successful."

Brobst notes that a nonprofit with limited resources may need to employ some out-of-the-box thinking to get a VNR produced. It may be possible to partner with other departments in the organization, and with other organizations, by offering to shoot footage that can be used not only for the VNR but for other purposes as well, such as for PSAs or informational and tribute videos and for B-roll that can be supplied to the media.

To keep production costs down, you may want to consider approaching video departments at community colleges and four-year colleges and proposing your VNR as a class project. Another option is to connect with the in-house video production facilities maintained by many major corporations. Approaching a corporation by way of an organizational board member, or with a direct appeal to the company's public affairs department, may result in access to some high-end equipment at little or no cost to the nonprofit.

Lamoureaux offers a word of caution here. "While costs can be contained by using in-house resources or college students, the success of most VNRs depends heavily on providing expert advice and counsel from a journalist's perspective. Many VNRs fail due to lack of 'newsworthiness' or production values that don't match the news look and feel. It is always advisable to involve someone with newsroom experience to avoid these pitfalls."

Corporate facilities can be quite impressive, as I learned when I spent several days producing a video at the Bristol-Myers Squibb studios in Princeton, New Jersey. The company had top-of-the-line studios and equipment, and the in-house production staff—the camera operators, lighting and sound people, makeup artists, and editors—were all first-rate professionals who knew their craft thoroughly and were committed to creating a first-rate product.

CHAPTER FOURTEEN

PRODUCING VIDEOS AND DVDS

Videos are an excellent vehicle for nonprofit organizations to tell their stories. Videos can be shown at major fundraising galas and at less grandiose chapter events and small fundraising meetings. They can be sent through the mail as audio-visual brochures and downloaded from Web sites. The footage shot can also be used for public service announcements, B-roll footage, and video news releases on broadcast, cable, and satellite television. With the advent of digital technology, videos are being phased out by DVDs, which are a superior vehicle for conveying images and sound. But the basic purpose remains the same—to tell a story with impact.

Determining Objectives

Before starting to produce a video—and for the purposes of this chapter, the word *video* will stand for DVD as well—you need to be clear about the purpose. Why are you making the video? How does it fit into your overall public relations campaign? How does it fit into your fundraising campaign? Who is going to see it? How are you going to show it? What do you want people to do after they've seen it? In what other ways can the video be used? What related materials will be used in conjunction with the video?

Such decisions are rarely made by the public relations practitioner alone, nor should they be. Fundraisers and other people "in the trenches" who will be using the video should be consulted in the early stages. Their input can be invaluable.

The Production Process

Video production, like filmmaking, takes place in three stages. Everything that goes into preparing the way for the shooting is called *pre-production*. The actual shooting is called the *production* stage. Once the shooting is done, *post-production* starts; here the footage is edited, and music, titles, voiceovers, and special effects are added.

Preproduction

The moment producing a video is first discussed as a serious option, the pre-production stage has begun. Everything from that point on, until the actual shooting starts, can be considered part of that process.

An important early choice concerns format. To be effective, videos need to be shot professionally. The professional format has been and, for many production companies, continues to be Beta SP, which is a broadcast-quality analog videotape. The advent of digital technology has resulted in the increasing use of digital video, or DV, which comes in a variety of formats, including the high-end Digital Beta, the less costly DVCam and DVC Pro, and a format of somewhat lesser quality, MiniDV.

According to Doug Katz, president of Blue Plate Productions (www. blueplateproductions.com), a New York–based video production company that produces promotional videos for the National Basketball Association, the Leukemia and Lymphoma Society, and CancerEducation.com, "Most people can't tell the difference between video shot on Beta SP and video shot in one of the professional digital formats. And no matter how the footage is shot, everything, including analog Beta SP tape, is edited digitally, so there is no difference in cost there. With the exception of the high-end Digital Beta format, digital cameras and editing decks tend to be less expensive than Beta SP equipment. They may offer a more economical alternative for a nonprofit with a limited budget."

The Budget. Nonprofits can sometimes arrange to have the entire budget for a video funded by an advertising or PR agency or by a dedicated supporter. A credit line on the video, thanking the funder for the generosity that made the video possible, is all the recompense asked. If you can fund your video by way of pro bono work or donations, count yourself fortunate.

Whether someone else is funding the project or it is coming from the public relations budget, you will need to calculate costs very precisely. Work with a production company closely to develop a line-by-line budget for the project. Include everything, every expense, no matter how small. Total it all up, and add 10 percent as a contingency line for the things that will run over budget.

Researching the Project. In producing a video the first step is to find out everything possible about the organization that you can draw on in telling its story. Learn about its history and current projects, the people it serves, and the people who make it work. Talk to the people, including staff people and fundraisers, who will be using the finished video. Find out what images they feel will have the greatest impact on the people they are "selling" the organization to. Which projects and what aspects of those projects elicit the strongest responses? Talk to supporters and find out what they find fascinating and compelling and, most important, what sets the organization apart from the competition.

Whenever possible, you should visit the shooting locations in person. Talk to people, look around, get a feel for things. Start thinking in terms of camera angles and things that would look good on camera.

Read up on the subject, browsing the organization's own literature as well as books and magazine articles about the area the organization works in. The Internet is an invaluable source of information. The better acquainted you are with the issues the organization deals with, the more you will be able to appreciate the things you see and hear.

Developing the Concept. Television is a visual medium. The audio is there to enhance and augment the pictures. If you doubt that, try turning off the sound on your television set and watching a few commercials. You may be surprised at how much you understand with the sound off.

Your organization needs to tell its story in pictures. Think in simple, clear, powerful images. Look for images that you can put on the screen to move and motivate a viewer.

When I produced a video for the League Treatment Center (www.leaguetreatment. org), a Brooklyn facility that works with children and adults with mental retardation and autism, I spoke to teachers, social workers, administrators, doctors, nurses, psychologists, and residence workers. I watched the children with mental retardation playing, and the children with autism closed up in their own worlds. I visited each adult residence and spoke with the adults with mental retardation, who always greeted me—and everyone else they met—with big, warm smiles.

A number of powerful images stayed with me: men at a residence, grinning and leaning on their rakes as they proudly showed off the little vegetable garden they had created in their backyard; choir members loudly singing together, off key, but with faces filled with joy; third graders giggling as they learned to use sign language to enhance their communication skills. I made notes about each of the images and put a star next to those I felt were the most powerful. But one image stayed with me more than the rest. A six-year-old girl named Cara was in the indoor playground, being encouraged by her teacher to go down a small slide. Cara paused at the top of the slide, fear etched on her features, afraid to risk it. Finally she closed her eyes and took a deep breath, and she was on her way, sliding down the slide and scattering the big colored cushions at its base, laughing with delight as the cushions bounced around the room. That was the image that stayed with me: Cara's face as it went from scared to beaming. She was cute, the teacher's smile was warm, and the slide and the cushions were bright and colorful. It would all make for wonderful visuals. I put that image on my list and gave it *two* stars.

The concept of the video evolved into a guided tour conducted by the actor Eli Wallach. We would begin with a medium close-up of Wallach, who really was a long-time supporter of the League Treatment Center, introducing himself on camera and inviting the audience to join him on a personal tour. As Wallach shared his very real pride in the place and its services to disadvantaged children and adults in Brooklyn, he would encourage viewers to join him in supporting its wonderful work. With that framework in place, we would show off each of the half-dozen facilities and the various programs.

Writing the Script. Surprisingly, when you bring a camera crew on site, people tend to just go about their business as if the crew weren't there. Despite the presence of a camera operator, a sound man, and a director all moving around the room with their equipment, despite the occasional request that something be repeated for a different camera angle or to get better audio, people will almost always just ignore the camera and go on about their daily lives—allowing you to shoot some great natural scenes.

We captured scenes of people in classrooms, workshops, therapy sessions, on the playground, in the garden, at the doctor's office, and in staff meetings, and in every case, after a few seconds, everyone was comfortably ignoring the camera. Perhaps that explains why reality TV shows work; in any case, it is something to keep in mind when writing a script and preparing to shoot on location.

The Storyboard. Once you have the concept for the video, it is time to start developing the script. You may be able to write the script yourself, and that can mean a welcome cost savings. If that isn't a possibility, you can connect with a video production house and ask for a referral to a good video scriptwriter. Ask to see samples of her work, to get an idea of how well she has handled similar projects in the past.

If you decide to try writing the script yourself, the best way to start is by doodling pictures. You can use a storyboard—a big pre-printed sheet a yard long, with little cartoon boxes spaced out on the page—or you can just scribble on any piece of paper.

Using stick figures, create a series of simple drawings that tell the story. For the League Treatment Center video, I just drew some cartoonlike boxes on a sheet of paper and started filling them in with simple stick-figure drawings. My first was a stick figure of a little man with a very big head looking directly out of the box. This was my "artist's rendering" of Eli Wallach introducing the video. Luckily, he never saw it.

I soon filled other boxes with a stick-figure Cara sliding into the cushions with a big grin that stuck out of the box altogether, a stick figure Boy Scout standing next to an American flag, several stick figure gardeners leaning on rakes, and other images that had caught my eye, or the eye of one of the people I had spoken to in the planning stage.

After I had the pictures more or less in place, I added words—not too many words. When it comes to video scripts, less really is more. Because video is such a visual medium, the pictures matter a lot more than the words. Now that I had a rough idea of how I wanted the story to unfold, I went to the next stage and started working on a more fleshed-out version of the script.

The First Draft. There are a number of software scriptwriting programs available, and some, like Final Draft, have become industry standards. I like to start scribbling in long-hand, dividing a page of 8½-by-11-inch paper down its length and writing the word *Video* at the top left and *Audio* at the top right. I leave a narrow column in the center headed *Instructions,* which is generally used for instructions for the camera or the later edit. It's a very low-tech and easy thing to do.

Always remembering that video is a visual medium, you make your first entry under the *Video* column, indicating what the audience will see (for example, Eli Wallach standing in front of the main League Treatment Center building in Brooklyn).

Next to it, in the Instructions column, you note the kind of shot you have in mind, such as "medium close-up." You may want to leave decisions on camera instructions for later. In the right-hand *Audio* column, you write what the audience will hear (in this example, "Hello, I'm Eli Wallach, and I'd like to tell you about something remarkable in Brooklyn—the League Treatment Center").

You continue in that vein, sometimes deciding on the video first and then the audio that will accompany the image and sometimes working the other way around. But always have at least a general idea of what members of the audience are going to see as they hear the words.

Start at the beginning, and work your way through to the end. Indicate where you will use what shots of which operations, where you will insert photos, and where you will put interviews. Use the Instructions column to indicate where you want to use any special effects.

It is a lot like assembling a jigsaw puzzle, first one piece and then another. Don't be afraid to shift the pieces around. Try different ways until the elements fall into place. Don't worry too much about getting everything absolutely right. You're going to keep changing the script and moving things around. Leave it alone for a while—a day or two if you can, a lunchtime break at the very least—and go back to tinkering with it.

When you have the script pretty much the way you want it, stop. Type it up on a word processor, and you have a first draft of the script.

Having written the first draft of my script, I met with heads of the League Treatment Center to review it. Each staff member had her own suggestions for

Photos, Documents, and Interviews

The preproduction stage is the time to gather archival photos, documents, and film footage that you may want to use in your video project. If you are going to incorporate historical elements into the video, you may want to contact a historical society to arrange for appropriate photos. There is usually a fee, but the dramatic impact of a good historical photo can be well worth the expense.

When I produced a video about a man who was being honored by the Anti-Defamation League, I wanted to include photos of his Brooklyn neighborhood as it had looked when he was growing up there in the 1930s. I contacted the Brooklyn Historical Society, explained what I was looking for, and soon received faxes of about twenty 8-by-10-inch photos from that era. I chose a half-dozen of the best photos and worked specific references to them into my script. I ordered the photos I wanted and was told to expect them in a couple of weeks.

One particularly great photo was of a Coney Island beach scene, complete with people wearing old-fashioned bathing suits. Because the honoree, as a boy, had helped support his family by selling frozen candy bars on the beach, the photo was perfect. When the video was shown at the Pierre Hotel in Manhattan and that scene came on the screen, the room erupted in laughter, right on cue.

A word of caution: when you order photos and other materials from museums and historical societies, be sure to follow up. The person I ordered the photos from went off on vacation without sending them or assigning the task to anyone else. With time in the editing suite already scheduled and the screening date for the video fast approaching, her forgetfulness caused me some anxious moments. She returned from vacation in the nick of time, and I had the photos I needed to properly tell the story. After that, I learned to always place my orders for archival materials as early as possible, to allow for possible glitches.

If you plan to include on-camera interviews, you need to arrange them with the interview subjects and work in the logistics of getting a camera crew to their locations. You can also opt to interview some people by telephone or via audio recordings. If you do, you'll want a photo of the person to show on the screen while her voice is heard.

Arranging all these elements takes time, so it is a good idea to start dealing with them as early in the process as possible, usually after the first draft of the script has been approved.

additions, subtractions, and general tweaking. By the end of the meeting, I had enough notes to begin work on the second draft.

The Second Draft. With the second draft it's time to get more precise. Up to now you've kept things loose to let ideas move around and come together. Now it's time to nail them in place. Incorporate the suggestions that came out of the meeting, fine-tune the wording, and finalize the actual narration.

When it comes to the script for a narration that will be read as a voice-over to the video it is best to use short, simple, easy-to-pronounce words. And to assemble them in short, easy-to-read-into-a-microphone sentences.

Because of the nature of the League Treatment Center's work, there were certain words and terminology that had to be included. Wallach was the consummate pro. When it came time to read the voice-over, he smoothly handled even the most multi-syllabic words without breaking a sweat.

Once the second draft has been approved it's time to prepare the shooting script.

The Shooting Script. The script you've written outlines the order in which the scenes will eventually be seen and heard by the audience. The shooting script lays out the order in which the scenes will be shot by the camera crew. They are not necessarily the same thing. Exhibit 14.1 shows a sample page from the shooting script used in the ORT video described in Chapter Three.

In the League Treatment Center script, the first scene was set at the main building in Brooklyn Heights, just across the Brooklyn Bridge from Manhattan. Other scenes were shot at various locations throughout Brooklyn. The last scene in the finished video was also set at the Brooklyn Heights center. It would have made no sense to set up and shoot at that location on day one and then come back to do a separate shoot at the same place on day two or three. Once we were there, we shot all the scenes set at that location. The scenes were later put into the proper sequence, during the editing (or postproduction) phase. Most films and TV shows are shot out of sequence in the same way. The order of the scenes to be shot is worked out in the shooting script.

Shooting scripts bear out the adage "the devil is in the details" because there are so many details to take into account, and it is so easy to mess them up. The trick is to mentally walk through every aspect of the shoot and try to thoroughly imagine every step in advance. Once you have the shooting script down, you may want to adjust your original script to cut something out that now appears to be too difficult or time-consuming to shoot, or you may want to add something that occurred to you as you went over the detailed shooting script.

EXHIBIT 14.1. SAMPLE PAGE FROM A VIDEO SCRIPT.

Production: "The Highest Level"   Page 1 of 32

Video	Instructions	Audio
Fade in from black		Music up
Elliott Gould standing in classroom among many students working at computers.	Establishing shot: Int. L.A. ORT	Music fades
Gould smiles at camera	Medium shot	Hello. My name is Elliott Gould, and I'd like to tell you about ORT.
Gould moves down line of students.	Medium shot	
Stops at last student in line; they exchange smiles.	Medium shot	Here at the Los Angeles ORT Technical Institute, and at ORT schools in 50 countries around the world, students learn skills that open doors to the future.
Gould puts hand on computer.	Zoom in to CU	
Gould looks into camera.	Dissolve to B-roll	Let me show you.
Morning. H.S. student with backpack walking on city street.	Dissolve to ext. school	Music up. The day starts early for students at ORT.
Greets other students at school entrance.	Dissolve to int. school	There's a lot to learn.
Walking in corridor, greets teacher; exchange smiles.		Committed teachers are ready to help.
Students in classroom.	Dissolve to classroom	The work is hard.
Teacher writing on board.	Medium shot	(Teacher explaining the material.)
Students focused on board.	CUs of students	It takes a lot of work.

Source: Page 1 of video script "The Highest Level" reprinted courtesy of American ORT.

Ask someone—preferably a detail-oriented someone with experience in the field—to review the shooting script, looking for details you may have missed. Definitely share it with the camera crew in advance, to make sure that what you have scheduled is doable.

You can save yourself a lot of trouble if you plan things out thoroughly. Of course, there is always Murphy's Law to contend with, but thorough planning does at least give you a fighting chance.

Surveying the Site and Hiring the Crew. I had already done a site survey—something that is often done together with someone from the production company—when I visited various League Treatment Center facilities throughout Brooklyn. I had an idea of what images I wanted to capture at each facility, and where I thought the camera should be positioned to get the shots. I had a sense of the lighting and sound possibilities, the power sources, the ambient noise, access to the buildings, and how much time would be needed to set up each shot. The setup, even for a simple shot, can be very time-consuming. It is always important to check with the location in advance, to be sure you have permission for the camera crew to come on site. You don't want a store manager or warehouse foreman barring the crew's way because no one passed on word that they were coming. Be sure to be at the shoot to handle details and deal with any problems.

I had also hired a video crew. I was already familiar with several video production houses. Video production houses can be found online or in the yellow pages. You can also ask people who have worked with camera crews for recommendations. Ask for demo reels. Find out how much experience a video production house has had with the kind of job you have in mind.

Make sure the camera crew includes, at the minimum, a camera operator, an audio technician, and a gaffer to handle the lighting and other details. If you don't have experience directing, hire a director. There must be someone on site running the show. Costs vary, but a competent production crew with equipment can be hired at rates of from $1,500 to $5,000 a day.

You'll want to make a list of the names and direct phone numbers of all the people you will need to connect with during the shoot. You will also need the names of people to call when things that you thought were all worked out suddenly turn out not to have been.

Consider food and transportation needs for everyone involved in the production, and work out all schedules in detail, leaving extra time to accommodate things that may end up taking longer than expected. And remember, things *always* take longer than expected.

Production

The day before the shoot, call everybody involved. Even if everyone has already sworn to you that all the arrangements have been made and double-checked, call anyway. Tell people you're just touching base and looking forward to seeing them the next day.

It never hurts, and one detail caught and corrected in advance can save a lot of grief the next day.

On the day of the shoot, bring bagels, sandwiches, muffins, and plenty of water for the crew. Maybe it isn't your responsibility, but your thoughtfulness will be appreciated, and a happy, well-fed crew is a more efficient crew. The setups will go faster, and the shots will be better.

As the producer and director of the shoot, your job is not to worry about the equipment. Your job is to worry about the people. You need to be a "people mover." You are the one who makes sure people are where they need to be when they need to be there. It is your job to see that the people who will be interviewed are comfortable and at ease. You are a facilitator.

With all that is going on, it is easy to lose focus. Come to the shoot with detailed notes about what you want to walk away with at the end of the day. That includes what you are looking for in the interviews.

Often during the preproduction site survey you will speak to someone who says something about the organization that is just wonderful. It may be a certain phrase or a way of describing things or an anecdote that perfectly captures the message you are trying to convey. You will have noted, with great forethought, what she said so that you don't forget that great quote or anecdote. When you return to interview her on camera, if she doesn't happen to say it again, be sure to gently remind her, and get her to say it again on camera.

Some of the most memorable statements, the things that make for the most powerful sound bites when recycled in TV ads and PSAs, are there thanks to some diligent prompting by the interviewer. Always remember that the purpose of the on-tape interview is to capture people saying things that will help you convey your message.

Work with the camera crew to follow your shooting script. But be flexible and open to possibilities. If you or one of the crew should spot something that grabs your attention, don't hesitate to use it, even if is not in your script. It may be just the thing you need to drive your message home. And if it's not, you can always cut it in postproduction.

Keep a log of the shots, noting which went well, which can be scrapped, and so on. That log will help when it's time to find the scenes you want to include in the final edit.

When you are shooting footage for the video, it is a good idea to try to shoot some extra footage for PSAs and B-rolls. You have the camera crew there; it makes sense to maximize the crew's time and make full use of all that equipment. Seize the opportunity to obtain some extra footage that can be put to other uses.

Ask the production company for a talent release form. You can also find sample forms in books on video production. Typically a simple, one-page document, it grants to the organization that has commissioned the video the "absolute right and permission to use" the subject's image. Be sure to bring along plenty of copies of this form to the shoot and get them signed by anyone who appears in the video. Parents can sign releases for minor children. During shooting of the League Treatment Center video, several parents asked that their children's faces not appear on camera. To accommodate them, we simply shot those kids from the back, keeping their identities anonymous but making use of their physical presence on the playground.

Postproduction

When the shooting is done, you're ready for postproduction: editing and revisions.

Editing. Editing suites charge by the hour. You can sometimes get a better rate as a nonprofit, and you can usually get a cheaper hourly rate if you are prepared to edit in the off hours, especially after midnight. If budgets are really tight, you can find low-end studios or arrange with someone just starting out to do the editing for a nominal fee in return for being able to use the finished product on a demo reel.

However you decide to proceed, the less time you need to spend in the editing suite, the less money you will spend. The key to saving time, energy, and money on the editing process is to create what is called a *paper edit* or *edit list,* a shot-by-shot list of how the final video is to be assembled.

During the production phase, you will have shot much more footage than you can use for the final video. There will be several takes of the same scene, scenes shot from different angles, and interviews that got flubbed and had to be reshot. Even with a carefully kept log of the shoot, you are going to have to shuttle back and forth through the footage to find the best scenes and decide which parts of those scenes you want to use in the video. If you do that preliminary scanning in the editing suite, where the meter is running, your costs will quickly mount. It is better and considerably cheaper to have a VHS copy made of all the footage, which can be watched in your office or at home on a standard VCR-TV arrangement.

For a nominal fee, the production company can prepare *window dubs,* which are VHS copies of the footage with a visible counter—something like a taxi meter running along the bottom of each frame. The counter tracks each frame, and there are thirty frames per second, so you can identify fairly precisely the starting and ending points of each scene that you want to use. Alternatively, you can keep track on the VCR's built-in counter, but window dubs make it much easier. Someone is going to be spending a lot of time scanning the videos, and that extra visibility will save a lot of eyestrain and fatigue. When you have viewed all the footage that was shot, and when you have compiled your inventory of favorite shots, you number them in the sequence you want them to be assembled. The result is an edit list, or paper edit.

In the editing suite, you instruct the editor on the order in which to assemble the scenes. You can also e-mail the edit list and let the editor do it without your being there.

But editing is a work-in-progress kind of process, and if you are there when the shots are being assembled, you will often get an idea for a new combination that you hadn't considered before.

After all the footage and stills and interviews are in place, you add the titles, the music, the narration, and any special effects, such as wipes and dissolves. What you have now is not the final video. What you have created is the *rough cut*.

Revisions. It is the rough cut that you show to committees for their review. You should explain that it is a rough cut; it's preliminary, and not polished. Invite comments and suggestions. Take careful notes. Confer with the decision makers about which changes to make, what things to move, and what things to leave as they are. Then go back into the editing suite and fine-tune the video.

Use your judgment either to proceed to making the final version or to make a revised rough cut for another review and critique. Obviously, the process eventually has to be finalized, and usually a second rough cut is enough to get the final approval, pending a little tweaking. But not always. If you don't establish a limit on how many times you will revise the video, you will literally never finish it.

Eventually, the video is approved by everyone who has to approve it, the finishing touches are made, and it is ready for its premiere. When the final version of the video is completed, it is copied onto Beta SP or the best available digital format. That tape is known as the *edit master*. The edit master should never travel. It should remain securely tucked away in the production studio or in the organization's offices. A second edit master can be made and used to make copies for screening at large functions. VHS copies should be made for distribution and showing in smaller, more intimate settings.

The Premiere

Often the world premiere of a new video will be at a gala fundraising dinner in a hotel or conference center. The video will be projected onto a large screen at the front of the room, or, if attendance is very large, onto two large screens, one at each end of the room. In an even larger room, more screens are added. (A simple device called a *splitter*, because it splits the signal, sends the video image and sound from the videotape deck to several screens simultaneously, with no noticeable loss of quality in either the image or the sound.)

Because the images are projected so large and the sound has to be of professional quality, it is usually best to use a Beta SP tape or a good digital format for showing the video, which means arranging for a Beta SP or digital deck. Prior to the event, make sure to check the quality of the playback. If the image is out of focus or the colors cannot be correctly balanced, insist on a replacement deck. You should always bring along a VHS copy of the tape, so if all else fails, you can use it as a backup and play it on a VHS deck. The VHS tape won't provide comparable image and sound, but it is better to show the video and introduce it with a mild disclaimer about technical difficulties than not to be able to show it all.

After the Premiere

The video on the large screen has just conveyed its message to a large and probably very important audience. It helped prime the pump for a fundraising campaign or to motivate supporters and get them rallied to the cause. Now it's time to consider other purposes and other audiences.

The video can be duplicated onto VHS tapes and sent out to chapters nationwide for use at monthly chapter meetings. DVD looks better, but not everyone has a DVD player, and VCRs are fairly ubiquitous. The video can also be included in the information packages sent to major supporters, current and potential, and it can be used for solicitation purposes in one-to-one meetings as well as meetings with small groups. As a tool for speakers making presentations to civic and governmental groups, a well-produced video can be an invaluable asset.

Videos are also a great way to tell the organization's story with impact at conferences and expositions. Copy the latest video, as well as recent TV interviews with organizational leaders and older videos and footage from programs about current programs and projects, onto a two-hour VHS tape for continuous showing. Place the VCR and the TV monitor, or a single compact unit that combines them both, on the information table along with brochures and informational material. As people browse and chat with organizational representatives, their eyes will be caught by the images on the screen, which offer an added way to get the message across. The two-hour video can be made at a production studio, or you can do it yourself by simply copying the various elements onto a standard VHS tape, using two VCRs and a couple of inexpensive cables available anywhere video supplies are sold. When the two-hour tape is finished, it will automatically rewind, and it remains only for someone at the information table to remember to press the "play" button to start the next two-hour cycle.

Although not everyone has a DVD player, videotapes are steadily being replaced by DVDs, which, in addition to providing superior video and audio quality, offer the added benefit of being much lighter and consequently cheaper to mail. DVDs can also be played on many computers, which makes them ideal for screening in an office environment.

If the audience you are dealing with is computer-savvy, the DVD format is definitely worth considering. Any full-service production house can produce a DVD.

Especially when you are dealing with a younger, more technically proficient audience, a DVD can be a welcome vehicle for conveying your message. A DVD can also be set to automatically repeat the program indefinitely, which makes it an ideal medium for showing at expos and conferences.

"This Is Your Life": The Honoree Video

One type of video that is relatively simple and inexpensive to produce and that can at the same time do a great job of selling the organization is the biographical tribute, or the "This Is Your Life" video. Usually made to highlight the accomplishments of an honoree, the video is designed to be shown at a tribute dinner in her honor.

Some organizations produce a tribute video for an honoree every year, and the video becomes one of the perks of being so honored. Extra VHS copies are made and given to the honoree for presentation to friends and family members. Sometimes the footage is recycled in later tribute videos also made about the honoree, perhaps by her company, her professional association, or a community group.

Producing a biographical video is not complicated. Writing the script can be a matter of recording an interview with the honoree about her life and then editing it down to capture the highlights. The point of the video is to make a link between the honoree and the organization's programs and needs.

Many honorees don't really know much about the organizations that are honoring them, and they may need some prompting. Rather than having an honoree read from a prepared script, which can sound stiff and forced, guide her with questions that allow her to state in her own words what aspect of the organization and its projects especially appeals to her. You don't need much. The entire video should run no more than four or five minutes.

An easy way to record the interview is to bring the camera crew to the home or work location of the honoree. Find a room where the phones can be turned off and where interruptions can be nipped in the bud, and shoot the interview on video. Have the cameraman vary the shots during the interview from close-up to tight close-up, with one long establishing shot to set the scene.

Later, in the studio, you can edit the footage down to the required length. What you will have now is several minutes of the honoree speaking as she looks into the camera— a talking head—and that can be very boring. Worse yet, because you have cut from close-ups to tight close-ups as you arrange the interview segments, you also have what are called *jump cuts*, where the speaker's face jumps from one size to the other and back again. You cover those jump cuts, and a lot of the rest of the talking head, with photos, film and video footage, and other materials that help tell the story.

When you begin preproduction of the video, ask the honoree for photos of her early life as well as diplomas, certificates, awards, citizenship papers, and anything else you can use to illustrate her life story. To catch the flavor of her younger years, especially if she doesn't have many photos, you can contact the archival collections of neighborhood historical societies and museums. For a fee and a credit line at the end of the video, you can get some great photos.

Choose which audio portions you will use on the basis of the visual images that you will be able to project to go with the audio portion. Again, the emphasis in video is on pictures. Concentrate on putting good images up on the screen, and find the audio portions that go with them. Similarly, if the honoree tells a great story, find photos that illustrate the words. What you are producing is called a "video," not an "audio." Without pictures, long stretches of words are boring.

Keep in mind that you are not producing a searing exposé. You are producing a warm and touching tribute to a person whom everyone in the room has gathered to honor. With some nice effects and the right music, you can create a very positive atmosphere in the room.

Honoree videos can provide added benefits for the organization's fundraising effort. Gary Perl, senior field director at American ORT, likes to use an appearance in an honoree video as an added incentive to major donors. Contributors who increase their gifts to the campaign by a designated amount are invited to appear in the video paying tribute to the agency's mission and to the honoree.

"Not everyone wants to be in the video," Perl says, "but many people do, especially since they often have business relationships with the honoree. They like the idea that in the years to come, every time the honoree watches the video, they're going to be on the tape, saying nice things and reminding the honoree of their relationship."

CHAPTER FIFTEEN

USING THE INTERNET

Every nonprofit organization should have a Web site. Today not having a Web site is like not having a telephone number. No one is going to take seriously any organization that does not have one.

A Web site offers immediate benefits for nonprofits, according to Aaron Janowski, president of Wellsley Corporation (www.wellsley.com), who has designed Web sites for nonprofit organizations like the the Jewelers Security Alliance and the arts group Jazz at Noon. "Perhaps the most important benefit is the ability to maintain ongoing, interactive communication with supporters."

It can cost thousands of dollars to have a Web site designed professionally. At the other end of the spectrum, a serviceable Web site can be created for a few hundred dollars with the templates in a simple program like Microsoft FrontPage. Whatever route you choose, it is essential for an organization to have an online presence. Once it has been established, the Web site address should appear on all printed materials: business cards, stationery, newsletters, brochures, invitations, souvenir giveaways—everything.

The site should be visually compelling and easy to navigate. It must also download quickly, within eight seconds, or you risk losing your audience. If your Web site is slow to download or difficult to use, people may choose to go somewhere else.

To counter that, Web sites are designed to maximize "stickiness." The term *stickiness* refers to the length of time a person stays on your site. The longer someone sticks around, the more time you have to capture his interest and influence his thinking. Obviously, stickiness is a good thing.

Your Web site must be easily findable as well. Search engines, whose "crawlers" and "spiders" scour the Web for indexable text, must be able to find your site readily, advises Ilise Benun, president of a marketing company called The Art of Self Promotion (www.artofselfpromotion.com) and author of the book *Designing Websites for Every Audience.*

"Sometimes Web site designers are so intent on designing a Web site that is creative and visually appealing," says Benun, "that they will render the text as a graphic which is unsearchable by users, who may want to search a page for a particular word or topic, and unindexable by search engines that control where you come up in the rankings. It is a matter of sacrificing function—usability and findability—for form. It is easy to lose sight of the purpose of the site, which is having the ability to communicate with your target market."

For nonprofits, the ability to communicate is essential. In addition to connecting with current supporters, a Web site can be key to reaching out to potential supporters. The Web site should have an easy-to-complete registration form that captures the e-mail addresses of visitors to the site and asks for permission to add their names to a newsletter distribution list. A visitor to the Web site completes the form, grants permission, hits the "Submit" button, and automatically begins receiving the newsletter.

Indispensable Elements of a Web Site

Certain elements should be on every nonprofit organization's Web site:

- Information about the organization's history
- The organization's mission statement
- Biographies of officers and key staff members
- Information on funding sources and current projects
- Policy statements
- Reports on the organization's activities and achievements
- Frequently asked questions ("FAQs") about the organization, along with their answers
- An archive of news stories that have appeared about the organization
- The current issue of the organization's newsletter and archived issues of previous newsletters
- The organization's current annual report
- An online brochure

- An outline of planned giving opportunities for supporters
- A regularly updated calendar of upcoming events sponsored by or related to the organization

Audio clips and video clips that can be viewed via streaming video are additional strong components of a Web site. They can include virtual tours of organizational projects, enabling visitors to see and hear the organization in action.

Make it easy for people to contact the organization by including the address, the main phone number, the fax number, and the main e-mail address on every page of the Web site. The Web site can also provide an opportunity to capture visitors' e-mail addresses. By offering visitors the opportunity to sign up for free content (for example, to receive weekly updates), you can add their contact information to your database. A survey page can also be provided, where visitors to the Web site are asked for more detailed information.

Nonprofits should look for ways to use their Web site that are particularly suited to the nature of the organization. The Public Theater in New York, for example, posts critical reaction to their plays. Although complete reviews of their plays cannot be put on the Web site due to copyright limitations, the theater company does regularly post excerpts, also called *pull quotes*, from reviews that have appeared in the press.

Chat Rooms and Bulletin Boards

Once you have a Web site, you can set up a chat room, where people interested in the field in which the organization operates can share their thoughts and feelings and latest news of interest to like-minded folk. By becoming a kind of virtual community center, you can raise the presence and visibility of your organization in the public eye.

A virtual bulletin board, or message board, works in much the same way. People post messages and react to them as they would to an actual physical bulletin board. But, again, because it is based on your Web site, the virtual bulletin board helps to establish your organization as a source and a hub for information in that area of concern.

The Virtual Press Room

No organization should be without a "Press Room" link from its home page. Journalists have learned to go to an organization's Web site as the first stop in their search for information.

As described in Chapter Six, it is becoming increasingly the norm to contact journalists with a simple press release or a minimal press kit consisting of a folder with just a single news release and a photo and then direct them to visit the organization's Web site for more information by including the Web site address.

Everything that might go into a traditional press kit (see Chapter Six) can be downloaded from the Virtual Press Room: half a dozen of the most recent news releases, bios of major leaders, fact sheets, organizational backgrounders, a calendar of events, brochures, testimonial letters, photos of people and projects, logos and other graphics, and speeches by leaders. You can also scan and post, after getting permission, articles that have appeared about your organization in newspapers, magazines, journals, and newsletters of other organizations. Again, streaming audio and video can and should also be featured.

An noted in Chapter Six, it is becoming common practice for organizations to send journalists electronic press kits (EPKs) via e-mail and to post them on their Web sites. An EPK features the same elements as a more traditional press kit, in downloadable form.

Webinars

Another way the Internet can be used to rally support for projects and programs and generate news is for the organization to host online seminars, sometimes called *Webinars* (contact www.webex.com). Webinars combine the Internet, the telephone, and e-mail to deliver data, voice, and video via real-time chats in a virtual seminar environment.

Online Newsletters

An online newsletter, also called an *electronic newsletter, Web newsletter, e-newsletter,* or *e-zine,* serves the same purposes as the old-fashioned printed newsletter (see Chapter Eight) but has the advantage of saving on both printing costs and postage. It also has the virtue of providing up-to-date content. By the time a traditional newsletter is printed and mailed and reaches the subscriber's mailbox, some of the information may no longer be timely. A printed newsletter also lacks the instant feedback capability that is routinely provided with an e-newsletter by the inclusion of a "Contact Us" button. The instant feedback option simply cannot be matched by the slower pace of mailed-in letters to the newsletter editor. That interactivity makes e-newsletters a wonderful vehicle for maintaining ongoing communication with organization supporters.

For all their virtues, however, e-newsletters may not work with older audiences. "In my experience, many contributors still prefer to respond to traditional mailings and newsletters," says Gary Perl, senior field director for American ORT. Perl works with industry-based ORT chapters in the fields of real estate, jewelry, engineering, banking and finance, and construction.

Perl tries to serve both audiences. He prints hard-copy newsletters for those who prefer them and also creates online versions for members and supporters who are comfortable with the Internet.

Like e-mail releases, e-newsletters can be created in simple, plain-text format or in the more elaborate HTML environment. Either way, the newsletter can be e-mailed directly to members and supporters. Alternatively, it can be posted on the organization's Web site, and an e-mail alert can be sent out, inviting supporters to read the new issue online. The message should be brief and should include a direct link to the Web site and to the specific newsletter site so that visitors can navigate to it with a single click of the mouse. There should also be a page on the Web site where visitors can view the latest issue of the newsletter and sign up to receive it.

An e-mail newsletter may just be a simple one-pager in plain text that goes out to members and supporters to keep them informed of the latest developments. More elaborate e-newsletters can be created with HTML. These can be longer, but probably not more than four pages.

With the flood of spam and unwanted e-mail bombarding people's computers, it is both good manners and legally required to include an opt-out option in notices sent to supporters—something along the lines of "If you do not wish to be notified when future issues of the newsletter are posted on our Web site, please simply reply to this e-mail with the word *Delete* in the subject line." In addition, every issue of the e-newsletter should have a similar opt-out line along with a statement like "This newsletter is being sent to you at your request. If you no longer wish to receive it, please reply to this e-mail with the word 'delete' in the subject line." Once people have subscribed to a nonprofit newsletter, however, they tend to stay subscribed—another reason why an e-newsletter can be a good way to maintain communication with supporters.

Every issue of the e-newsletter should include an embedded Internet address that the recipient can click to go directly to the organization's Web site. The standard contact information should also be prominent, including a "Contact Us" button, to make it easy for visitors to the Web site to communicate with the organization.

The ease with which an e-newsletter can be kept timely enables an organization to quickly inform supporters about new developments in a specific area of interest. That in turn makes it possible for the organization to position itself as the primary expert in the field, notes online marketing guru Ilise Benun. "Readers come to count on the organization for expertise in the field. That helps it to stand out from other organizations working in the same area."

The same rules of design and layout that work for printed newsletters hold true for e-newsletters, such as avoiding big blocks of type and allowing plenty of white space to make the newsletter easy to read. The same elements that can be included in a printed newsletter can also be included in the online version.

An example of an excellent e-newsletter is the *AMD Update* (www.amd.org), which, with twenty-five thousand subscribers around the world, describes itself as "Your one stop for information on age-related macular degeneration (AMD)." Offering news and information for people dealing with this condition, the e-newsletter provides a wealth of material, which ranges from reports on a recent annual conference of the American Academy of Ophthalmology to reviews of the *I Love Spinach* cookbook featuring recipes for spinach, which can help preserve vision. Millions of people have AMD, which is the leading cause of legal blindness and vision loss among seniors. Editor Judith Delgado notes that the e-newsletter also offers updates on clinical trials and new treatments, reminders to have regular eye examinations, and a request for donations to support its work—all typical newsletter items that might be found in a print version, but all delivered quickly, and at no cost to the organization for printing or postage.

The last line on the e-newsletter's cover page is a required notice inviting the recipient to point and click to unsubscribe if not interested in receiving further e-mailings. The recipients of the *AMD Update* apparently consider it an excellent vehicle for news and information, Delgado notes, and so the "unsubscribe" option goes largely unused.

E-Mailings

Less elaborate than a newsletter, a simple letter can also be sent via e-mail. A letter from the president of the organization, an announcement of an upcoming event, a recent article, and an online survey requesting feedback on issues of concern to the organization can all be sent to an e-mail list on a regular or occasional basis. Letters can be sent in lieu of a newsletter or in addition to it. Like an e-newsletter, the e-mail should include the organization's Internet address as a link that will take the recipient directly to the Web site. It should also include the standard contact information and instructions on how to unsubscribe from future mailings.

At Hebrew Union College–Jewish Institute of Religion, Jean Bloch Rosensaft, senior national director for public affairs and institutional planning, prints *The Chronicle*, the school's forty-page glossy magazine, twice a year. In addition, she produces a semiannual online newsletter for alumni, faculty, board members, staff, and students. For ongoing, time-sensitive communications, she does a regular "e-mail blast" to a list she has developed of stakeholders that includes students, faculty, alumni, board members, donors, supporters, and staff. Some people from the media who have signed up for the e-mail are also on her distribution list.

In her more or less daily e-mailing she includes news and information about upcoming events and also informs subscribers about faculty who have been quoted in the media and about other relevant news stories. She always includes links to the news stories in her e-mail so that subscribers can read more if they're interested.

Her regular e-letter is not a formal e-newsletter, Rosensaft points out. A newsletter would be more structured and would be a more comprehensive roundup of news items. Rather, it is a small daily bulletin, and as such it is relatively easy to manage and keep current. She believes that short, single-subject e-mails allow subscribers to get the information quickly and are read more readily than longer, compiled e-newsletters.

When, for example, Rosensaft placed a story about HUC-JIR in *The New York Times*, she announced it in her daily e-mail and included a link to the story. She also placed the story on the school's Web site, giving people another way to digitally access the information. Her e-mail blasts also direct readers to HUC-JIR's Web site for news and information about the institution.

Tracking and Disseminating Stories

The Internet and related new technology are also changing the way organizations monitor the exposure they receive in the media. At the United Service Organizations (USO), Donna St. John, director of communications, uses Insight, a Web-based media monitoring system to track, organize, and analyze all her media coverage on her computer. She can instantly see where stories about the USO have appeared in print, in broadcast media, and on the Web. The system makes it possible to evaluate and report results of the coverage and provide actual clips of the stories themselves. St. John also uses QuickView Video Monitoring Service, which provides both a summary and a clip from news stories. Both services are products of BurrellesLuce Information Services.

"The new technology saves a lot of wasted time and effort," notes St. John. "In the past, I would read the news summary, then request a transcript of the program that did a story on us. I would receive the transcript and read it, and if I liked it, then I would request the tape. We lost a lot of time and immediacy that way. Now I can see the clip right away and order it immediately."

For example, when actor Gary Sinise mentioned his support for the USO on *The Late Show with David Letterman* and *The Oprah Winfrey Show*. "The summary of electronic news media coverage included a news clip of the stories," St. John says. "I was able to place my order immediately and post them to our Web site and make them available for distribution while they were still very timely. That heightened the immediacy and the impact."

New Media

In October 2004, Alex Herrmann, global communications lead for IBM's communications sector, spoke at a United Nations conference of nongovernmental organizations, exploring ways nonprofit organizations can use new technology to communicate their messages to the media. He talked about "new media," which is, he said, "a generic term for the expanding range of electronic communications made possible by computer technology. The term is generally used to distinguish the 'new media' from the 'old media,' things such as print newspapers and magazines that are static representations of text and graphics."

Technology has dramatically changed the way people communicate with each other and with the media, Herrmann observed. If nonprofits are to communicate with the media effectively, it is essential that they know how to use the new tools available.

Herrmann noted that "some of the things usually included under the heading 'new media' are no longer all that new." Among the items he cited were Web sites, digital press rooms, electronic press kits, and e-mail used to deliver press releases and electronic newsletters.

After reviewing a mind-boggling roster of new technologies, tools, and devices, Herrmann summed up what the term *new media* means for people involved in getting the word out about their nonprofit organizations.

"The new media and technology provides great opportunities and lots of fancy new tools. But," he stressed, "the content is still more important than the channel."

It's nice to know that, old media or new media, what you have to say is more important than the communications tools used to say it. It is still essential to know how to tell a story that the media will find compelling.

CHAPTER SIXTEEN

PLANNING DINNERS
AND SPECIAL EVENTS

For most nonprofits, the need to raise money is paramount. When it comes to fundraising, dinners remain the perennial favorite. Sooner or later, every organization does a dinner.

Raising money may be the prime reason for a dinner, but it is typically not the only one. Dinners and other special events provide an opportunity for supporters to socialize with one another, to build esprit de corps and to share a sense of pride in working together for a common goal. Events also provide a good platform to acquaint supporters with the organization's latest developments and to motivate them for the next step in a campaign. Dinners and other special events afford an opportunity for publicity. They become news events, something that can be framed within the framework of *who, what, where, when, why,* and *how.*

Because dinners—sometimes called "rubber chicken events," with some justification—are so commonplace, many organizations have opted for alternatives. Favorites include events built on walking for the cause, running for the cause, and riding bicycles for the cause. Other popular activities include golfing, boating, barbecuing, reading, rowing, theatergoing, bowling, baking, and holding auctions and yard sales. Many organizations offer a range of events spread out over the course of the year. All represent prime platforms for public relations.

Typical is YAI/National Institute for People with Disabilities, which runs a wide range of events during the year, including a family dinner-dance every spring, a golf outing in May, the Central Park Challenge in June, and a black-tie gala in November.

Leslie Goldman, who manages corporate support for YAI special events, notes that these activities serve several purposes for the organization: "The events raise a lot of money for us. The Central Park Challenge alone raises $800,000 each year. They also keep us in the news. That helps us bring in the money we need to maintain a margin of excellence in our programs. The stories in the news also help us let people know about the services we offer so we can reach out to more people."

In addition to the more sophisticated marketing and public relations tools used to promote events, YAI relies on some more old-fashioned methods, such as enlisting four thousand staff members and volunteers to distribute posters and banners at locations throughout the city each spring, announcing the Central Park Challenge. The banners and posters start appearing two months before the event, hanging from lampposts and in neighborhood restaurants, delis, salons, building lobbies, and stores. All that activity creates a "buzz" that supplements the stories in the news and gives them added resonance.

Before the Event

In event planning, as in the rest of life, timing is everything. When you begin to plan an event, it is always a good idea to consult a calendar of upcoming community events so that you do not schedule your event at the same time as that of a competing organization. You do not want potential attendees to be forced to choose between two worthy causes, especially when your event may not be the one they choose. Also consider holidays, vacation schedules, and the possibility of bad weather.

In the first stages of planning for a special event, you should be very clear about the goals you want to achieve. A common goal is to generate publicity for the organization. Publicity about an event provides an opportunity to tell the public what your organization does, and why it is important.

Rick Frishman, president of Planned Television Arts, an independent division of Ruder Finn, Inc., advises nonprofits to stage events for just that purpose: "Holding an event gives the media something to say about you. The media loves talking about awards, so give an award to someone."

Another common goal is to recognize a contributor or an individual working in the field or the achievements of the organization in a challenging area. Obviously, one by-product of a recognition event is publicity. Yet another is to provide members with opportunities for networking. Cocktail parties are a familiar vehicle for achieving this goal. Any event, whatever its ostensible goal, can also provide a good platform for networking. Showcasing the organization to prospective members and, of course, providing a vehicle for fundraising are other common goals. In the initial planning stages, you should also consider who should attend the event, how much it will cost, and how much you plan to raise.

Dame Judi on Broadway

Effective public relations is often a matter of being clear about the organization's mission and then thinking creatively about how to accomplish it. That can be especially true in the area of special events.

When she worked for the British Broadcasting Corporation in New York, communications vice president Ronni Faust was put in charge of promoting the newly released BBC video of *As Time Goes By,* the comedy TV series starring Dame Judi Dench.

Faust did some out-of-the-box thinking. At lunch with the UK deputy consul general in New York not long before, he had mentioned his love for the theater.

She approached her boss with a suggestion. Dame Judi was appearing on Broadway that summer. Why not throw a gala party in her honor while she was in town and accessible? Her boss liked the idea immediately. But he told Faust that she could spend no more than $10,000. For the major party she had in mind, that budget was totally inadequate.

"What," she wondered, "can you do in New York City for that kind of money?" Having contacted Dench's agent, Faust knew there was tremendous competition for her time. Everybody wanted to entertain Dame Judi.

Faust knew she would need a hook, and a pretty serious hook at that, to get Dench to agree to the party. Faust got in touch once again with her theater-loving friend, the deputy consul general. Would the UK consul possibly be interested in cohosting a party to honor Dame Judi Dench?

The answer was an immediate and enthusiastic "Yes, indeed."

The invitation list was prepared, and invitations were extended to all the Brits on Broadway (of which there were many that summer), as well as to all the directors Dame Judi had worked with during her long career.

"Judi Dench is one of the best-liked and most highly respected actors in the UK," notes Faust, "so it was a good bet that we would have star-studded attendance—and no surprise when we did."

The presence of the many notable celebrities drew considerable coverage in the press. Perhaps even more important, from Faust's perspective, it elevated the image of the BBC in the eyes of those who received the exclusive invitation. The point of the whole exercise was to get publicity for the BBC and for the newly released BBC video starring Dame Judi Dench, and Faust's out-of-the-box thinking accomplished that goal admirably.

Making her triumph all the sweeter was the fact that she accomplished it with minimal expense. Because the consulate not only provided the location but also picked up most of the tab for the food and drink, the event put only a $4,000 dent in Faust's PR budget, spent largely on the invitations and the photographer. Faust pulled off an impressive PR coup, and she did it on a shoestring.

The PR role in holding a dinner can be readily applied to other special events as well. A detailed checklist of public relations elements should be developed, indicating the date by which each task will be completed and implemented. The tasks discussed in the following passages are typically key elements of a dinner or special event.

"Hold the Date" Card

One of the first things that will go out to the public is a "hold the date" card. Even before an honoree has been selected or the venue chosen, a simple postcard should be sent out to members and supporters, alerting them to put the chosen date on their calendars. How soon before the event should it be sent out?

"The sooner the better," advises Gary Perl, senior field director at American ORT. Each ORT chapter with which Perl works has its own annual cycle, including a succession of philanthropic events that take place every year. To be effective, Perl has to carefully consider the timing of the many events he runs.

"Send out the 'hold the date' a year, even a year and a half, before the event, if you can," Perl advises. "Getting the event onto calendars as soon as possible is important. Of course, you may not always have that much lead time, but whatever time you do have, use it."

If a specific theme, graphic, color scheme, or slogan will be featured throughout the event, this is a good time to begin using it. Work with the person who will be designing the invitation and related materials so that the look is consistent. But even if the details have not yet been finalized, it is important to let people know that the date has been set, and to ask them to reserve it. People live busy lives, and calendars fill up quickly.

Once the "hold the date" card has gone out, informing people about the event, it should be followed up, Perl says, with further reminders, in the form of letters, newsletter announcements, and e-mail alerts. Other letters should be sent to targeted groups, inviting people to join a committee, attend a preliminary planning meeting, and so on. Planning for a successful event begins early and continues up to and after it takes place.

News Release

Once the honoree has been selected, you need to get her photo and biographical information for news releases and the invitation. If the honoree doesn't have a photo, it is worth having a professional photo taken. Sloppy, amateurish materials send a very poor message, suggesting that the organization does not take itself or its mission seriously.

The goals of the news release are to stimulate interest in the upcoming event, maximize attendance, and augment the fundraising campaign. A media list should be developed for every honoree. It should include publications and electronic media that connect in some way to the honoree's profession, interests, hobbies, geography, and community affiliations. A release should be sent to all the honoree's local publications, neighborhood newspapers, and magazines. Other possibilities should be explored as well.

If, for example, the honoree is an accountant, then the release announcing that she is to be honored should be sent to all local, regional, and national trade publications dealing with the field of accounting. Ask the honoree for the names of the professional accounting organizations she belongs to. Go to their Web sites, and find the contact information for their national, regional, and chapter newsletters. Contact editors of the various association newsletters, and send them the release and the photo.

If the honoree is active in other community groups, clubs, associations, or religious organizations, send the release to those organizations as well, and to the alumni associations of every school the honoree ever attended. Highlight the appropriate aspect of the honoree's interests for each group of publications, slanting the various versions to suit the focus of that particular audience.

Confer with the honoree to find out if she has any special connection with anyone in the media who might be induced to do a feature story. If she does, pursue the lead with a phone call, a news release, a photo, and more phone calls.

When the honoree finds that being honored by your organization is considered newsworthy by so many publications, she cannot fail to be impressed. When friends and business acquaintances start calling with congratulations, your stock will rise even higher. People talk, and word gets around. If you do a good job for your honoree this year, the person you tap for the honor next year is more likely to be favorably disposed from the outset. All that publicity gives your organization visibility in areas it might not otherwise have penetrated. Doors to additional sources of support may be opened that were not previously accessed, providing potential new leads that can be developed by the fundraising staff.

Timing. The news release should be timed to appear fairly close to the event. Regional magazines may publish on a monthly or even quarterly schedule, which means a relatively long lead time for getting the release and photo to them. The story should appear in monthly publications the month before the event, which usually means getting the release to the publication the month before that.

In the case of weeklies, the story should ideally run the week of, or the week before, the event. Weekly newspapers may need a couple of weeks' lead time because the story may not make it into that week's issue and may get bumped to the following week. When Gary Perl places stories with *Real Estate Weekly*, the key trade publication of the New York real estate industry, he likes to send releases three weeks in advance of the date of the event. He follows the same rule for industries served by a range of publications that includes *National Jeweler*, *New York Construction News*, *Women's Wear Daily*, and *Engineering News*.

Dailies feature specific sections and columns covering different areas of the news. If you are targeting a section or column, know when it appears and when its deadlines are.

For radio and TV, consider arranging an interview with the honoree, especially if she is a newsworthy draw. Be sure to prep her with the basic information about your organization that you want her to convey. Talking about your organization may be only a very small part of the interview, but you want to make sure the honoree gets it right. (Preparing guests for radio and TV interviews is covered in Chapters Twelve and Thirteen.)

Two weeks before the event, fax a press release to the regional office of the Associated Press (AP). In the cover note, ask that the event be listed in the AP Daybook of upcoming events. The added benefit of sending the fax is that AP sends its Daybook information to broadcast media subscribers every morning.

Format. A streamlined format works best for a news release about a special event. Similar to a media advisory or an AFI, it lists key information in easily accessible indented-paragraph form.

The head of the release remains the same, with the organization's name and the personal contact information, the date, and FOR IMMEDIATE RELEASE appearing at the top of the page. The headline is centered immediately under that. The word WHAT appears in all caps at the left of the page, and that information is presented in a brief sentence. Then the word WHO appears on the left, followed by that information. Next come WHEN, WHY, and WHERE and the related information. The release easily fits onto one page, with all the key information readily accessible to reporters and editors. The simplicity of the format makes it easy to use for assignment editors, who may be more likely to assign someone to cover the event in person—always a plus for news coverage.

Feature Articles

Lori J. Greene, director of special events, Relay for Life, Eastern Division at the American Cancer Society, believes strongly in the ability of articles in the local press to act as what she calls "word-of-mouth PR."

"When we hand out brochures and posters," Greene says, "and hang banners on light poles to promote our annual Relay for Life event, it's great, but that's not the main thing that gets people to come to the event. What gets them to come is word of mouth, hearing about it beforehand from other people. And reading about it in human interest stories in the local press. People read those stories and see the pictures of people from the community, and it's as if someone spoke to them face to face. It makes them care and want to participate, to do something."

Greene, who heads up Relay for Life in New Jersey, advises making personal contact with reporters and editors at local publications and cultivating those relationships.

Once a journalist sees the potential for a good story, it is only a matter of providing the material she needs in order to write it. Getting several good feature stories in the *Montclair Times*, a suburban New Jersey weekly, played a big part, Greene believes, in helping the organization raise $150,000 at its annual event.

Invitation Package

Invitations to dinners and special events typically have four elements: the outside envelope, the invitation itself, the response card, and the response envelope. If the response card is a postcard that is intended to travel back to the organization on its own, which precludes enclosing a check, a response envelope may not be needed.

Design matters. An attractive, creative, professional look conveys a sense of professionalism and sophistication about your organization. The various elements of the invitation package should be coordinated and work together with the same design, graphics, and color scheme. A subliminal message conveyed by a well-designed invitation is that you are an organization that knows what it is doing, an organization that can get the job done.

Outside Envelope. People are inundated with mail. They have learned to quickly toss unwanted mail into the trash. Your first goal when preparing the outside envelope is to see that it survives the initial cut. You do not want your carefully designed and printed invitation going into the garbage unopened, unread, and unanswered.

Ideally, the name of the organization alone will be enough to catch the recipient's eye. Printed clearly in the upper left-hand corner of the envelope, in dignified black or dark blue for easy legibility, the name alone may be enough to get the recipient to put the envelope in the "important mail" pile.

Using an envelope of an unusual size is another way to catch the eye. But these can be expensive to create and costly to mail. The familiar 5¼-by-7¼-inch A-8 envelope remains a popular standard. Using a color other than white can help the envelope stand out from the crowd but runs the risk of making the invitation look to some eyes too frivolous, lacking in the seriousness and prestige conveyed by a dignified white envelope.

One technique that works well is to imprint an image on the face of the envelope. The organization's return address has to be printed on that side of the envelope anyway, so the image can be added at relatively little cost. Typical images printed on the face of the outside envelope include faces of the people the organization helps, animals it protects, or historic buildings it preserves. If the image is likely to arrest the attention of the recipient, printing it on the face of the outside envelope may be worth considering.

Invitation. When it comes to invitations, creative designers can offer a seemingly infinite number of variations on a theme, with possibilities that include four-panel, six-panel, and eight-panel designs, gatefolds, inserts, foldouts, blind embossing, and innovative uses of papers, colors, graphics, and photos. Whatever the design, it is the invitation that makes the lasting impression; the invitation is the most important part of the package. A first-class invitation suggests a first-class event. Make sure the invitation has impact and represents your organization appropriately.

The *who, what, where, when, why,* and *how* of the event should appear clearly in the invitation, as should the name and photo of the honoree (or each honoree if there are more than one), the names of the committee members, some brief background information about the organization, the reason for the specific event, and the name of the award being presented, if any. Other things that frequently appear in invitations include names of past honorees; listings of the organization's national, regional, and chapter officers and board members; directions to the event (often included as an insert); and a pledge card or solicitation vehicle inviting the recipient to make an extra contribution beyond the cost of the dinner or special event itself.

Response Card. The response card should conform to the look and design of the rest of the invitation package. At the very least, it should be white or a neutral, unobtrusive color. It is intended to be returned with the name and contact information of the person who is reserving a place at the dinner or event. If people are expected to fill in that information themselves, leave enough room on the card for them to do it legibly. Countless frustrating hours have been wasted by people trying to decipher illegibly scrawled names and addresses on response cards. You may want to affix a label with that personal information already on the response card, leaving it to the responder to simply check off the appropriate boxes.

The response card typically offers a selection of contribution choices, with a rising scale of prices ranging from one seat at the dinner to an entire table. Often a brief "thank you" message appears on the card, to remind the person as she makes her commitment that her generosity is appreciated.

Often included as part of the response card, or as a separate item, is a reservation blank for the journal that is being prepared in conjunction with the dinner or special event (see "Journals" later in this section). Requests for special dietary provisions are also a frequent element of response cards.

Many organizations code their response cards to indicate from which mailing list they took the invitee's name. This technique can be helpful for future fundraising efforts. If it is used, a simple code number or letter is unobtrusively added at the bottom of the card.

Response Envelope. The response envelope brings the response card, along with any accompanying checks, back to the organization. Favorite sizes are the 6½-by-4¾-inch A-6 and the 5¾-by-4½-inch A-2, both of which fit comfortably inside an A-8. The response envelope should also conform to the design of the entire invitation package or at least be white or a neutral, unobtrusive color. The organization's address should be clearly printed on the face of the envelope. This makes it easy for the invitation re-cipient to respond by simply dropping the card and a check into the envelope, and it avoids the problem of the envelope being misaddressed. Some organizations also affix first-class postage, to make it even easier, but most rely on recipients to find their own stamps.

Some organizations favor using a business reply envelope (BRE). The advan-tage over using stamps is that the organization pays postage only for those envelopes that are actually returned. BREs look businesslike, however, and may detract from the elegant tone being set by the invitation.

Response envelopes can also be coded, to simplify the process of keeping track of response rates from various lists. In that case, codes for departments or desks are indicated on the face of the envelope, away from the address area.

Mailing Weight. Early in the design process, have the designer prepare a mockup or "dummy" of the invitation package, using the actual paper that will be used for the final invitation, response card, and envelopes, all cut to the exact dimensions of the final package. Include any enclosures, such as additional pledge cards, journal ad reserva-tion forms, personal notes, business cards, and so on, and take the package to the post office for weighing.

A nonprofit can arrange with the post office for a special indicia, to be imprinted on envelopes, that allows the organization to take advantage of special nonprofit postal rates. But these are generally not used for invitations to dinners and special events. The invitation usually travels by first-class mail. That ensures speedy delivery, but it can be expensive, especially if you let your invitation package become overweight.

With all the elements that go into it, the package is possibly going to weigh in at just under two ounces. Be careful not to add so much to the package that it goes over the line into three ounces. Over the line by a hair is still over the line and kicks you up to the next level of postal costs. Multiplied by the large quantity of invitations you are sending out, that extra ounce can hurt, boosting the costs of your mailing and cutting into the net profits of the event. Be sure your package weighs in below the line, and by more than a hair.

Reminders to Guest Speakers and Honorees

Your event checklist should include a section with the names and contact numbers of all the main players, speakers, celebrities, and featured guests. Two weeks before the event, it is always a good idea to contact all of them to remind them of their roles. Make sure they have the details of the location, including entrances and who to look for when they arrive. Ask if they need anything to facilitate their participation. A let-ter, fax, e-mail, or phone call will all work, but however people are contacted, they should be asked to confirm that they have the latest information about their roles and the timing of their participation. If they don't confirm, you may want to make an additional connection, to double-check that they have all the information correct and that there are no previously unforeseen problems in their arriving on time. If necessary, you can always juggle schedules, but only if you have all the information.

Journals

Another fundraising tool that is commonly produced by public relations is the event journal. Prepared for distribution at dinners or special events, journals are an excellent way to maximize fundraising potential. At first glance, producing a journal may seem like a waste of time, effort, and money because journals are almost universally left behind at the event—torn, stained, and trampled underfoot. In fact, however, they can generate considerable money because they are excellent vehicles for advertising.

A journal can be printed in an 8½-by-11-inch format or smaller, saddle-stitched (with staples through the spine, like a newsmagazine), perfect-bound (with pages held in place by glue alone, like a larger magazine), or held together with a spiral binding, like a college notebook. It can be printed with a glossy or a matte finish or with any combination of the two.

Typical elements of the journal include a letter from the president, often with a photo, and pages of information about the organization's history, mission, and current projects, accompanied by appealing photos. The same information that appears in the invitation may also appear in the journal, such as listings of previous honorees and the roster of organizational officers, board members, and members of the dinner committee as well as information about the event and any awards being presented.

Letters of congratulations from a mayor, a governor, congressional representatives, and the White House, with the appropriate municipal, state, and presidential seals at the top of the page, can also be impressive additions to a journal. Such letters can generally be had for the asking; contact the appropriate press office several months in advance. Accompanying the request should be the organization's annual report, a brochure, and a recent newsletter, to demonstrate the organization's legitimacy. Printing too many such letters in a journal lessens the effect, but a few well-placed congratulations can enhance the organization's standing in the eyes of supporters.

As a related project, the original letters, as well as letters solicited from past honorees, community leaders, and notable figures, can be collected into an "appreciation album" for presentation to the honoree at the dinner—a second award to commemorate the occasion.

The letters and information pages are the editorial elements of the journal. These elements are nice to show off to the guests at the event, but the editorial component is not the reason why an organization produces a journal. The reason is the advertisements.

Early in the process leading up to the dinner, journal ad reservation forms are mailed to the entire invitation list. Like a "hold the date" card, a journal ad reservation form can be sent out as much as a year before the event.

American ORT's Gary Perl notes an important advantage to early mailings. "It's all about budgets and timing," he says. "Corporations like to be philanthropic; it's always good public relations to be perceived as giving back to the community, especially at times when the news is full of stories of corporate greed. A corporation will make contributions until its annual allocation is used up. Requests that come in after the funds have already been allocated to other charities may have to wait for the next fiscal year."

Additional mailings may take place in the months leading up to the event, and an additional ad reservation form is often included along with the invitation. The reservation form offers a range of choices. The most expensive choice is typically a full-page ad on the outside back cover or inside front or back cover. It is the most expensive choice because virtually anyone who picks up the journal will see it immediately. It is hard to beat that kind of exposure.

Next are a full "gold" page, a full "silver" page, and a full "bronze" page. Some organizations complicate matters by offering a "platinum" option as well, with platinum one step above gold in the hierarchy of value. The pages in the journal may be coated with a metallic finish or may simply be white with the appropriate colored border printed around the edges. Next up is the full white page, and then, in descending order of cost, come the half-page ad, the quarter-page ad, the ad that covers one-eighth of a page, and the ad the size of a business card.

Contributors supply the camera-ready artwork for their ads and send it to the organization or sometimes directly to the printer. They may also supply a few words, typically congratulations to the organization and the honoree, that the organization checks for errors and then passes on to the printer, to be turned into simple ads. The preparation time and effort is minimal and, depending on the rates charged for the ads, the profit to the organization can be considerable. Sometimes the printer will cover the cost of printing the journal as a donation, or a supporter will underwrite the cost, in which case all the proceeds of the journal go to the organization.

When the guests arrive at the dinner, they typically find a copy of the journal on their chairs. A kind of captive audience, they have to pick it up if they want to sit down. Some will simply drop it on the floor and forget about it. But most will actually leaf through it as they wait for the rest of the guests to take their seats and for the program to begin.

The first thing people usually look for is their own ad. Then they look to see who took the big-ticket ads on the covers and the metallic pages. A quick flip through the impressive letters at the beginning and a glance at the photos of current organizational projects, and they are probably done with the journal. Even if they take it home with them at the end of the evening, as they are always urged to do, in all likelihood they will not look at it again.

But even in the limited time they have spent scanning the pages, they have gained an impression of the organization and the people it works with. That impression becomes a building block in the public image of the organization. It is part of the ongoing public relations campaign and an element that will lay the groundwork for more messages about the organization, which will be conveyed in the future.

Printed Program

Also, very often, at every place setting at the dinner or on the reception table are printed programs listing the schedule of the event. The names of the people on the program committee responsible for the event also typically appear in the program, giving credit where credit is due. Photos and brief biographical information about the honoree, special guests, and speakers are often featured as well.

Proclamation

A great addition to almost any event is a proclamation. As much as a year prior to the event, contact the mayor's office, the city council, or the borough president's office (if you live in a city that has boroughs) and request that the day of the event be officially proclaimed the day of your organization. You will usually be asked to send a letter on organizational letterhead, and perhaps an invitation and an annual report, to establish legitimacy—all pretty routine.

Politicians love issuing such proclamations, which provide favorable visibility for them with virtually no effort. The proclamation can be reprinted in the journal and presented, nicely framed, to the honoree. It also makes for a nice mention in news stories about the event.

The Event Itself: Dos, Don'ts, Divas, and Best Practices

Public relations practitioners have varying degrees of responsibility for dinners and special events. At large nonprofits, they may concentrate on working with the media. At smaller organizations, they may be the people running an event. Familiarity with some of their responsibilities and with how to handle them can be useful in either case.

Coordinate, both in advance and during the event, with the venue where the event is being held. If possible, do a site survey in advance, to check out the space in detail. Get the names of the people you will be working with and their direct contact numbers. Be courteous, and recognize that this is their turf, but keep in mind that things have a tendency to go awry. Rely on the local professionals to know their jobs and to do them properly, but be prepared with contingency plans in case they don't.

Know where to find the light switches, the outlets, the audio hookups, the exits, and the house telephone. Know the names and numbers of the house engineer, the maitre d', the head captain, and the audiovisual people. Check out the microphones and lights in the ballroom before the dinner, to make sure they are set at the correct levels.

Decide in advance what you will do if, for example, the lights fail to dim at the appropriate moment, or if they fail to go up again. Who will you call if the audio doesn't work? What if there are problems with the air conditioning or the heating and people are complaining that the room is too hot or too cold? What if the entrée is unexpectedly delayed, and the schedule for the event is completely thrown off? (It happens: hotels run simultaneous functions, and your dinner may not be the highest priority.)

You don't have to fix everything yourself. But it's good to know you have the numbers of the people to call who can get them fixed.

Because speakers come in different sizes, the position of the microphone that is ideal for one may not work for another. When necessary, arrange for a platform to boost the height of shorter speakers. A person at a microphone often can't tell if her voice is being picked up properly by the microphone or not, so monitor the microphone during the speeches, and be prepared to come to the podium to reposition the microphone so that the speaker can be heard, and to reposition it for subsequent speakers.

In October 2004, I had the opportunity to work with Suzanne Hemming and Kay Gilman on a dinner for the Brooklyn College Foundation (www.brooklyn.cuny.edu/bc/offices/bcf). Hemming and Gilman joined forces in the 1970s to found an event-planning company. Today, Hemming + Gilman (www.hgnyc.com) is one of the nation's premiere event planners, working on everything from the celebrations after the Grammy Awards telecast to a Frank Sinatra event at the pyramids in Egypt to the four-day centennial celebration of the Statue of Liberty.

The dinner event took place at the Rainbow Room at Rockefeller Center. Titled "The Best of Brooklyn," it honored a Brooklyn College alumnus—Murray Koppelman, class of 1957—and was emceed with warmth and charm by the actor Jimmy Smits—also a Brooklyn College alumnus, class of 1980—who is involved with a number of nonprofits and cofounded the National Hispanic Foundation for the Arts (www.hispanicarts.org) in 1997 to promote Hispanic talent in the performing arts. After the event, Smits offered some advice for anyone called on to play the role of emcee.

"You have to remember that it's OK to laugh and make jokes," he said, "to put people at their ease. Most organizations are engaged in pretty serious business, and you'll get to that during the event. But people also deserve to enjoy themselves as they celebrate their accomplishments."

Planning for the event was a months-long process, and the evening's schedule went through several drafts on the way to being finalized. All the elements were listed and timed to the minute, including food service and audiovisual components. The schedule allowed for some flexibility, in acknowledgment of the fact that things don't always go exactly according to plan in the real world. But even when things are running late, it is important for all the people involved in the program to know exactly what they are supposed to do, and for everyone to be, literally, on the same page.

The evening was a great success, with each segment flowing smoothly into the next. That success was due in no small measure to the detailed plan reproduced in Exhibit 16.1.

Dos and Don'ts

In three decades of staging events for nonprofits, you learn a thing or two. Kay Gilman offers some of those hard earned lessons in this list for planning an event. The following items, according to Gilman, are *dos:*

- *Get commitment and motivation from your chairpersons and honorees.* Leadership is key. Your chairpersons and honorees are the event's stars. You need commitment and motivation from both. The chairs are the people signing your outreach letters; the honorees should give you access to their lists of friends and business associates. If they are reluctant to take an activist stance, or if they ask to be involved "in name only," say "Thank you" and move on.
- *Personalize your fundraising outreach.* The more you can personalize your fundraising outreach, the more successful your event will be. All letters should be personalized with a handwritten note, if possible; ditto for the invitation. Follow-up phone calls, particularly from those who know the target donor, are invaluable.
- *Showcase your cause—briefly.* A succinct, well-focused video highlighting your cause, or a testimonial from someone tangibly helped by the organization, can be a plus, both for the occasion itself and for ongoing postevent fundraising and awareness. But keep it short. People pay to attend fundraising events—don't make them pay twice!
- *Time everything.* The entire event should be timed down to the last millisecond, from the moment the first guests arrive for cocktails through the serving of the meal, the program and speeches, the dance sets, the distribution of gift bags, and the departure of the guests.
- *Create an upbeat ambience.* A feel-good atmosphere should reign from the minute the guests walk in and should last until the moment they leave. Accomplish this effect with flattering ambient lighting, upbeat music that drives the mood, a well-planned and delicious menu, a brief focused program or entertainment, and, again, flawless timing. Celebrity participation is a crowd pleaser as well, if you can make it happen. People should leave saying, "What a great event this was! I want to be here next year."

EXHIBIT 16.1. PLAN FOR "THE BEST OF BROOKLYN" EVENT.

A	6:30 PM	**VIP reception**	
B	7:00 PM	**General cocktail reception**	
C	7:00 PM	**WAITERS: Preset appetizer**	
D	7:45 PM	**BARS CLOSE**	
E	7:50 PM	**GUESTS MOVE TO DINING AREA:**	*Montage*
F	7:55 PM	**Voiceover:** —Ladies and gentlemen, please take your seats. (Repeat as necessary.)	*Homeslide*
#1	8:00 PM	**Voiceover:** —Intros. Emcee Jimmy Smits	*Homeslide*
#2	8:00 PM (4 min)	**Jimmy Smits:** —Welcomes Guests —Personal connection to BC —Intros. President Christoph Kimmich	*Title Slide/IMAG*
#3	8:04 PM (2 min)	**Christoph Kimmich:** —Remarks —Intros. Brooklyn College Video	*Title Slide/IMAG*
#4	8:06 PM (3 min)	**BROOKLYN COLLEGE VIDEO**	
#5	8:09 PM (1 min)	**Jimmy Smits:** —Intros. Dinner Chair Howard Wohl '64	*IMAG*
#6	8:10 PM (2 min)	**Howard Wohl:** —General remarks —Thank Board, Dinner Committee —Announces $ raised	*Title Slide/IMAG* *Ack. Slides*
#7	8:12 PM (1 min)	**Jimmy Smits:** —Segue to dinner	*IMAG*
#8	8:13 PM (30 min)	**WAITERS** **—PICK UP APPETIZER** (10 min) **—SERVE ENTREE** (10 min) **BAND PLAYS SIMULTANEOUSLY** **GUESTS DINE** (10 min) Once waiters off floor, program resumes . . .	

| **#9** | 8:43 PM | **Voiceover:** | *Homeslide* |
| | | —Welcomes back Jimmy Smits | |

| **#10** | 8:43 PM (1 min) | **Jimmy Smits:** —Intros. Roy L. Furman '60 | *IMAG* |

| **#11** | 8:44 PM (3 min) | **Roy L. Furman:** —Tribute to Murray Koppelman '57 —Intros. tribute video | *Title Slide/IMAG* |

| **#12** | 8:47 PM (7 min) | **KOPPELMAN TRIBUTE VIDEO** | |

| **#13** | 8:54 PM (1 min) | **Roy L. Furman:** —Welcomes Koppelman to stage/photo op | *Title Slide/IMAG* |

| **#14** | 8:55 PM (4 min) | **Murray Koppelman:** —Acceptance remarks | *Title Slide/IMAG* |

| **#15** | 8:59 PM (1 min) | **Jimmy Smits:** —Welcomes back President Kimmich | *IMAG* |

| **#16** | 9:00 PM (4 min) | **President Kimmich:** —Promotes BC 75th Anniversary —Promotes capital campaign —Thanks Jimmy Smits/welcome Smits back | *75th Logo* *Campaign Slides* |

| **#17** | 9:04 PM (3 min) | **Jimmy Smits:** —Endorses 75th/Capital Campaign —Remarks on volunteerism/philanthropy —Segue to dessert | |

| **#18** | 9:07 PM (30 min) | **WAITERS** **—PICK UP ENTREE** (10 min) **—SERVE DESSERT/COFFEE** (10 min) **BAND PLAYS SIMULTANEOUSLY** **GUESTS DINE** (10 min) | |

All programs vary by 10–15 minutes, based on start time and speakers' remarks

Source: Brooklyn College Foundation at the Rainbow Room, NYC, event schedule courtesy of Hemming + Gilman Productions.

Gilman's *don'ts* include the following points:

- *Avoid endless speeches.* It can't be over-emphasized: people hate long, droning speeches and award presentations that seem eternal. If you bore your audience into a stupor, you are ensuring that next year's invitation will have a place in everyone's rotary file.
- *Keep the menu simple.* Forget the sorbet intermezzo and a separate salad course. Long menus can make an evening drag on interminably. Stick to three courses, with the first course attractively preplated and on the table when the guests walk in.
- *Don't overeconomize.* Yes, the purpose of a fundraising event is to raise money for your organization, and no, you do not want the evening to project 1980s-style opulence. But don't scrimp to the point where people feel they are unwanted, uncared for, and ill fed. Budgets should be carefully monitored, but your guests should feel that someone was focused on showing them a first-class evening. And, yes, sometimes you do have to spend some money to make more—both now and in the future.
- *Don't be sloppy.* Sloppiness is anathema in any area of event planning. This is true from the first fundraising letter to all written materials (typos are death!) to every aspect of the event itself. The devil is definitely in the details when it comes to planning a first-class event.
- *Avoid glaring lights.* Ambience can't be overemphasized. Nothing kills a mood like harsh, flat lighting. Conversely, subtle ambient lighting in shades of pink or amber makes everyone look (and feel) youthful and glamorous. And proper lighting is not a killer expense.

Divas

Kay Gilman offers a personal note that may provide encouragement to anyone dealing with "difficult" personalities at a special event: "We have also dealt with the full gamut of divas—male and female. One well-known female recording artist demanded a menu of an elaborate buffet of delicacies and vintage wines in her dressing room, at great expense to our client—only to leave it totally untouched. We have endured countless client tantrums—no names, please. But virtually all of these backstage explosions and potential glitches have stayed right there—the mark of a skilled event producer is to ensure that these could-be volcanoes are confined to the back of the house and are never realized by the audience/paying guests."

That is a lesson to be learned by all harried public relations people involved in putting on a special event. Professionalism means keeping the problems "confined to the back of the house."

Best Practices

Positioning Banners, Signs, and Photos. Whatever the event, it represents an opportunity to tell the organization's story and rally support. An information table with brochures and other literature should be located in a central area, usually near the welcoming/registration table, where people can pick up information. This can be a good place to dispose of last year's annual report and past issues of newsletters. A TV/VCR should be set up as well and primed to play a continuous video composed of past videos, TV interviews with organizational leaders, and footage of current projects.

A banner with the organization's name and logo should be prominently displayed at the information table. A banner or sign with the organization's name should also be displayed on the speaker's podium. Photos taken of speakers will thus include the organization's logo rather than the name of the hotel, benefiting the organization rather than the hotel's marketing department.

The easiest way to display a banner is to put a stickpin in the wall and hang the banner from it on a cord, but most hotels frown on people putting even small holes in their walls. An alternative is to drape the banner on an easel. Hotels routinely provide half a dozen easels upon request.

The easels can also be used for displaying mounted, poster-sized photos of the organization's projects. The photos should be prominently displayed in the reception area, where people can see them. When the crowd moves into the main ballroom for dinner, the easels and photos can be brought into the ballroom and positioned along the edges of the room during the meal. If there are breakout sessions after the dinner and meetings in other rooms, consider relocating the photos again, or, better yet, switching them for new photos. A hospitality suite is also a good place to display attractive photos of the organization's projects. A good picture can be worth a thousand words in telling your story. Opportunities should be found for using pictures to tell it.

Screening a Video. Chapter Fourteen looked at producing videos for showing at a dinner or special event. Fitting the showing into the right place in the program can contribute significantly to the overall effect of both the video and the dinner.

If you show a video early in the evening, people will still be relatively awake and alert. If you wait too long, the lateness of the hour and the openness of the bar may combine to sap energy and curtail the attention span of even the most dedicated audience.

If you can avoid it at all, never screen a video after the meal. However compelling your message and urgent your cause, the fact is that many people are going to leave after the meal. Unless you have an appearance scheduled by a celebrity who everyone is dying to see, a considerable part of your audience is not likely to stick around. If you show the video after the meal, you are courting disaster. That darkened room makes it all too easy for people to duck out early—or to doze off, overcome by the effects of food and wine. When the video ends and the lights come back up, there are likely to be far fewer people in the room than there were at the beginning. And some of them may be snoring.

There is a lot to be said for showing the video before the main speaker's presentation. The fact is that not everyone in the audience actually knows, or deeply cares about, what the organization does. Some are guests of supporters, others may be filling in spaces at a table purchased by a major supporter, and still others just don't read their mail. Showing a brief video prior to the main speaker is a good way of bringing everyone in the room up to speed on what the organization does. It also gives the speaker the added option of referring to scenes in the video during her remarks. It all works together nicely.

If the video being shown is about the honoree, it can work even better. In that case, the event chairperson introduces the video about the honoree, the video is shown, and then, as the lights come back up and some people in the audience are applauding the video, the honoree comes out on stage. The applause swells as the honoree, whom the audience has just come to know from seeing the video, is warmly greeted by the chairperson. The chairperson turns to the audience and enthusiastically announces, "Ladies and gentlemen, this evening's honoree."

Those people who began to applaud at the end of the video will continue applauding and lead the rest of the audience along with them. Amidst the applause, the honoree steps to the microphone and begins to give her speech—a lovely setup for her presentation.

Presenting an Award and Taking Photos. When the honoree finishes her speech and the audience applauds, the dinner chairperson or whoever has been assigned the task should come forward to present the award. The photographer shoots the photo of the beaming chairperson handing the award to the beaming honoree. Holding the award close, the honoree says just two words—"Thank you"—and retires from the stage. The chairperson adds some brief praise and announces the next speaker, or the dinner.

You will want to get a good photo of the award being presented to the honoree, for sending to the press. Keep in mind that glass, Lucite, and polished metal all reflect light, which means that the photographer's flash is liable to produce a starburst reflection off the award that will make the photo unacceptable for publication.

As the photographer moves into position to take the photo, ask her to wait a moment as you quickly step in to remove the Lucite cover from the award. Have the photographer take several shots of the presentation, to increase the chances of getting a nonreflective, usable photo for the press.

Photos showing organizational leaders shaking hands with the honoree as they smile stiffly at the camera are often disparagingly referred to as "grip and grins." But, stiff and artificial as they may be, such photos bring together several key elements: the organization, the membership, and the honoree. Such photos may not win any awards for photographic originality, but they do the job.

Similarly, "firing squad" photos are even more harshly criticized. These feature four or five or more people, all standing stiffly in front of a banner as they stare glassy-eyed at the camera. Besides being painfully dull to look at, these have the added drawback of requiring an impossibly long caption that lists the name and title of everyone in the picture. It may seem a crime against aesthetics to run such photos, but they serve the purpose of highlighting the people that the organization should be highlighting. Many supporters of the organization will actually find such photos interesting, especially if their own faces are among those smiling out from the page.

Steve Friedman, the photographer we met in Chapter Four, may have taken more "grip and grin" and "firing squad" photos than any other living human being. Literally thousands of honorees have posed before his cameras at dinners, galas, and other special events. His photos have appeared in *The New York Times* as well as in a huge range of local and trade publications.

"The most important part of the picture is the eyes," Friedman says. "It's essential to get their eyes to respond. Often when people look at a camera, they feel self-conscious. They get that 'deer in the headlights' stare—definitely not a good look for photos. You have to keep in mind that when the picture appears in a newspaper, those people are going to be looking out of the page at the reader. If there is no energy, if their eyes have a flat, dull look, that is what the reader is going to see. I always banter with my subjects to keep them lively and engaged. Part of my job is putting energy into the people I photograph so that I get the energy back in the photo. Someone once described what I do as 'making tired people look happy for one-sixtieth of a second'. That's really not a bad description."

Friedman typically fires off a series of shots in quick succession, in case one of the subjects blinks at an inopportune moment. The whir of the rapid-fire shutter clicks, combined with Friedman's lively banter, helps to keep the energy level high—and the eyes alive.

After the Event

After the event is over, it's time to deal with the postevent publicity. If you have prepared properly, you have the names and titles of the people whose photos you have taken, and you have written the appropriate captions. You have also made a note of where the people in the photos come from, and you have identified the local press outlets in their areas. It is now a matter of matching things up.

Trade publications are in this sense "local" publications. According to Steve Friedman, when *Real Estate Weekly* runs a full-page layout of photos he has taken at a nonprofit event, with plenty of pictures of industry "familiar faces" smiling out from the page, the prestige of the organization is enhanced by association. The good feelings generated by the people in the photos can also serve as a springboard to future events and continued support.

Association magazines and newsletters will also frequently run such photos because the people in the photos are association members. Local chapters of national organizations like the photos because they demonstrate the national presence of chapter members. These photos require some effort to prepare and disseminate, but the coverage can be worth it.

The caption should be introduced by a brief headline and should include a sentence explaining where the photo was taken and the significance of the event so that the photo and caption can stand alone in the publication, without any further explanatory information.

The accompanying news release should explain everything in more detail. Usually included are the number of people who attended, the amount raised, the impact on the cause, highlights of the event, and a quote or two from prominent leaders of the organization. If the release and photo get picked up, that's terrific. If the photo alone gets picked up that's great. If only the release gets printed, that's not as good, but it's still nice. Any postevent publicity can earn the organization some much-appreciated recognition.

The releases and captioned photos can also be posted on the organization's Web site for viewing and downloading by members and supporters. They can be recycled in the organization's newsletter and sent to online newsletter editors, or to anyone else who may have an interest in the event and its participants. When it is time to compile the annual report, the photos can be a good way to showcase the organization's activities during the year.

Clipping services, such as those offered by BurellesLuce, will find and send you articles that appear about your organization. It is the best way to track how many of your stories get picked up and where they appear. Because many nonprofits find the subscription rates for clipping services out of their league, you may want to request that people in outlying chapters of the organization send you copies of stories that are picked up by the local press. When you have a collection of clippings from an impressive array of sources, you can put together an informal clip book. Photocopy the clip book—see Chapter Five for guidelines on getting permission from the publications—and circulate copies among leaders and board members, especially the public relations committee, to show off the fruits of your labors. It never hurts to let people know that the organization is getting good press, thanks to its excellent public relations.

Success Stories

City Harvest's Bid Against Hunger

October is a popular month for special events in New York. As the Brooklyn College Foundation was holding its dinner with Jimmy Smits in the Rainbow Room in midtown Manhattan, another local nonprofit, City Harvest (www.cityhrvest.org), was staging its own event two miles to the south, at the Puck Building, another New York landmark.

The nature of a special event is often dictated by the organization's focus. City Harvest works to combat hunger, and its annual Bid Against Hunger event, timed for the start of the harvest season, included food stations operated by forty of the top chefs in New York City. At the event, which was attended by six hundred people, there was also a silent auction as well as a live auction conducted by an auctioneer from Christie's.

The Hip-Hop Summit Action Network Gala

Later that same week, the Lighthouse at Chelsea Piers, approximately halfway between the Rainbow Room and the Puck Building, was the setting for an event with a different style, a gala mounted by the Russell Simmons Hip-Hop Summit Action Network (www.hsan.org). According to Jody Miller, president of JLM Public Relations (www.jlmpr.com), a New York public relations firm specializing in clients in the entertainment industry that worked on the event, honorees included hip-hop stars Mary J. Blige, Ludacris, the Ludacris Foundation, Anheuser-Busch, and MTV's "Choose or Lose" Campaign. The event featured a keynote speech delivered by the Reverend Al Sharpton.

Attendees received gift bags with products donated by the event's sponsors, including L'Oréal, Baby Phat, Phat Farm, and PepsiCo. Contents of gift bags are typically provided by event sponsors in exchange for the exposure, but this gift bag included something a little different, notes Dupe Ajayi, a writer and producer for BET Radio, who covered the event for the station. One of the HSAN board members, celebrity Sean "P. Diddy" Combs, head of Bad Boy Entertainment, added his own preelection gift: a T-shirt reading, in big black-and-red letters, "Vote or Die!" The T-shirts, noted Ajayi, were a big hit with the guests.

"Live on Our Stage"

Ojeda Hall-Phillips is director of the Women's Business Center of the nonprofit Local Development Corporation of East New York (LDCENY), which operates in a depressed area of Brooklyn. The organization's mission is to encourage local entrepreneurship, and to that end each year it holds a series of three special events. These include its Total Woman Business Conference in May, a forum for Women's History Month in March, and the "We Can!" seminar on small-business loans in October.

To promote its events, the organization regularly makes use of public access radio and TV. Funds for PR usually come from private foundations or corporations or from the organization's own earned income, which LDCENY draws on to run paid ads on popular local radio stations and in local newspapers, as well on bus shelters. In addition, the organization partners with Brooklyn Congresswoman Nydia M. Velázquez, who is a frequent guest speaker at LDCENY events and whose office handles sending out press releases to the media by e-mail and fax.

To make the seminar on the nuts and bolts of small-business loans more appealing to attendees at the "We Can!" seminar, Hall-Phillips looked for something different. She decided to bring in a cast of actors to perform interactive scenes that would dramatize how to approach a loan officer to secure a small-business loan.

That was where I came in. I own a theater company, Access Communications (www.access-comm.com), that sends professional actors into major corporations and nonprofits to perform skits on topics like sexual harassment awareness, diversity, and conflict resolution. Access Communications has performed all over the country and in Canada for companies like AIG–Sun America, Bristol-Myers Squibb, HSBC Bank, and Playtex. For the "We Can!" seminar, a cast of actors from Access was at St. Francis College in Brooklyn, dramatizing for an audience of several hundred local entrepreneurs the wrong ways and the right ways to borrow money.

One young actress played a sweet but naive entrepreneur who was determined to open up her own "Dessert Shoppe." With no clue about how to approach a bank, she made humorous misstep after misstep as the rest of the cast, and the very involved audience, advised her on how to go about securing the loan. With drama, laughter, and a lot of audience input, the key learning points of the seminar were conveyed in a way that held the audience's attention and gave attendees the confidence to try it on their own.

Hall-Phillips was delighted with the results: "The attendees all got involved, and they really seemed to get the lessons that were being presented. It was a very successful seminar." A little creative thinking can have a disproportionate effect on the success of an event.

The Canine Cotillion

In creating an event, it is always a good idea to find innovative alternatives to holding just another luncheon, dinner, cocktail party, barbecue, boat cruise, tour, or wine-and-cheese tasting. With some creative thinking, an event can often be created around the organization's mission. A case in point is the Canine Cotillion.

Every spring, St. Hubert's Animal Welfare Center, in Madison, New Jersey (www.sthuberts.org), hosts its annual event. This popular black-tie gala fundraiser typically draws 225 attendees from throughout the state. Guests are invited to bring their dogs, and about eighty canines are typically in attendance, many arriving in tuxedos and evening gowns. Canines and humans share in the evening's festivities.

Advance promotion includes sending out hold-the-date-cards accompanied by refrigerator magnets featuring photos of appealing pets all dressed up for the ball. As they hold shopping lists and grocery coupons to local refrigerators, these attractive magnets keep the shelter on the mind of St. Hubert's supporters. The invitations to the cotillion, as well as flyers, newspaper ads, and the program journal, continue the theme, prominently featuring a photo of an irresistible canine (see Exhibit 16.2). To keep costs down, the development associate at St. Hubert's, Jennifer Schulz, turned to her husband, graphic designer Jeff Schulz (www.command-z-design.com), to create the invitation package, flyers, program, and journal. The photos themselves are contributed every year on a pro bono basis by a local photographer, Joe Galioto of The Image Maker.

St. Hubert's annual Canine Cotillion is just one of fifteen similarly imaginative events that the shelter runs each year, all marked by the creative flair and whimsy that have become St. Hubert's hallmark. Other popular events offered annually include ice-cream socials, held outdoors at the shelter during the summer, at which humans get ice cream and the dogs get "frosty paws," and a "Meow Luau," at which cat lovers gather to hear lectures on the subtleties of feline behavior. The events regularly get full-page photo spreads in the Morris and Somerset County weeklies and have also been covered in the *Star Ledger*, the major area daily, as well as *Woman's World*, *Dog Fancy*, the *New Jersey Monthly*, New Jersey Cable News 12, and the New Jersey section of *The New York Times*.

Events liked the Canine Cotillion and the rest play to the streak of whimsy in everyone and have a particularly strong appeal for animal lovers. St. Hubert's PR director, Kelly G. Vanasse, president of Kelly Communications, (kelly communication.com), notes that the events are in keeping with the philosophy and mission of the organization: "We offer creative events that nurture the human-animal bond and help raise the crucial funding to further our mission."

The publicity generated by the events establishes a brand for the shelter that helps it stand out from the competition. The publicity also attracts many people to St. Hubert's to adopt pets, thus helping the shelter to fulfill its mission.

Murder Mysteries

For the annual fall Parents' Day celebration, the activities board at Assumption College (www.assumption.edu), in Worchester, Massachusetts, wanted something different to entertain some five hundred students and their parents gathered in the college gym. The board invited Mostly Murder (www.mostlymurder.com), a New

EXHIBIT 16.2. CANINE COTILLION SAMPLE INVITATION COVER.

Source: Courtesy of St. Hubert's Animal Welfare Center.

York–based murder mystery company, to come to the campus and stage a live, interactive murder mystery.

The cast of professional actors arrived with information about the guests already worked into the plot, and the actors entertained the guests by "discovering" at the scene of the crime golf clubs, ties, and tennis racquets bearing the names of students and parents. As one "suspect" after another was incriminated, interrogated, and applauded by everyone present, the guests solved the mystery, and those with the best solutions were photographed with the Super Sleuth trophies they received as rewards for their detecting.

In Port Washington, New York, the Friends of the Library opted to have a local resident write an interactive murder mystery that was performed for three hundred guests on two successive weekend evenings in the library auditorium. I was the writer, producer, and emcee for the event. I was also in charge of publicity, and in that capacity I made it a point to cast the editor of the local *Port Washington News* in a prominent role as an investigative TV reporter. As a result, the murder mystery was front-page news in several issues of the paper that appeared prior to the event. A press release sent to the Long Island daily *Newsday* included the names of every local resident involved in the production. The pagelong list of names, along with a photo from a dress rehearsal, appeared on the front page of the weekend North Hempstead edition, *Guide to Community News and Events,* under the headline "Mystery Play Offers Sinful Amusement." The coverage in the local papers generated a lot of interest and helped pack the house for the live performances.

Partnering

Holding a special event is often a matter of partnering with other people and organizations whose interests complement your own. Alicia Evans of Total Image Communications and the National Black Public Relations Society worked on a national church outreach program to present a series of health fairs in African American churches throughout the country. The fairs were sponsored by the pharmaceutical company Ortho-McNeil.

In each city where Evans staged an event, she partnered with nurses from the local chapter of the Black Nurses Association. In addition to providing their professional skills, the nurses brought another asset to the fair, their friends, ensuring not only a substantial turnout but also an interested and receptive audience.

"Word of mouth helped spread the word that we were providing free health check-ups for members of the community at local churches," Evans recalls. "What was especially gratifying was the fact that we were actually able to save the lives of several people who, the examinations showed, were just inches away from a heart attack."

Raffles and Lotteries

A raffle is often included as part of an event schedule. Prizes are typically donated to the nonprofit by businesses that, in return, receive exposure for their products when they are mentioned at the event and a "thank you" in the journal or program. One popular raffle technique is to invite people to enter by dropping their business cards in a bowl. This is an excellent way for the organization to later "harvest" names and contact information, including e-mail addresses. Before adding people's names to an e-mail list, however, it is important to get their permission (see Chapter Fifteen).

Lottery tickets can be a creative variation on the raffle theme and can also add a note of excitement to an event.

Local Appeal

When Lynn Silverman, founder and president of Creative Event Planning, in New York (www.creativeeventplanning.com), was hired to run a twenty-sixth anniversary gala dinner for the St. Nicholas Preservation Corporation (www.stnicksnpc.org), her goal was to generate a large turnout for the organization's annual fundraising event. Proceeds of the gala would go to maintaining affordable housing for the poor.

Silverman came up with the idea of inviting the popular former mayor Ed Koch to be the featured speaker, and she arranged for another popular figure, local CBS Channel 2 anchor David Diaz, to introduce him and to emcee the evening. The presence of the local celebrities emphasized the note of civic pride that was a key element of the event.

During the cocktail reception, guests were invited to be photographed with the former mayor. After the event, each photo was personally autographed by Koch and sent to the guest. To emphasize the "bridge to the future" aspect of the gala, Silverman hired a local designer to create an archway of the Williamsburg Bridge under which guests passed as they made their way from the cocktail reception to the dinner. Continuing that theme, she commissioned a toy designer to make a twelve-by-twenty-four-inch replica of the Williamsburg Bridge as the centerpiece for each table, a refreshing break from the standard roses in a cylindrical vase. One guest at each table found a "lucky penny" under his or her dinner plate and got to take the bridge home as a memento of the evening.

The following year, for the twenty-seventh anniversary gala dinner, Silverman again called on a local celebrity, this time Yolanda Vega, the very popular "lottery lady" who announced the lottery winners each week on TV. At the cocktail party, guests posed with Vega for photos to which a Williamsburg Bridge background was digitally added. Guests left the gala that evening with a photo souvenir of the occasion.

With the popular "lottery lady" on board for the gala, Silverman did some out-of-the-box thinking and bought one hundred lottery tickets. "At the dinner," she recalls, "we hid the lottery tickets all over the room—under plates, beneath chair cushions, behind drapes. When it was announced that, in honor of Yolanda Vega, the guests were invited to keep any tickets they could find—and that one of the tickets might be worth several million dollars—the room just *erupted* with excitement. People were scrambling all over the place, looking for those lottery tickets. It was a big hit and the guests loved it."

Because the event was for a worthy cause, Vega had refused to accept any fee for her participation. Looking for a way to say "thank you," Silverman did some sleuthing and discovered that Vega was an ardent Yankees fan. As a token of appreciation, Vega received a lovely crystal baseball ornament for her Christmas tree and an autographed Yankees baseball shirt. The "lottery lady" was as delighted as the St. Nicholas guests.

VIP Visits and Tours

A tour of organizational facilities by supporters and VIPs has many things in common with a dinner or other special event. Many of the same rules of preparation apply. Photos taken of the visit can be used in news releases and in the organization's newsletter. Video footage can be incorporated into PSAs and promotional videos. It is especially important to assign people to ensure that visitors are made to feel welcome. Much goodwill can be garnered by a well-run tour.

It is always a good idea to arrange for someone from the organization to serve as the personal host for a special guest or celebrity. When the celebrity arrives, the appointed host should take her under his wing, introduce her to organizational leaders, show her to her seat, and generally make her feel comfortable and at home. At least that is how it is supposed to work.

Gracious hosting needs to be carefully planned, as I learned when I was working as public relations consultant for the Mental Health Association of Nassau County (www.mhanc.org) for its annual fundraising event held at a botanical garden on Long Island, thirty miles east of New York City. The guest of honor was to be the late film and television star Tony Randall. As the evening unfolded, all the guests were mixing and mingling, enjoying a lovely June twilight. I was looking for Tony Randall.

Traffic on the Long Island Expressway was reportedly backed up, and he was late. No one seemed to mind as people strolled among the plants, enjoying the evening breeze. But I was getting nervous. I needed a photo of Randall with the committee for the local papers.

I had positioned an organizational banner near some lovely flowering plants, to highlight the setting of the botanical garden. But I was quickly losing both the light and the dinner committee, whose members were starting to head for their seats. Still no Randall.

Then I happened to notice a slight man in a blue blazer wandering along the pebbled pathways, smiling and nodding to people who smiled back but who made no effort to engage him in conversation. Apparently Randall had arrived unheralded and unnoticed. He was looking a little lost when I went up to him, introduced myself, and welcomed him to the event.

A charming, elegant man, Randall told me he had begun to think he had come to the wrong botanical garden; no one seemed to want to talk to him. I assured him that everyone was just shy in the presence of such a famous celebrity, and he chuckled as he agreed that I was probably right.

I led him by the arm to find one of the two cochairwomen. I wanted to turn Randall over to her so that I could round up people to pose with him for the publicity photo.

I finally found one of the chairwomen and introduced her to Randall. She smiled, said hello, and immediately rushed off into the gathering twilight to attend to a last-minute detail. This was not helping me get the photo I needed. Pulling Randall along like a kid towing a wagon, I went in search of the other chairwoman, finally found her, introduced her to Randall, and watched as she, too, disappeared, even faster than the first one. It was getting darker, and I was still no closer to getting the picture I needed.

Then one of the veteran members of the organization, a woman named Helen, strode up to us, her hand outstretched and a big, welcoming smile on her face. Randall took her hand warmly as I made a quick introduction. I knew from preparing his biography that Randall was interested in Native American art, and I knew from our earlier discussions that Helen had an impressive collection in her home. I informed them of their common interest and turned Randall over to Helen to "babysit" as I hurried off in pursuit of the disappearing chairwomen.

I eventually rounded them up, along with the photographer and Randall and Helen and several other key people, and guided the group to where I had positioned the banner. The photo caught the last of the fading light, and it looked great when it appeared in the papers the following week.

As soon as the photo had been taken, the vanishing chairwomen vanished again. Luckily, Randall and Helen were delighted with each other and continued to chat away happily, like long-lost friends. Had Helen not come forward of her own accord and proved to be such an accomplished hostess, it could have been a very long and uncomfortable time for Randall.

When he came to the microphone later that evening, he was in fine spirits and had many nice things to say about the organization—comments that found their way into the press release that went out the following day.

Special Events Come in Many Shapes and Sizes

For the fourteen-hundred-kid-strong Watchung Hills Soccer Association (WHSA) in New Jersey, the year's main special event is an awards night at which the community's young athletes are honored. According to Steve Finkel, WHSA president, "We don't have a 'gala dinner,' but we honor the kids by calling each team to the podium and then having their coaches announce them individually. They all get trophies of some sort, including for participation, and we usually serve a dessert like ice cream." The names of award recipients are posted to the WHSA Web site and published in the local weekly newspaper, the *Echoes-Sentinel.*

For Freya's Sensory Center, a facility serving infants with severe brain damage on Long Island, the keynote event one year was a kid-friendly rock-and-roll concert performed at Huntington High School by the local Bubblegum Band.

For the American Airpower Museum in Farmingdale, New York, the annual Labor Day event includes offering visitors an opportunity to take a step back in time by climbing aboard an actual World War II B-17 or B-24.

For the Richard David Kann Melanoma Foundation of West Palm Beach, Florida, a signature special event is bringing out 650 children from kindergarten through twelfth grade with their families to attend a skin cancer screening at the Palm Beach Zoo. Thanks to public awareness and appreciation of the foundation generated by this and similar events, it was awarded a $1.5 million grant from the Cancer Division of the National Institute of Health to conduct a five-year research project, in conjunction with the University of Miami, on ways of combating melanoma—a serious step on the road to accomplishing its mission of making people "sun smart," facilitated in large measure by the practice of good public relations.

Whenever possible, a special event should fit with the organization's mission. Girls Incorporated offers a good example of this principle. On the day before its annual luncheon, the organization, as part of its media literacy program, gives young girls a chance to match wits with seasoned media pros. The organization invites media professionals to pair off with girls from the program and brainstorm ideas for the following year's PR campaign. Called "Girl Pitch," the event has proved so popular with the media that every year some media professionals have to be turned away.

PART THREE

MONITORING THE PR CAMPAIGN

Part Three consists of two chapters. Chapter Seventeen, "Reviewing and Revising the PR Plan," looks at methods for measuring how well your plan is working. The PR plan must be carefully monitored, realistically evaluated, and then revised as necessary. Some elements of the plan may need to receive added emphasis, and others may have to be dropped altogether.

Chapter Eighteen, "Reporting to Stakeholders," looks at the importance of keeping senior staff, the organization's leadership, and others informed about how the organization is being represented in the media. The chapter also reviews how PR practitioners at a variety of nonprofits handle the vital reporting aspect of the PR process.

The follow-up outlined in this final part of the book is essential. A PR campaign is not something you can wind up and send on its way. It must be carefully monitored and regularly reviewed and revised. As when you are driving a car, your steering must be continually adjusted if you are to reach your destination.

CHAPTER SEVENTEEN

REVIEWING AND REVISING THE PR PLAN

Calculating Results

To respond to the challenge of measuring the success of a public relations campaign, the PR industry has developed formulas to calculate results. The best known of these are *advertising equivalency* (AE) and *media impressions* (MI).

Advertising Equivalency

AE considers the media outlet in which a PR placement appears and compares it to an ad of the same size in the same position in the same outlet. What would have been the cost of those column inches in a newspaper or magazine, or of those seconds and minutes on TV or radio, in a paid ad? Applying AE to the placement of the full-page ads that Teach For America was able to get without cost in many leading national magazines, such as *Time, People,* and *Fortune,* yields an advertising equivalency of several hundred thousand dollars. That is what the cost would have been if the organization had paid for running those ads.

For the free fifteen- and thirty-second PSAs that YAI/National Institute for People with Disabilities ran on New York television stations to promote its annual 5K Central Park Challenge, you calculate the AE by tallying what it would have cost the organization if it had paid for placing the same number of spots of the same length, in the same time slots, on the same programs. One estimate sets the value at $300,000.

Reckoning what the nonprofit Guiding Eyes for the Blind would have had to pay for the radio spots that ran as free PSAs on major rock stations in the New York area also makes for an impressive AE. By comparison, the cost of the public relations efforts it took to get all that exposure is considerably less.

The AE concept has some obvious flaws. For one thing, Teach For America, YAI, and Guiding Eyes would not have been able to afford the actual price of all that advertising, so the comparison is, in that sense, unrealistic. In reality, they would never even have considered undertaking such high-priced ad campaigns; it simply would have been beyond their budgets. If the ads had not been free, they would not have appeared at all, and certainly not on the scale and frequency that they did.

Nevertheless, AE serves as a nice yardstick for measuring, and reporting to the organization's leaders, the dollar value of the PR achieved. Since the PR cost to generate all that publicity is usually so much less than the equivalent advertising cost, AE makes the money spent on public relations look like a great bargain—which, of course, it is.

Another problem with AE is that it understates the value of PR. A media pickup tends to be far more effective than a paid ad in conveying a message to the public. The public is understandably skeptical of advertising, assuming that any message communicated in space that has been paid for is self-serving for the advertiser and of dubious credibility.

Most people, however, do not realize that much of the other material they encounter in the print and electronic media is placed there by someone doing public relations. It is perceived as presented by a neutral source, the news media themselves, and so is seen as carrying an implied editorial endorsement. That material has much greater credibility than advertising.

As a result, a message placed via public relations has more intrinsic value than a message that is conveyed through advertising. That value is missed in a statement of advertising equivalency that merely measures the cost of comparative advertising space and time. Despite its flaws, however, AE is frequently used to measure the success of a public relations campaign.

Media Impressions

The number of people who actually see your message is counted by media impressions, or MI. This, too, can be a tricky number. Say, for example, a news release from your organization is picked up by a local newspaper that has a circulation of 20,000 readers. To calculate the number of media impressions generated by your release, you multiply the circulation figure of 20,000 by 2.5 for a total of 50,000 media impressions.

The reason for the multiplication goes back to the days when it was routinely assumed that the reader gave his newspaper or magazine to someone else to read after he had finished it. It was further assumed that approximately half the people who received the secondhand newspaper would in turn pass it on to a third person, so the total "pass-along" circulation for a newspaper with a circulation of twenty thousand is calculated at fifty thousand.

That pass-along phenomenon may have represented reality in the days before television and niche marketing publications—people really did share their copies of *Life* and *Look* with family and friends—but today such pass-along readership figures are not realistic. Despite that fact, they continue to be used.

Figuring MI for radio and television is simply a matter of tallying the number of people who listen to or watch the program on which the spot appears, using figures provided by a national rating agency like Arbitron or Nielsen. A guest on a radio talk show with an audience of two million listeners has made two million media impressions. If your organization is featured on a TV evening news program with a viewership of half a million, the MI is half a million.

Of course, there are obvious problems with MI as well. A publication may have a certain circulation, but that does not mean that every reader gives every inch of every page equal attention. Your organization may have been mentioned in a column or a letter to the editor that gets more attention, or less, than other sections of the magazine or newspaper, and not every member of the computed audience for a radio or TV program will necessarily be tuned in to every show or paying attention to the segment in which your organization is featured.

MI shares a built-in failing with advertising equivalency in that it assumes ads and stories placed via public relations have the same impact on the public. Again, that assumption shortchanges the value of public relations, which tends to have far greater credibility with the public than advertising.

Still, the MI calculation provides some standard of measurement, however flawed, and continues to be used by advertising and public relations agencies to impress clients with the effectiveness of their campaigns.

Neither AE nor MI is a totally realistic tool for measuring the success of a public relations campaign, but both can be used to compare one public relations campaign or strategy with another. Tracking AE and MI can provide a sense of whether one campaign is doing better or worse than another and can thus serve as a guide for making needed adjustments.

Evaluating the PR Campaign

How can you evaluate your public relations efforts? How do you know if you're doing a good job?

How can you measure your success? One way is to begin by measuring your accomplishments against your goals. If you are clear about your goals, shouldn't it be a simple matter to measure your accomplishments, compare them to the stated goals, and see how well you've done? Well, maybe.

When it comes to measuring PR success, not all goals are created equal. Did you set as a goal increasing attendance at a major event by one-third? That would be a fairly easy goal to evaluate. Count the heads, do the arithmetic, and you have your answer. Similarly, if your goal was to increase recruitment from a certain area, you could take a look at the numbers and see how well you did.

What about a goal like increasing name recognition or achieving greater visibility for your organization? How do you measure that? It isn't so easy. For such goals, common to virtually all nonprofits on the planet, a look at the situation before and after the campaign can be a good way to evaluate the success of your PR efforts.

The classic approach to a PR campaign begins with extensive pre-campaign research, to provide a benchmark that defines the level of awareness about your organization to the public at large or among specific segments of the public. Later, a post-campaign analysis is conducted to determine the degree to which the level of awareness has changed. This kind of research can be expensive, and many nonprofits simply can't afford it.

An alternative is to conduct focus groups before and after a PR campaign, to determine what changes in public perception the campaign has accomplished. By carefully monitoring responses, you can get a sense of the impact your efforts have had. For example, are people more aware of your organization than they were before the campaign? Do they better appreciate what you do and why it is important? Can they express in a few words what your organization is all about? Positive answers may indicate that you have successfully communicated your key message points.

Another way of measuring before and after is to compare press clippings received before the campaign was launched with those that come in six months or a year later. Examining news clips can also be a good way to make adjustments for your next campaign. News clips can reveal whether the organization's key message points are being communicated effectively. A survey of media coverage can also indicate whether the news items are appearing in media outlets read, listened to, or viewed by your target audience.

If you see that something important about your organization is being ignored or misunderstood, you can focus your efforts on correcting the problem. Developing and successfully conveying a key message point that addresses the problem may resolve the confusion.

If a review of print and electronic media coverage reveals that your spokesperson is not doing an effective job of telling the organization's story, it may be time to send that person for professional media training. As a rule, no one should be allowed to represent your organization to the media without some sort of media training—at the very least, to rehearse interviews (see Chapter Thirteen). Alternatively, it may be time to find a new spokesperson.

When PR Isn't Working: Making Changes

What if you've done everything right and you still aren't getting coverage in the media? Imagine that you've put together an impressive media contact list, assembled a dynamite press kit, sent press releases, called radio and TV stations, and . . . nothing; no one cares about your story. If that happens, it is time to take stock.

If the target markets you have selected do not respond, you may want to reconsider your selection of target markets. Maybe you are approaching the wrong markets. Maybe the people you assumed would be your natural support base don't find your cause all that appealing. It may be time to try reaching out to a different audience.

If the message is not coming across clearly, then the message or the message points or the way the message is being communicated may need to be revised. Reexamine your written materials and your Web site. Look for boring writing or unimaginative presentations. If you're putting people to sleep before they can learn about your organization, you need to rethink your approach.

If the selected media outlets are not receptive to your message, you may need to shift focus to different media. Consider your media contact list. Is it current and accurate? People change jobs, get promoted, and get transferred. If you're sending your material to someone who is no longer there, it may be going directly into the trash.

Are you sending things to the right section or department at the media outlet? Should you be targeting the religious editor rather than the editor of the business section? It is usually a mistake to assume journalists will pass your material on to a colleague. They may, but they very well may not. It's up to you to get it to the right person.

Review your media list carefully. Consult media guides and go online to the outlets' Web sites to be sure you have the right names and contact information. Call and ask who handles your kind of story.

If you do have the right names, give some thought to the media targets you have selected. Maybe you're reaching too far too soon. Often you'll do better to approach local media and establish a track record before going after the bigger national media outlets. New publications and programs are constantly being launched, and you may be able to get in on the ground floor with some of them.

Renew your contact with journalists you contacted earlier. Keep the focus on the newsworthiness of the story you are pitching. Try pitching it from a slightly different angle. Unless you have already established a relationship with a reporter or an editor, it is not a good idea to beg for coverage with the plea "We really need the publicity." Journalists like to see themselves as professionals who report the news; show them that your story is news.

Try repackaging your story. Reporting the results of a survey, holding an event, and presenting an award are all things that look and sound like news. When you hold an event, at the very least make sure that you get into calendar listings by observing each outlet's particular requirements. If time is short before an upcoming event, concentrate on just a few of the major media outlets, and stress the urgency of the story.

If your special events are not generating enthusiasm in your target audience, consider offering different kinds of events. Try coming up with creative, unconventional events that tie in with your organization's mission. Then promote them like crazy.

If you are being ignored, shift your emphasis to something that cannot be ignored. Look for things that are new, challenging, controversial, or unprecedented, even if they are tangential to the main emphasis of your project. If something will get you coverage, use it.

If you're still not getting media coverage, it may be time to consider the messenger. Are you dealing with the media properly? Are you hostile, rude, and impatient, or do your treat journalists with respect for their time and professionalism? When you meet them face to face, are you well groomed and well put together? Do you look and sound like a professional? Personal impressions can have a big influence on your success with the media.

Your credibility is key. The cardinal sin, as far as the media are concerned, is to lie to a journalist. Being caught in a lie can instantly ruin your credibility and wreak havoc with carefully nurtured relationships. If you find that you accidentally misled a reporter, however, it does not have to mean that you have forever destroyed any chance of ever getting coverage in the media again. Be honest and forthright and apologize, and then be very, very sure to get all your facts right in the future.

Dealing with a PR Crisis

The only thing worse than getting no press is getting bad press. If you are faced with a crisis in which the media are clamoring for comments about an alleged issue of misconduct, impropriety, or misstatement, the first thing to do is to respond immediately. How you handle the bad news will affect how your good news will be handled by the media in the future.

You should prepare to deal with crisis situations in advance, well before a crisis ever arises. Consider some worst-case scenarios; imagine some possible issues, and then plan how you would respond so that you will be ready when a hostile press knocks on your door. Camera lights and microphones thrust into your face can be very unsettling. Do your best to remain calm, and try to project as relaxed a demeanor as possible.

If you don't know the answer to a question, it is all right to say so and promise to get back to the journalist with the information that was requested. You should try to avoid saying, "No comment." There is a harshness to that response that makes some journalists smell blood. Better to say something like "I'd prefer not to comment on that at this time."

However difficult it may be to deal with the media in a crisis, keep in mind that all stories eventually fade from the news. Be patient, remain calm, and keep your head, secure in the knowledge that this, too, will pass.

Tracking PR Success

It can be tricky to measure the impact of a public relations campaign. Public perceptions and attitudes are difficult things to quantify. But public awareness of an organization, and the public's understanding of and appreciation for what the organization does, are very much affected by how often people encounter the organization in the media.

The more an organization is in the news, the more opportunities it has to convey its key message points, and the greater its impact on public awareness. The amount of exposure an organization is getting in the media *can* be measured.

Many nonprofit organizations employ a clipping service, such as Bacon's Information (www.baconsinfo.com) or BurrellesLuce Information Services (www.burrellesluce.com), to cite the two best-known ones, to track their appearances in the news. For a regular monthly "reading fee" of approximately $300, and an additional per-clip charge of about $2, the service will collect and forward clips of every story about the organization that appears in the press. Similarly, stories that appear in the electronic media and on Web sites can also be tracked and reported. The search areas can be customized by region, interest, kinds of media outlets, and other criteria. With regular reports of media placement, it is possible to measure the degree of visibility generated by a public relations campaign.

Benchmarks and Media Logs

At the American Red Cross in Greater New York, Leslie Gottlieb, director of communications and marketing, uses the BurrellesLuce clipping service to track media coverage.

"We have benchmarks," she says. "We keep a media log, and we look at key media outlets and key messages. We analyze our appearance in the media over a period of time—say, from June to October—and we compare coverage over the previous two years. We also look at what percentage of the coverage we receive is positive and what percentage negative. For example, out of 244 mentions in the local media in the last six months, only 2 were not positive. That's not a bad ratio."

Donna St. John, director of communications at the United Service Organizations (USO), says, "It's hard to measure the success of a public relations campaign. You don't always know why some journalists contact you. But sometimes they'll say, 'I saw your release.' Or our clipping service will pick up a story somebody ran about us. And sometimes you're getting coverage out there, and you just don't know about it."

St. John makes use of a media monitoring system provided by BurrellesLuce and its affiliate, Video Monitoring Service of America, as well as a related tracking system called Quick View. The USO gets daily print and electronic media reports, including a Web-media report. At one time, the organization used a fax distribution service to send out news releases. Media pickup has increased significantly, St. John says, since the USO began using PR Newswire, a media distribution service.

Random Successes

Sometimes PR success can be a random thing. St. John remembers getting a call from *The Today Show*, asking permission for someone from the program to accompany a USO tour. As she answered the producer's questions, St. John sensed an opportunity. She started gently pitching the story *she* wanted to tell, about the various ways people could help the USO support American troops overseas.

"We'd been getting a lot of calls and e-mails from individuals, organizations, and corporations, asking how people could help. I pitched the idea of our USO president, Edward Powell, coming on *The Today Show* to answer those questions. *The Today Show* bought it, and he was on the show a few days later, explaining how people could help and telling them how much it mattered. Response to his appearance was terrific. We were flooded with offers of support."

That great placement came about because St. John saw a possibility and acted on it—a PR coup that made a nice highlight in her report to stakeholders. Effective PR is often a matter of being able to spot, and seize, a promising opportunity.

Lynn Uhlfelder Berman, senior media relations manager at YAI/National Institute for People with Disabilities in New York, recently found herself measuring her PR success at the racetrack. It happened as a direct result of a story she had placed in *The New York Times*'s "Job Market" column that highlighted the organization's success in finding jobs for fifty disabled workers (the previous year, the number had been forty) among the fourteen hundred staff hired by Restaurant Associates, the company that operates the food village at the U.S. Open tennis tournament.

"The story got a lot of attention," Berman says, "and it also caught the eye of a man at Yonkers Raceway, who said that, after reading the article about us in the *Times*, he might be interested in hiring fifty of our people to work at the racetrack. That was great news to hear. Helping our people get jobs is one of our major goals."

Like St. John at the USO, Berman has capitalized on opportunities to maximize PR for her organization. While scanning the Web for information on health care for people with mental retardation, she discovered that the U.S. Surgeon General's Office was planning an entire conference on closing the gap in medical services for that population. When she saw that, a light bulb went on.

Berman immediately contacted the Surgeon General's Office and was able to arrange a phone interview with two of the conference organizers and YAI's CEO, Dr. Joel M. Levy. The organizers were impressed with what Levy had to say and invited him to serve on a panel at the conference.

"As a result, the Surgeon General's report cited our Premier HealthCare medical practice as a national model for the provision of medical services for people with mental retardation," Berman explains. And that, in turn, has helped us reach a new, powerful, and influential audience. Being mentioned in the report also has been helpful in attracting media attention to Premier HealthCare. We use it in all our marketing materials. I would consider that a PR success."

CHAPTER EIGHTEEN

REPORTING TO STAKEHOLDERS

A Primary Focus

Chapter Seventeen looked at evaluating the PR campaign. It asked the questions "How can you measure success?" and "How do you know when you are doing a good job?" This chapter looks at an equally important question: "How can you let the people you report to know you are doing a terrific job?"

Kathryn Kimmel is vice president of marketing and communications for the Gemological Institute of America, a large nonprofit in the jewelry industry. Her duties include responsibility for the organization's considerable public relations campaigns. She emphasizes the importance of maintaining an ongoing flow of information to an organization's stakeholders.

"Keeping the internal audience of stakeholders informed of the organization's accomplishments is vital," she says. "They must be your primary, though not your only, focus of communications. Some of your greatest advocates and communicators are within your organization. By ensuring that the internal audience is frequently updated, they can help form a significant sphere of influence. Members of the organization should be the first to know, as much as is appropriate."

Ben Nivin, director of professional information at YAI/National Institute for People with Disabilities, believes that regular reporting to stakeholders is essential to motivating and maintaining leaders' involvement, and that their involvement translates into concrete results.

"There must be a realization that for an organization to be successful in public relations, the leadership needs to appreciate, be supportive, and be involved in the process," Nivin says. "Without that support and vision, we could never be generating so much positive publicity about our organization."

Clips, Clip Books, Updates, and Testimonials

When stories about YAI appear in *The New York Times, The Wall Street Journal, Crain's New York Business,* the *New York Daily News,* and *Newsday,* Lynn Uhlfelder Berman, YAI's senior media relations manager, makes a point of keeping the organization's leaders informed. "Whenever we get a major hit—and this is not unique to YAI—we send out copies of the clip, with a cover memo from the CEO or president (or both), to the appropriate board members. If, for example, the story is about our medical practice for people with disabilities, we send it to our Premier HealthCare board members, who have a particular interest in that area. If it's a story on people with disabilities working at the U.S. Open, we will probably send it to the YAI and the Corporate Source board of trustees and everyone on our board. We also put together every year a book of media hits covering newspapers, TV, radio, and the Web. It's a pretty comprehensive clip book, divided into separate tabbed sections for our different organizations and different kinds of hits. We give it to a distribution list that includes board members, visitors, staff, officials, potential donors, and foundations. We also try to post links to articles on our Web site, as many nonprofits do. One problem is that links to some publications, such as *The New York Times,* are free for only a week, and you don't want visitors to have to pay to view the story."

Donna St. John, director of communications at the United Service Organizations (USO), also makes it a priority to keep stakeholders informed, which she does by preparing monthly reports of all print, electronic, and Web-based media coverage. In addition, twice a year she also sends stakeholders a statistical report that summarizes all the media coverage the USO has received in the previous six months.

Alicia Evans of Total Image Communications and the New York chapter of the National Black Public Relations Society agrees about the importance of regularly reporting public relations achievements to the board. "PR people are always working under the pressures of deadlines, and it is sometimes easy to forget the internal audience," Evans says. "But it is very important to prepare reports on a regular basis, with photocopies of news clips and summaries of placement in the electronic media. People must know how the organization is being presented in the media."

At the Gay and Lesbian Alliance Against Defamation (GLAAD), notes Cathy Renna, a spokesperson for the organization, major supporters are kept informed by way of news clips that are regularly disseminated, on a quarterly basis. The media receive an

A Tale of Two Seminaries—*Continued*

To continue the "tale" begun in Chapter Two, the people responsible for PR at the Episcopal Theological Seminary of the Southwest (ETSS), in Austin, Texas, and at Hebrew Union College–Jewish Institute of Religion (HUC-JIR), the seminary of Reform Judaism in New York City, may be separated by two thousand miles, but they have similar goals for their respective seminaries.

ETSS trains Episcopal priests; HUC-JIR trains Reform rabbis, as well as cantors, educators, and communal professionals. Both Bob Kinney in Austin and Jean Bloch Rosensaft in New York work to keep their seminaries in the public eye, to promote their school's identity, and to keep their boards of trustees informed and enthused. When it comes to managing the PR function, they say pretty much the same things; they just say them in different accents.

As director of communications at ETSS, Kinney does not use a clipping service but instead relies on himself as well as people who spot articles in the press and online and forward the clips and links on to him. So far, he says, the system has worked well.

"We keep track of what appears in the press," he says, and adds that he photocopies and passes on clips, as well as e-mail links to articles, to the school's trustees and supporters so that "they can see how we're being presented in the media."

At HUC-JIR, Rosensaft, whose title is senior national director for public affairs and institutional planning, subscribes to the BurrellesLuce clipping service. Like Kinney, she sends clips of newspaper pickups to the school's stakeholders: board members, supporters, and alumni. She also prepares a collection of clips in a clip book for periodic reports to the president, trustees, and top administrative personnel.

Rosensaft has heard certain nonprofits called "the best-kept secret in the world" by their stakeholders, and she notes that the practice of public relations comes with its own set of challenges. "More is more. People are always convinced that there could be more PR, that it could be better and more persuasive. In reality, you can get a great piece of news in a major paper, but your stakeholders may miss it. It's kind of like a Zen question: 'What is the sound of a tree falling in the forest if no one is there to hear it? What is the impact of getting the organization in the media if no one knows about it?' Your institution may get substantial coverage in one locale, but stakeholders who miss that particular day's paper or TV clip or reside in another locale may never experience it."

HUC-JIR has campuses in New York, Cincinnati, and Los Angeles in addition to one in Jerusalem. Rosensaft says that it is only realistic to expect that the media in cities with an HUC-JIR will be more likely to run a story than the media in, say, Chicago or Atlanta, where there is no HUC-JIR physical presence. A local hook, such as a visit there by the provost, a special event honoring alumni in that community, or the local presence of a traveling exhibition organized by HUC-JIR, is essential in capturing local media attention.

In addition to sending photocopied clips and clip books to supporters by "snail" mail, Rosensaft does a more or less daily e-mailing to stakeholders, including students, faculty, board members, alumni, donors, supporters, staff, and some media. In her one-page e-mail, she typically highlights upcoming events as well as breaking news stories. When she places a story in *The New York Times* or on ABC, CBS, or CNN, for example, she mentions it in her daily informal "e-mail blast" and includes a link to the story. She also posts a notice and a link on the bulletin board of the school's Web site. When a member of the faculty is quoted in the press, she provides a direct link to the article. When an HUC-JIR leader is speaking to Congress, her e-mail alerts people to the fact and tells them when to tune in to C-SPAN.

In New York, as part of her "internal PR" campaign of reporting to supporters, Rosensaft publishes, twice a year, *The Chronicle*, a two-color newsmagazine about her school that also includes recent articles by faculty scholars. In Austin, Kinney publishes the ETSS counterpart, *Ratherview*, also a two-color newsmagazine, annually. The publication includes updates on the school, major sermons, and news about projects and activities going on at the school. It is intended, Kinney says, to give friends and supporters up-to-date information about ETSS—the same purpose served by *The Chronicle*, according to Rosensaft. The two publications feature photos of students and supporters, and both have donation envelopes folded in and readily accessible.

eight-page GLAAD update every quarter. GLAAD has a monthly e-newsletter as well, *Media Spotlight*, which is also sent out in a two-page hard-copy version. The organization posts updates and announcements to members on its Web site, and additional updates are frequently sent both electronically and in hard copy. "It is very important that people have current information about the organization and the issues we deal with," says Renna. "We definitely make it a priority."

Keeping stakeholders informed is also high on the list of priorities for Leslie Gottlieb, director of communications and marketing for the American Red Cross in Greater New York. In addition to a regular distribution of news clips and reports on radio and TV coverage, Gottlieb does a daily limited distribution of three or four representative clips to senior management and selected board members. This effort is augmented by a more comprehensive report, compiled every six months, which receives a more general distribution to a wider selection of stakeholders.

"It is crucial that the leadership know how we are being represented in the media," Gottlieb says. "That awareness serves as a starting point for discussion and planning."

At the Public Theater in New York, director of communications Arlene R. Kriv also considers keeping stakeholders informed a priority. She puts together a weekly press update for board members that includes industry news and stories about the New York theater scene as well as clips and summaries of stories that have appeared about the Public Theater itself. At quarterly board meetings, a summary is distributed featuring highlights of the previous three months.

When it comes to reporting on the success of a PR initiative, says publicist Cynthia Horner, "It can be a good idea to include a report on the number of hits on your Web site and the number of people who have requested information. I also like to include testimonial letters from people who have attended an event or who have been positively affected by the organization. The reality is that success can be measured not only in the number of press clippings you get but also by the impact you have on people's lives."

Legal Issues

Many nonprofits seem to have no hesitancy about making photocopies of published articles, letters to the editor, and op-eds, for distribution far and wide. Even with some appreciation of the fact that they may be involved in clear violations of copyright, many nonprofit organizations, perhaps acting on the idea that they are working for the greater good, assume they are exempt from such legal considerations. They are not. The use of clippings very often involves questions of copyright; see Chapter Five to review copyright issues and the need to obtain permission for the use of previously published pieces.

CONCLUSION: BRINGING
IT ALL TOGETHER

Public relations is really very simple. It requires basic communication skills, a little creative thinking, and a lot of perseverance.

Identify your target markets, select the tools you will use to reach those markets, add a little creative thinking and as much perseverance as you can muster, and launch your PR campaign. Your organization will be on the way to getting the recognition and support it deserves.

This book has been designed to enable nonprofit organizations to create, implement, and monitor a successful public relations campaign. As outlined in Part One, it all begins with careful planning.

My personal favorite tool for the initial stage of the planning process is nothing more sophisticated than a pen and a piece of paper. Some of my most successful projects have begun with random notes scribbled on a napkin, often while sharing a meal with someone who had a vision.

That's one of the nice things about people at nonprofits: they tend to have a vision of how things can be better. They truly want to "fix the world." I wrote this book to help them do it.

What Does Successful PR Look Like?

Public relations guru Rick Frishman, president of Planned Television Arts, an independent division of Ruder-Finn, Inc., speaks to the excitement of the chase after media coverage when he asks, "What are the six nicest words in the English language for a publicist?" He answers his own question as he ticks off the six words on his fingers: "Nice to see you again, Oprah." If you are getting your organization on *The Oprah Winfrey Show*—again—you are clearly doing something very right.

But, although getting a hit of that magnitude is always nice, day-to-day PR for most nonprofits tends to be a bit lower-key. PR for nonprofits is an ongoing process of telling the organization's story, conveying its message, establishing its identity, and maintaining its image in the hearts and minds of the public.

You Never Can Tell . . .

Any PR person will tell you, in the same or similar words, "Sometimes PR is like playing the lottery."

Anyone who has ever worked in public relations has a tale to tell about a story he just knew was going to get terrific play—except nothing happened. Nobody picked it up. Nobody printed it, nobody put it on the radio, and no TV station even wanted to consider it. Nothing. Why? Who knows? That's the thing with PR. Sometimes it really is like playing the lottery.

The same people also have tales to tell about stories they were sure no one would want—and guess what: those stories got picked up. Everywhere. Maybe something happened in the news that made those stories timely, but, for whatever reason, the media just ate them up.

You do all the right things, these people will tell you, all the things you always do, and sometimes you just get lucky. And that is part of what makes the practice of public relations so frustrating and so fascinating at the same time. It's a head game, an ongoing attempt to come up with exactly the right angle and just the perfect pitch that will have the media begging for the story. There is always that lottery-ticket rush: maybe this time, with this story, you'll hit the jackpot. Well, you never know.

Changing Times

In order to touch people's hearts and minds, you have to be able to reach them. Part Two of this book presents a variety of ways to do that, many requiring an ability to handle new technologies. Anyone who intends to use PR effectively must master new technologies as they become available. To avoid them it is to guarantee failure, both for yourself and for your cause. I've seen what that looks like, up close and personal.

Earlier in this book, I touched on my father's confrontation with changing technology. A closer look at his story underscores the importance of flexibility in the face of change.

My father, you'll recall, was a Linotype operator. He learned his trade as a young man, in the 1940s, before he enlisted in the U.S. Army and went off with the rest of his generation to fight World War II. When he returned to the Bronx, in 1945, he hung up his sergeant's stripes and the Bronze Star he had earned for courage under fire and the Purple Heart he had earned courtesy of a German sniper whose aim was just a bit off, and he took up his trade again.

As a Linotype operator, he possessed the cutting-edge skills of the communications technology on which the world depended. Thanks to my father and other men like him (in those days there were only men) who sat at their massive, clattering machines, pounding away at their keyboards, setting type on gray lead "slugs," newspapers and magazines were able to roll off the presses and bring knowledge to the world.

It was a trade with a heritage that went back to the Gutenberg press and the first days of movable type. Down through the centuries, printers had always considered themselves an elite among workingmen. They knew how to read, in an age when most people did not. They knew how to keep their big machines going, feeding the presses. They were the very bone and sinew of the world's communications network.

And then it all came to an end, pretty much overnight. Linotype machines went the way of the dinosaurs they resembled in their massiveness, to be replaced by computerized typesetting. My father never got over it. His trade vanished while he still had years to go before retirement.

There were only a few jobs left, a very few, for Linotype operators. A staunch union man all his life, my father had the drill down cold. Every morning he got up and dressed and waited by the phone for the call from the union, assigning him a job for the day. If he didn't hear from the union by ten o'clock, he could assume he was not going to be called that day. He would be free. Only he didn't want to be free. He wanted to go to work, to do the only job he knew how to do.

My father hated waiting by the phone. He was a man who had been a master of high-demand skills for the four decades of his professional life, and now he suddenly found himself effectively "unskilled." He knew he should learn the new skills, and he tried to learn them, but somehow he just wasn't able to.

He came to dislike and distrust and even fear anything that smacked of new technology. When he bought a VCR, he bought it "with installation," convinced that he would never be able to master the "technology" required to hook it up to his TV. A man who had spent his life working with complicated machines, he paid a kid from the store to come to his home and plug in the cables for him.

No one in PR can afford that attitude today—not for himself, if he wants to be effective as a PR practitioner, and not for the organization he cares about. The proper practice of PR means the constant learning of new skills. But, although the skills may change almost beyond recognition, the basic PR task remains the same: getting the message to the target market with maximum impact.

My father, so competent at his mid-twentieth-century skills, so totally at a loss as the technology of communications changed around him, is very much on my mind when I consider the staggering pace of technological change and how it affects the field of public relations. The changes come so fast that there is a temptation to hang on to the familiar just a little while longer. And maybe a little while after that.

New technology means new learning curves, new challenges to overcome, and new applications to master. When my head starts spinning, I want to holler "Whoa!" That's when I think of my father, who couldn't keep up with the pace of change and spent the last years of his working life sitting next to a phone that never rang.

In order to be effective, public relations practitioners must be prepared to adapt to changing technologies. There simply is no other choice. If you don't adapt, sooner or later you find yourself sitting by a silent phone, waiting for it to ring. And it never will.

Missions Accomplished

Nonprofits have important missions to accomplish; effective PR can help accomplish those missions. Not every pitch will succeed, and rejection is part of the PR process, but if an organization has a compelling message, clearly expressed, and if it has targeted the right individuals at the appropriate media outlets, it will get into the media.

Success does not happen overnight. As the preceding chapters have illustrated, much of good PR involves establishing relationships with the media, and that takes time. A story in a local paper or on a local TV or radio station can be a springboard to coverage by larger media outlets with greater reach. Publicity truly does beget publicity.

A PR campaign that is carefully planned and properly executed will bring results. It really is that simple. May you have much success, for you and your cause, practicing good public relations.

Index

A

Access Communications, Inc., 6, 274
Adoptive Parents Committee, 197
Advertiser's kits: circulation and readership information in, 178–180; ordering, 178; rate card included in, 179–180
Advertising: calculating PR equivalency to, 285–286; comparing public relations and, 171; cost per thousand (CPM), 173–175, 181, 187–188; crafting headlines, subheads, body copy, 177; event journal, 262; print, 175–180; reach and frequency concepts of, 180; ROP (run of press) concept of, 179; ROS (run of station) concept of, 181, 185; rule of AIDA on, 172; staying on message with "big idea," 172–173; testing your target market, 175; Wanamaker quote on, 12. *See also* PSAs (public service announcements); Publicity; Radio advertising; TV advertising

AE (advertising equivalency), 285–286
AFI (available for interview) notice, 33, 89–91, 110
AIDA rule of advertising, 172
Ajayi, D., 273
All-purpose news release, 77
AMD Update (newsletter), 249
American Academy of Ophthalmology, 249
American Airpower Museum, 60, 281
American Cancer Society, 28
American Heritage magazine, 164
American Jewish Public Relations Society, 35
American ORT, 5, 37, 44, 51, 52, 151, 243, 247–248, 262
American Red Cross, 63, 291, 297
American Speakers Bureau, 54
American-Statesman, 22
"Anglo-Jewish press," 35
Annan, K., 153
Annual reports: described, 145–146; elements of, 149–155; on fundraising efforts, 146–147; letters from

chair/professional head included in, 149–150; media as audience of, 148–149; recipients of, 148
Anti-Defamation League, 234
AP (Associated Press) Daybook, 210, 257
Apollo Theater, 23
Ardoin, M., 146–147
Art of Self Promotion, The, 245
Art of War, The (Sun Tzu), 15
Articles: annual report inclusion of, 151, 152; copyright issues of, 102–103, 298; feature, 101–106, 257–258, 298; press kit, 113; reprints of, 152
As Time Goes By (British TV series), 254
ASPCA (American Society for the Prevention of Cruelty to Animals), 161
Association for Women in Communications, 40
Association of Junior League International, 14–15
Assumption College, 275

CPSIA information can be obtained
at www.ICGtesting.com
Printed in the USA
JSHW021252231220
10514JS00002B/90

9 781118 336076